ANTHROPOLOGICAL PRAXIS

About the Book and Editors

"This book provides us with valuable insight into the different ways in which anthropologists have associated themselves with human groups in need and with institutions and agents of change. . . . It describes very well the present status of applied anthropology and yet, in the enthusiasm of contributors, leaves us much to anticipate for the future."

—from the Foreword
by Erve Chambers

This text presents twenty-five original case studies that show working anthropologists solving problems in government and industry. The chapters are expanded versions of the 1981–1983 winning entries from the annual Praxis competition. In each chapter, the author describes the targeted problem or issue, his or her role as an anthropologist, the specific anthropological skills or knowledge used, and the results of the work. These in-depth studies demonstrate ways in which anthropological knowledge is applicable to real-life situations.

The introduction, by coeditors Robert M. Wulff and Shirley J. Fiske, sets the agenda for understanding the dimensions of applied anthropology today. The editors examine the anthropologist's role in public management and the policy process.

This provocative text is a must for any introductory applied anthropology course, graduate or undergraduate, used alone as a casebook or in conjunction with a more theoretically based applied anthropology text. It is an excellent guide for anthropologists hoping to work outside academia or for the mid-career anthropologist thinking of a career switch as well as for students embarking on internships.

Robert M. Wulff is deputy development director, Urban Development Action Grants, U.S. Department of Housing and Urban Development. **Shirley J. Fiske** is program director for social science and marine policy, National Sea Grant College Program (National Oceanic and Atmospheric Administration).

ANTHROPOLOGICAL PRAXIS

Translating Knowledge into Action

edited by
Robert M. Wulff
and Shirley J. Fiske

Westview Press / Boulder and London

Copyright © 1987 by Westview Press, Inc.

Published in 1987 in the United States of America by Westview Press, Inc.; Frederick A. Praeger, Publisher; 5500 Central Avenue, Boulder, Colorado 80301

Library of Congress Cataloging-in-Publication Data
Anthropological praxis.
   "Award winning entries from the first three Praxis
Award competitions of 1981, 1982, and 1983"—P.
   Bibliography: p.
   Includes index.
   1. Applied anthropology—United States.   I. Wulff,
Robert M.   II. Fiske, Shirley J.
GN27.A67 1987   306   87-9300
ISBN 0-8133-0313-3
ISBN 0-8133-0314-1 (pbk)

Printed and bound in the United States of America

The paper used in this publication meets the requirements of the American National
Standard for Permanence of Paper for Printed Library Materials Z39.48-1984.

10   9   8   7   6   5   4   3   2   1

Contents

PART 3
PLANNING AND IMPLEMENTATION: DECIDING WHAT TO DO

PART 4
EVALUATION: ASSESSING WHAT HAPPENED

Foreword

Anthropological Praxis: Translating Knowledge into Action is a collection of case studies in the application of anthropology. As such, it follows a fairly distinguished tradition. The case study has been a favored mode for communicating the work of applied anthropology and has become a particularly important tool for classroom use. As crucial as they might be, abstract generalizations and theories of cultural change and development cannot take the place of precise case examples that explore what happens when the knowledge and insight of anthropologists hit the hard ground of practical endeavor.

One reason case studies remain invaluable to us is that practicing anthropology is not solely a matter of being empirical or acting according to the best scientific tenets of our discipline. Our efforts are hedged on all sides by the happenstance of particular circumstances, by ethical and moral considerations, and by differing doses of good luck and misfortune. Applied anthropologists are always weighing the known against the unknown and are almost invariably forced to make recommendations and judgments under less-than-ideal research conditions. Thus, one thing we can learn from case studies such as those contained in this book is the virtue of flexibility—the wisdom that derives from being open to new possibilities and from being persistent in our pursuit of cultural understanding.

As essential as it is, the writing of case studies has been problematic in applied anthropology. Most earlier case reports on applied projects reflect the short-term involvement of the anthropologist. Such work was usually done under a consulting contract, and the anthropologist was involved in neither the planning of the research nor the final evaluation of its significance. Quite often in the past, anthropologists were employed by government agencies and others as troubleshooters when a project did not work. Although they provided valuable insight into the reasons for failure, their participation usually occurred too late in the decision-making process to have much impact on the project. Writing case studies under these conditions leaves unanswered the question of whether the anthropologist's advice was heeded at all, and if it was, what changes occurred as a result.

Another limitation of many case studies in applied anthropology is that they assume that the mere participation of anthropologists in a project means that anthropological knowledge and insight are being used to illuminate or solve the problem at hand. This is not necessarily so. Anthropologists have often worked in applied settings without drawing significantly on their anthropological background. These individuals have, in effect, been co-opted by their employers or by other disciplines. The work they do may be important, but it is difficult to argue that it is uniquely anthropological.

To some extent, co-optation in applied work is inevitable and even desirable. Applied anthropologists cannot afford to disregard the perspectives of other disciplines or to ignore the practical and bureaucratic constraints that normally attend applied research. On the other hand, applied anthropologists who are not constantly attempting to place their work within the framework offered by their own discipline are probably in danger of losing their professional identity. A degree in anthropology does not make an anthropologist. An ongoing commitment to anthropology usually does.

The critical reader of case studies will keep the following two kinds of questions in mind. First, what are the actual results of a piece of work? Did anything change as a result of the participation of anthropologists? Has the author of a case study had the opportunity to attend to both the short- and long-term effects of her or his work? Second, how can the participation of anthropologists be separated from that of other individuals working on a project? What has the author taken from anthropology and applied to his or her work? Is it likely that the effects of the project would have been different if anthropologists had not been involved?

These are not easy questions to answer. It is to the credit of the contributors to this book, and especially to editors Bob Wulff and Shirley Fiske, that they are answered here. I think this is, in large part, because of the special focus of the Washington Association of Professional Anthropologists' Praxis Award, which requires its jurors to pay special attention to questions like these as they judge each entry. These case studies are special in part because each passed a rigorous standard of proof that was judged independently by a diverse group of jurors.

I am impressed by the degree to which, in asking these questions of the case studies, we are able to arrive at worthwhile and accurate generalizations about the current state of applied anthropology. For example, it is clear that anthropologists have recently extended their reach to a great variety of human populations. More than half of the case studies in this book are based on work done in the United States. There are examples of work in the more traditional areas of applied anthropology, such as health, education, and international development. There are also cases based on new and promising areas of practice, such as legal planning, energy policy, housing, and welfare reform.

This book also provides us with valuable insight into the different ways in which anthropologists have associated themselves with human groups in need and with institutions and agents of change. Some of the work described here still follows the model of the relatively short-term consultation. But many of the contributors have based their activities on long-term association with another group. Several are full-time government employees. Others work with private, advocacy-oriented institutions or have used the university as a base for local-level collaboration. These differing modes of association reflect a pleasant reality. During the past decade anthropologists have shown considerable commitment to becoming involved in applied work on a full-time career basis.

I am especially heartened by the ways in which the contributors have responded to the question of how their work represents a distinctly anthropological contribution. In some cases, the contribution is methodological (e.g., the use of ethnographic research techniques) or epistemological (e.g., distinctions between "emic" and "etic" categories of knowledge or between "real" and "ideal" expressions of belief and behavior). But in a surprisingly large number of the cases, the authors linked their work to theoretical observations derived from general anthropology. Although such links between general and applied anthropology are often imputed, they are seldom described as well as they are in this book.

I must confess that this latter observation has caused me to reexamine the status of applied anthropology. For the past ten years, I have argued that applied work represents a distinct subfield in anthropology—an area equal in scope to the four traditional subfields of our discipline. I continue to believe this is true. Applied anthropology is that field of inquiry concerned with the standards and criteria that govern the uses of anthropological knowledge and insight. In this respect, applied anthropology has its own theoretical dimension and stands as a separate field of inquiry.

On the other hand, though it is important to recognize the unique status of applied anthropology, there is also a danger in this kind of thinking if it is used as a justification for ignoring or slighting the relations between applied anthropology and the rest of our discipline. In many respects, applied work has the potential to revitalize our appreciation of anthropology as a synthetic field concerned with the human experience in many dimensions. This book underscores how important it is for applied anthropologists to be well trained in general anthropology as well as in the special skills and insights of application.

Anthropology is a relatively small field. I have had the opportunity to meet most of the contributors to this book. They are mostly young people just entering the most productive stages of their careers. In final analysis, that might well be the most exciting prospect offered by *Anthropological Praxis*. It strikes me that this is a book that describes very well the present status of applied anthropology and yet, in the enthusiasm of contributors, leaves us much to anticipate for the future.

Erve Chambers

Preface

The chapters in this book are the award-winning entries from the first three Praxis Award competitions of 1981, 1982, and 1983. The Praxis Awards competition was established by the Washington Association of Professional Anthropologists (WAPA) to identify concrete examples of the successful application of anthropological knowledge to real-world problem-solving. As the discipline's applied arm grows in size and relative importance, examples of successful practice are essential feedback to ensure that practitioners, educators, and students of applied anthropology have access to state-of-the-art knowledge.

The entries were juried anonymously by outstanding applied anthropologists, who selected the winners and honorable mentions from the field of entries. Each chapter is a revision of the original award-winning entry and is an outstanding example of anthropological knowledge translated into action. We appreciate the time and patience required of all the authors to make revisions necessary to translate their entries one step further—into a format that communicates these valuable lessons.

The editors would like to thank first the jurors who spent their valuable time reading and judging the entries to identify the winners. The jurors have an impressive set of credentials in the field of applied anthropology. The jurors of 1981 were Sol Tax, Fred Richardson, Ruthann Knudson, Janet Schreiber, Erve Chambers, and Mary Elmendorf. For 1982 the jurors were George Foster, Erve Chambers, Annetta Cheek, James Wherry, and Setha Low. The 1983 jurors were Jean Schensul, Steve Barnett, and Dorothea Theodoratus. We would also like to acknowledge Carol Tyson, one of the initial Praxis codirectors (1981).

The Praxis Award competition is sponsored biennially by the Washington Association of Professional Anthropologists (WAPA). WAPA is a nonprofit association, incorporated in the District of Columbia. Its more than 200 members—the majority professional practitioners—include anthropologists working in the private sector, all levels of the federal governments, universities, and local government. The enthusiasm and foresight of WAPA in supporting the Praxis Awards was instrumental in its success. Thanks go to WAPA members and officers for their continuing monetary and emotional support. Last, we want to thank the general anthropology community for embracing the awards and making them a success.

Robert M. Wulff
Shirley J. Fiske

About the Editors
and Contributors

Robert M. Wulff is a practicing anthropologist working for the U.S. Department of Housing and Urban Development (HUD) in Washington, D.C., where he is a deputy director of development. Since arriving at HUD in 1978 as a specialist in neighborhood economic development, he has labored to combine the precision of a banker's underwriting with the wisdom of an anthropology perspective to create equitable and profitable community development projects. He is also an adjunct faculty member in the University of Maryland's Masters in Applied Anthropology program. Besides work in the corporate finance division of a New York investment bank, he has been managing partner in an urban planning consulting firm, faculty member of the University of South Florida's anthropology department, and research associate at UCLA's School of Architecture and Urban Planning. Contributions to the discipline include creating the Praxis Awards, helping found *Practicing Anthropology*, and participating on the inaugural Governing Board of the National Association for the Practice of Anthropology (NAPA).

Shirley J. Fiske is a practicing cultural anthropologist with the National Sea Grant College Program in Washington, D.C. Her work as a program director for social science and marine policy aims to increase the use of social science/anthropology in coastal resource development. The Sea Grant Program is a partnership between federal government and state academic institutions to develop the nation's coastal and marine resources through research, extension, and education. Since arriving in Washington, she has been active in the Washington Association of Professional Anthropologists (WAPA); she was also president of WAPA in 1985–1986. She has been codirector of the Praxis Awards since its inception.

Prior to joining the Sea Grant Program, Fiske was senior policy analyst with the Policy and Planning Office of the National Oceanic and Atmospheric Administration. Earlier she held faculty positions at the Los Angeles and Washington, D.C., campuses of the University of Southern California's School of Public Administration. Dr. Fiske received her Ph.D. in cultural anthropology from Stanford University.

Margaret S. Boone, Ph.D., is a social science analyst with the Program Evaluation and Methodology Division of the U.S. General Accounting Office. She also teaches part-time at Georgetown University in Washington, D.C., and is now at work on a book, *Capital Crime,* about that city's record-high infant mortality issue. Her interests are minority health and population issues, including Black infant mortality and teen pregnancy, the Black undercount, and health programs and policies for American refugees and other minorities.

Bridget Ciaramitaro received her M.A. (1981) at Memphis State University. Her M.A. practicum involved neighborhood organization and hazardous waste dumping. In addition to her role as codirector in the Center for Voluntary Action Research, she holds a position as research associate in the Department of Anthropology at Memphis State. Ciaramitaro is a charter member of the Mid-South Association for Professional Anthropologists and currently serves as president of the group.

Rosalind Cottrell was a graduate student during the neighborhood weatherization project and completed her M.A. in 1985. Currently she holds the position of research assistant for Aging, Education and Research at the Veterans Administration Medical Center, Memphis, Tennessee.

Judith R. Davidson was a consultant to USAID, Lima, Peru, and a doctoral candidate in the Department of Anthropology at University of California/Los Angeles at the time of her Praxis award. She received her Ph.D. from UCLA in 1984 and is currently manager of research and development, Center for Health Management Research, LHS Corp, Los Angeles. Her current research interests are innovations in treatment of depression among Hispanics, cost of noncompliance to diabetic therapy, Korean beliefs about health practices, and physicians as health educators.

Billie R. DeWalt is currently professor and chair of the Department of Anthropology at the University of Kentucky. He also holds an appointment in the Patterson School of Diplomacy at the same university. He is author of numerous publications and books in the area of economic development and social change, including *Modernization in a Mexican Ejido* (1979) and *Micro and Macro Levels of Analysis in Anthropology* (1985). He is coeditor of the series "Food Systems and Agrarian Change," published by Cornell University Press. He received his Ph.D. in anthropology from the University of Connecticut.

Kathleen M. DeWalt is currently associate professor of behavioral science and anthropology at the University of Kentucky. She is author of *Nutritional Strategies and Agricultural Change in a Mexican Community*

(1983). She received her Ph.D. in anthropology from the University of Connecticut.

George S. Esber, Jr., received his Ph.D. in anthropology from the University of Arizona (1977) and his M.S.W. from the University of Cincinnati (1984). At the time of his Praxis award, he was visiting assistant professor in sociology/anthropology, Miami University, Ohio; he currently holds the same position. His interests are applications of anthropology through interdisciplinary interaction.

David M. Fetterman received his Ph.D. in educational and medical anthropology from Stanford University (1981). At the time he wrote his Praxis essay, Fetterman was project director and senior associate at RMC Research Corporation in California. He is the author of *Ethnography in Educational Evaluation; Educational Evaluation: Ethnography in Theory, Practice, and Politics; Excellence and Equality: Reevaluating Gifted and Talented Education;* and *The Silent Scientific Revolution: Qualitative Approaches to Evaluating Education.* Fetterman was selected chair of the American Evaluation Association's Qualitative Methods Division and was recently awarded the Evaluation Research Society's President's Award for his contributions to ethnography in program evaluation. He is currently assistant professor in the School of Education and associate managing auditor in the Internal Audit Department at Stanford University.

Edward C. Green is senior research associate with John Short and Associates in Columbia, Maryland. He is currently involved in family planning and primary healthcare projects in the Dominican Republic and Nigeria. He received his Ph.D. at the Catholic University of America. After two years of dissertation fieldwork among the Maroons in Suriname, he spent five years teaching anthropology before beginning a career in development anthropology in 1980. He has since worked primarily in health and population in Africa, including four years in Swaziland working as a USAID contractor.

Stanley Hyland received his Ph.D. in anthropology from the University of Illinois/Urbana in 1977, where he and Charles Williams worked with Demitri Shimkin. His initial research in housing, community development, and policy planning has expanded to grassroots economic development and citizen participation planning. In addition to his work as codirector with the Center for Voluntary Action Research, he is associate professor in the Department of Anthropology at Memphis State University.

Thomas F. King received his Ph.D. in anthropology/archaeology from the University of California, Riverside, in 1976. He is the director of the Office of Cultural Resource Preservation, Advisory Council of Historic Preservation—a position that he held at the time he authored his Praxis chapter and that he continues to hold. The Advisory Council is an independent body whose primary responsibility is the administration of Sec. 106 of the Historic Preservation Act. His current work involves preparation of federal guidelines and supervision of "Sec. 106 review" (briefly summarized in his chapter) throughout the United States and Micronesia.

William L. Leap received his Ph.D. in anthropology with a concentration in linguistics from Southern Methodist University in 1970. He joined the faculty of the American University in 1970 and is now an associate professor and chairman of the department. He has worked with the Education Division of the Northern Ute tribe since 1978 and served as a research consultant to the division at the time of his Praxis award in 1983. He remains actively involved in efforts toward Indian language maintenance in several tribal contexts and has discussed technical, cultural, and political aspects of language maintenance and language renewal in numerous publications.

Richard N. Lerner is an anthropologist with the Environmental Branch, U.S. Corps of Engineers, San Francisco District, and has held that position since 1974. He received his Ph.D. in anthropology from University of California/Berkeley (1975). Lerner is the writer, producer, and director of the award-winning, 38-minute film, "The Environment and the Engineers at Lake Sonoma," which shows the plant preservation program on which his chapter is based.

John P. Mason received his Ph.D. in cultural anthropology from Boston University in 1971. At the time he wrote his chapter he was assistant vice president, Cooperative Housing Foundation, Washington, D.C. Presently he is an associate with Donnelly Roark and Associates, Washington, D.C. Formerly he was the director of the AID/University of Southern California Development Studies Program. Mason is a specialist in rural/urban planning, research, evaluation in shelter, squatter upgrading, institution development, and management participation. His area specialities are the Middle East/North Africa, Sub-Saharan Africa, and the Caribbean.

Gerald F. Murray received his Ph.D. from Columbia in 1977. He was instrumental in conceptualizing and designing the Agroforestry Outreach Project and eventually was director of field operations for the project. Murray received the Praxis Award for 1982 for his work with The Agroforestry Outreach Project in Haiti, described in his chapter. At the time he received the Praxis Award, he was director of field operations. He is currently associate professor of anthropology at the University of Florida in Gainesville. In addition to his Haiti work, he has done applied contract research in the Dominican Republic, Honduras, Guatemala, Costa Rica, El Salvador, Peru, Cameroun, and the urban United States.

Joseph Nalven received his Ph.D. in anthropology from the University of California, San Diego (1978). He was vice president and senior researcher for Community Research Associates, Inc., at the time of his activities estimating the population and impact of undocumented workers. Currently, Nalven is associate director of the Institute for Regional Studies of the Californias at San Diego State University. He is also finishing his law degree at the University of San Diego.

Patricia L. Parker received her Ph.D. from University of Pennsylvania in 1985. At the time she wrote her Praxis chapter she was a private consultant with the National Park Service working on historic preservation programs for local governments. She was also a doctoral student at the University of Pennsylvania. Currently she works for the Interagency Resources Division, National Park Service, where she is in charge of technical assistance on historic preservation to Micronesia and U.S. local governments. Under her previous married name of Pat Hickman, she coauthored the text *Anthropology in Historic Preservation,* with T. F. King and G. Berg (1977).

Kevin Preister has been a practicing anthropologist since receiving his M.A. in anthropology from Catholic University in 1979. As a research associate and program director for the Foundation for Urban and Neighborhood Development (FUND), Inc., based in Denver, Colorado, he has performed social impact assessments and impact management programs for a variety of development projects including recreation, water, oil and gas, urban redevelopment, and agriculture, both in the United States and abroad. He has conducted numerous training programs in socially responsive management for industrial and government clients. Mr. Preister is currently finishing doctoral requirements in anthropology at the University of California at Davis.

Edward C. Reeves is currently assistant professor of sociology and anthropology at Morehead State University, Morehead, Kentucky. He has published several articles on farming systems research and has participated and led workshops on this methodology and conceptual approach. At the time he wrote his Praxis chapter, he was assistant research professor, Department of Sociology, University of Kentucky. His Ph.D. is in anthropology from the University of Kentucky (1981).

Richard Scaglion received a Ph.D. in anthropology from the University of Pittsburgh (1976). He is currently associate professor of anthropology at the University of Pittsburgh. He served as director of customary law development for the Law Reform Commission of Papua New Guinea and was a consultant to the commission at the time he wrote his Praxis chapter. His interests include conflict management techniques in tribal societies and legal development in the Pacific.

Martin D. Topper received his Ph.D. from Northwestern University in 1972. He conducted postdoctoral work in American Indian affairs at the University of Chicago from 1972 to 1973 and undertook a second postdoctoral in the Anthropology and Psychiatry Departments of the University of California at San Diego from 1976 to 1978. At the time of his Praxis chapter he was assistant director of the Mental Health Branch of the Navajo Area of the U.S. Indian Health Service. He is currently the Indian Program liaison officer for the headquarters staff of the Environmental Protection Agency in Washington, D.C. Dr. Topper's applied interests lie in the areas of human communications, mass media, mental health care, and public health.

M. G. Trend, an applied anthropologist and documentary photographer, is a John Simon Guggenheim Memorial Foundation Fellow. He has been awarded the fellowship to study a group of Black farmers in Alabama and their urban descendants. Trend works for the School of Business at Auburn University, where he is project specialist for the Office of the Dean.

Robert T. Trotter II's current activities as a practitioner include analyzing migrant farmworker health needs in Arizona, working as head ethnographer for a nationwide project to assess migrant education recruitment processes, and participating in an economic development project for the Yavapai Apache Tribal Government in Arizona. Trotter was associate professor of anthropology and director for faculty research/development, Pan American University, Edinburg, Texas, when he wrote his Praxis chapter. He is currently professor and chair, Department of Anthropology, Northern Arizona University, Flagstaff, Arizona. He received his Ph.D. in anthropology from Southern Methodist University.

Allen C. Turner is currently attending law school at the University of Idaho. His goal is to practice Indian law. He is particularly interested in issues of Indian land tenure and Indian sovereignty. He most recently taught at Idaho State, Pocatello, and while there was a curator of the Idaho Museum of Natural History. Previous to that he was a principal in a private consulting firm called Community Resource Consultants, which conducted policy research for federal and tribal clients. He received his Ph.D. from the University of Kentucky.

Charles Williams received his Ph.D. (1981) from the University of Illinois/Urbana. His main research interests are community health, alcoholism, religion, and community development. He has done field research on Black Americans in Mississippi and Tennessee. He currently teaches and is an assistant professor in the Department of Anthropology at Memphis State University.

Introduction

Robert M. Wulff, Shirley J. Fiske

Anthropological Praxis is a collection of original case studies describing anthropological knowledge successfully translated into action. In each chapter an anthropologist demonstrates the utility of applying traditional knowledge to real world problem-solving. Such case studies are rare. Much of the literature in applied anthropology is neutral or negative reporting of the frustration of ignored or underutilized anthropological data—what "might have been" if we could only get policymakers' attention—and academically motivated research dissociated from real world problems and clients.

As an antidote to these pessimistic themes in the literature, the goal of this book is to provide optimistic case studies with benefits at two levels. For the professional anthropologist as well as students, they provide detailed, hands-on guidance for successful practice in government and industry.

This collection of successful examples of anthropological practice can serve to convince current and prospective practitioners of the utility and marketability of their anthropological knowledge to government and industry. To sell, one must be sold.

Each chapter explicitly describes the problem-solving process and the role of the anthropologist as a key player in the process. These first-hand accounts focus on "how to" lessons and on the many roles of the successful practitioner: implementer, mediator, coordinator, administrator, evaluator. The one-dimensional role of researcher, so common in traditional applied anthropology, is portrayed as only one of the many aspects of the successful anthropologist. The chapters highlight the area of practice in which real-world rewards are allocated: the use of knowledge, rather than solely the production of knowledge.

For teachers, practitioners, and students of anthropology the collective benefits of the chapters are both technical and psychological. The book provides (1) a new body of anthropological knowledge with tested problem-solving utility and (2) a level of confidence necessary to motivate anthropologists to market their discipline's problem-solving powers to government and industry.

Common Themes Across Chapters

To more clearly highlight the attributes of professional practice and to allow the reader to easily compare and learn from the diverse case study experiences, each chapter has been internally organized into four sections.

Problem and Client. Each chapter begins with a statement of the problem and an identification of the client. The scene is set succinctly, the important problems are identified immediately, and the clients and their needs are clearly established. The applied and problem-solving nature of the work is clear from the beginning.

Process and Players. The second section describes what happened. These rich narratives enable the reader to visualize the setting and the action. They are fascinating accounts of how practicing anthropologists work. Each author tells the story of what happened: how he or she got involved, what were the role and expectations of the clients, how the anthropologist balanced competing demands and established new directions, and how the process of working with clients snowballed into more widespread applications.

Results and Evaluation. We asked each author to assess his or her activities—to identify what worked, what did not, and how he or she knew they were successful. The authors present their results (intended and unintended) and their assessment of the project's success. Their valuable insights concerning what does and does not work in actual applications are useful lessons for current practitioners and students.

The Anthropological Difference. Finally, the authors discuss the most difficult to articulate and yet the most important aspect of their work: the anthropological difference. We asked them to imagine their projects without the involvement of the anthropologist. Would the outcome have been different? Was the solution to the client's problem significantly influenced by anthropological knowledge? Without such knowledge would the resulting solution have been inferior? From this hypothetical platform we asked them to define what it was about their knowledge, training, and approach to problem solving that contributed to the success of the activity. We asked them to be bold; their statements illustrate in clear terms why anthropology was necessary for the projects to succeed.

This section of the chapters addresses two related aspects of the anthropological difference: It specifies the anthropological knowledge used—the theory, methods, or concepts that made a difference—and it identifies the anthropological difference or the unique contribution the discipline's knowledge made to the success of the project. This discussion is critical for individuals thinking of entering the profession of applied anthropology because the authors identify what was most important for the intervention to work.

Organizing Principles for the Book

When organizing the chapters within the book, we rejected the obvious comfortable solution of using traditional subspecialties in cultural anthropology—urban anthropology, medical anthropology, and development anthropology—as too static and too inward looking. Such a traditional format would not have properly organized chapters that illustrate knowledge in action. The chapters describe dynamic processes (such as choosing a course of action), not static subspecialty areas (such as urban anthropology); and they all are examples of problem solving that often crosscut anthropology's divisions.

The anthropologists in this book are actively engaged in the processes of problem solving. They design research, identify and sample populations, pull together resources for a project team, recommend programs, and negotiate between cultural groups with different objectives and belief systems. We chose, therefore, to organize the book around stages of problem solving. Our emphasis is on the action—the purposeful use of knowledge—rather than on the disciplinary labeling or typology of roles for an applied anthropologist.

The stages of problem solving used in this book are (1) defining the need or problem by producing information, (2) formulating policy by choosing from alternative solutions, (3) planning and implementing interventions to achieve the chosen solution, and (4) assessing results through evaluation.

The stages and the model are not our invention. Disciplines like public management and the policy sciences have developed various iterations to describe the policy process (Anderson 1979) or the planned social change process (Rich and Zaltman 1978). They have recently been adapted for use in anthropology. In his discussion of the culture of policy, Chambers calls these "stages of policy decision making" (1985:41), and Van Willigen discusses anthropology as a policy science using similar stages (1986:41). Regardless of the pedigree, the stages are useful labels for understanding the complexity and context of action. Each stage identifies linked products in a transformation from unorganized knowledge to decisions about action choices and interventions to evaluation.

Many readers will undoubtedly see a strong similarity between our problem-solving stages and the policy process. This resemblance is expected because making policy is essentially setting general guidelines and forming a commitment to action at a macrolevel (organizational, national, institutional): Congress establishes laws, a corporation establishes a business plan, and state or federal agencies establish regulations. We have decided on the more generic label "problem solving" simply because not all the chapters illustrate policymaking per se; but all chapters illustrate some contribution to problem solving.

Let us add a quick caveat concerning our problem-solving model. Like all models this represents an ideal type problem-solving process rarely seen in actual practice. We are not proposing here that all problem solving must proceed by linear, one-directional stages. In reality problem solving is a set of interrelated processes that can be active sequentially or simultaneously or informed by activities occurring at other parts of the cycle.

Because our organizing model is an ideal type, not all our real-life chapters fit neatly into one problem-solving stage. Some chapters illustrate more complex pieces of action and have elements of several of the stages. For example, Robert Trotter's Chapter 11 cuts across stages of identifying the extent and nature of lead poisoning from folk remedies to assisting in the design of culturally sensitive publicity campaigns. We have placed any chapter that crosscuts stages in the section in which the anthropologist's role and contribution were most dominant.

Defining the Problem: Information Production

This stage may also be called problem identification, needs assessment, or policy research. The kinds of questions addressed at this stage of problem solving are

- What is the nature of the need or problem?
- Whose need is it?
- What is the extent of the problem? Where is it located? Who is involved?

This stage addresses first-order questions that establish basic data about a problem but not necessarily a causal link. Information production through research is the most common activity at this stage. Questions and activities typical of this stage are basic to a number of chapters. For example, the question, "How many undocumented residents are there, and what is their economic effect on the county?" demands a highly sophisticated research design and knowledge of and rapport with the undocumented community. In Chapter 2 Joseph Nalven describes the development of an innovative method to extrapolate such information in his consulting work for the Board of Supervisors of San Diego County.

The Swazi government and U.S. Agency for International Development (USAID) were concerned about disease caused by poor sanitation. Edward C. Green was hired as part of a team to investigate the practices, knowledge, and beliefs of rural Swazi—the ultimate goal of the project was to recommend a plan for health education. He describes how he planned and conducted the necessary research to lay the groundwork for the plan for health education.

Kevin Preister's work with issue-centered social impact assessment relies on a sophisticated and sensitive method of gathering information about community and corporate concerns that surround the development of a new ski resort in Colorado. The manner in which the problem was defined—through a unique, anthropologically inspired process of gathering information—promoted solutions to the concerns of both parties.

This problem-solving stage also addresses second-order questions establishing causality. That is, the problem is not only defined, its suspected cause is identified. Second-order questions become the leading edges of policy/solution formulation and program planning recommendations. Once one establishes or identifies causes of problems then the corrective actions become more obvious.

"What are the causes of high infant mortality and low infant birthweight among Black newborns?" The District of Columbia wanted to answer this question since it had extremely high rates of infant mortality. Margaret Boone's work showed a clear relationship between lifestyle/cultural variables and low infant birthweight. The medical model of postbirth treatment was not sufficient; programs to address prebirth lifestyle and cultural aspects of behavior were vitally important.

In Chapter 5 Ed Reeves and Billie and Kathleen DeWalt address the problem of lagging sorghum and millet production in developing countries. Through the farming systems research approach, they identified the constraints to production on farmers in Sudan and Honduras. These ethnographically collected data were paramount in establishing priorities for agricultural research on plant qualities that were important to farmers—such as drought tolerance, forage quality of stalks, and bird-resistant varieties. Concerns and priorities of low-resource farmers are extremely important in unraveling the mystery of low productivity in the agricultural sector.

Choosing an Alternative: Policy Formulation

This stage has also been labeled policy analysis, policy adoption, and the policy decision stage. As used in this book, this stage includes the analyses of alternative solutions, including their effects, and the selection of a preferred alternative. The result of this stage is the identification of a preferred direction for action. The key questions are

- What can be done? The answer can involve an extensive analysis of the range of alternatives that will address the problem.
- What are the expected effects or consequences of those alternatives? The answer can involve analyses of the costs and benefits to different groups, the analysis of externalities and distributional effects, the minimization of harmful effects, questions of equity and efficiency, capital flow and productivity.
- Is the solution feasible? Can it actually be carried out, or are there logistical, legal, religious, political, or other barriers?

Memphis Light, Gas and Water (MLG&W), a municipally owned utility company, was failing in its efforts to communicate an energy conservation program to low-income customers, the group most in need of assistance. In Chapter 8 Hyland, Ciaramitaro, Williams, and Cottrell describe how a team of anthropologists solved the communication problem through ethnographic research on both MLG&W policymakers and the Memphis low-income community. The ethnographic data revealed very different beliefs and worldviews concerning the concepts of energy and conservation, and the team's policy recommendations provided strategies for both sides to bridge this subcultural gap between service provider and recipient.

The National Parliament of Papua New Guinea grappled with the problem of a culturally inappropriate legal system bequeathed by the Australians when Papua New Guinea gained independence. The Law Reform Commission hired Richard Scaglion to advise on legal options through a Law Reform Commission. He organized and directed a team to conduct research on customary law and practices and recommended changes in the legal system to the parliament. His story is a fascinating account of policy formulation for the legal system of a newly independent nation.

At the request of the Swaziland Ministry of Health, Edward C. Green advised it on the feasibility of a national healers association and the likelihood that the healers would work together with Western medical doctors on some problems of health care. Chapter 6 on "The Integration of Modern and Traditional Health Sectors" documents his approach to the problem and shows how his work carries over to the program planning and implementation stages of problem-solving. He designed highly successful programs to bring together healers and Western doctors so that health care recipients could take advantage of the best of both sectors while conserving the skill and status of traditional healers.

The Tribal Council of the Kaibab Paiute in northern Arizona wanted to overcome the apathy of the tribal members for planning the tribe's economic future. The council's attempt to get citizen participation through a system of Western-style committees had failed. Allen Turner in Chapter 9 describes how he reintroduced traditional structures of communal Paiute decision-making and suggested alternatives to the tribal government to increase community participation.

Deciding What to Do and How to Do It: Planning and Implementing Interventions

Once a policy direction has been selected, organizations and individuals must determine the best mix of programs, services, or projects to carry it out. This stage of problem solving has been called implementation, program planning, and intervention strategies, and it usually involves decision-making activities at a level closer to the ultimate recipients of an intervention than the policy formulation stage.

In the field of management there is an enormous body of literature on implementation, and some authors argue that it is the most important stage of the problem-solving process. Because laws and regulatory mandates at the policy level are generally vague and indefinite, the planning and service delivery at the ground level becomes the most important manifestation of the original policy.

The kinds of questions addressed at this phase of problem solving are the following:

- What specific programs/actions should be designed to achieve the objectives?
- Which population groups should be targeted?
- What should be our priorities?
- What combination of activities will meet our objectives? Training programs? Services? Income transfer?

Each chapter in this section illustrates the importance of anthropological knowledge in successfully planning and implementing activities. Anthropologists have many roles at this stage: They are mediators between groups with culturally different beliefs and aspirations, as when Patricia Parker and Thomas King assist the Trukese to communicate their concerns to the Trust Territory of the Pacific; they provide technical assistance to groups on activities for which a general mandate already exists—as in Richard Lerner's work with the Pomo; or they manage the entire program effort, as in Gerald Murray's work with reforestation. The commonality is that a prior decision or policy has already been made regarding the optimal alternative. For example, the Haitian government and USAID had decided that reforestation of the denuded slopes was the appropriate action. Given this decision, Murray designed a successful agroforestry program, taking advantage of cultural value systems and organizational substrate that would not have been included in the program had there not been an anthropologist.

Lerner's chapter highlights the value of having an anthropologist as a part of an agency's permanent staff and the tremendous influence anthropological knowledge can have in designing social intervention strategies if wielded by a knowledgeable insider. Lerner was able to direct the Army Corps of Engineers' mitigation efforts on behalf of the Pomo to produce a culturally sensitive response to their potential loss of plant resources.

George Esber's role as a Janus-headed mediator required him to interpret between Anglo architects who were designing homes and Apaches who were to live in those homes. Applying his knowledge of Apache matrilocal social organization and the resulting social use of space, he was able to influence the architects' design solutions and ensure culturally appropriate homes.

The Indian Health Service (IHS) suspected that problems had arisen from the forced relocation of Navajo from the Federal Joint Use Area (FJUA). They hired an anthropologist, Martin Topper, to work on the problem from a health perspective. He gathered information on the problems experienced by relocatees and potential relocatees in the FJUA. His detailed knowledge of these problems allowed him to suggest to the Navajo area IHS and state, federal, and tribal groups programs to reduce the impacts of relocation.

Robert Trotter was initially contacted by the Region VI Office of the U.S. Department of Health and Human Services to determine if Mexican-Americans in Texas were using a dangerous lead-based folk remedy. The public health problem had received widespread publicity as the result of some recent deaths. Trotter identified the problem and helped to develop culturally sensitive programs for reducing the use of the folk remedies without interfering with the overall use of folk medicine by Mexican Americans in the Southwest.

Sometimes changes come from outside a planned intervention. The government of the U.S. Trust Territory of the Pacific Islands (TTPI) and the U.S. Navy planned to expand the airport on Truk. The Trukese objected to the expansion because it would destroy their fishing areas and important religious landmarks. Patricia Parker, who was working on her dissertation research with the communities involved, and Thomas King, who was a consultant in archaeology and historic preservation to the TTPI, collaborated in mediating the concerns of the villagers of Iras with the plans of the U.S. government for airport expansion. This chapter is an outstanding example of successful cultural mediation that changed the direction of a prior program decision of the government.

Assessing What Happened

Evaluation is a formal assessment of the process or impact of an activity. It is a part of the "good management" cycle of planning-implementing-evaluating and is written into almost all introductory management texts. According to the model, the results of evaluation then inform the planning process, and the cycle is enriched by this assessment. More than that, however, it is a common-sense response of any group or person to step back and take stock of what has just happened. Evaluation and assessment occur throughout the problem-solving process and not necessarily at the last stage.

The kinds of questions asked at this stage of problem solving are

- Was the process effective? efficient?
- What effects did the intervention have?
- Were there unintended consequences?
- Did the program meet its objectives? At what level?
- Did the effort adhere to its legal mandate?

The Peruvian Ministry of Health was dissatisfied with its midwife training program. Judith Davidson discarded the traditional "body-count" evaluation methodology for a user-oriented methodology and developed training curricula that effectively overcame the most important barrier to learning—culturally patterned behavior. Her chapter cuts across evaluation and program design.

Collecting qualitative data and integrating them into the dominant quantitative evaluation methodology are contributions in part from anthropology. David Fetterman describes his work on the evaluation of the Career Intern Program, a federal experimental program designed to create alternative high schools for drop-out students (interns). In the multisite evaluation the author played a key role in integrating ethnographic data into the traditionally quantitative evaluation methodology. In the same general tone, M. G. Trend's Chapter 19 describes the evaluation of a statewide welfare reform experiment that used an evaluation method that triangulated economic survey data with ethnographic data to reach conclusions with enhanced reliability and validity.

Concluding Remarks

Many students ask, "But what will I do with an anthropology degree?" or "What effect can anthropology have?" This book demonstrates the demand for anthropological services by clients who want the anthropological difference, and it shows what anthropologists can accomplish and how they do it. *Anthropological Praxis* lays out the fundamentals on which to build a professional practice arm in applied anthropology.

The anthropological difference is apparent at every stage of the problem-solving process: Anthropologists design programs that work because they are culturally appropriate; they correct interventions that are under way but that will be economically unfeasible because of community opposition; they conduct evaluations that contain valid indicators of program results. They provide the unique skills necessary for intercultural brokering; they collect primary and "emic" data necessary for planning and formulating policy; and they project and assess cultural and social effects of interventions.

This year for the first time, the American Anthropological Association's biennial survey of PhDs shows that the majority of 1985–1986 PhDs in anthropology went into practice outside academia (American Anthropological Association 1987). Even more astounding is that since 1984, in two short years, the proportion of PhDs seeking work outside academia has gone from 29 percent to 42 percent (Baba 1987:6). Clearly, more anthropologists will be seeking answers to the questions of successful practice.

The chapters demonstrate the challenge, complexity, and successes of the new frontiers in applied anthropology. Most important, the chapters demonstrate successful strategies of dealing with clients, the problem focus of their work, and the recognition of the anthropological difference that will help anthropology establish a practice arm in its own right. Taken together the book is a rich mine of new ideas and strategies for applied anthropology students and faculty at the crossroads in the discipline's future. We hope that the insights provided in each chapter will permit the next generation of practitioners to transcend our current efforts to forge a professional practice.

References

American Anthropological Association. 1987. Doctor Rate Update. *Anthropology Newsletter* 28(4):1.

Anderson, James E. 1979. *Public Policy-Making.* Second Edition. New York: Holt, Rinehart and Winston.

Baba, Marietta. 1987. Building on Our Strengths. President's Comments, National Association of Practicing Anthropology. *Anthropology Newsletter* 28(1):6.

Chambers, Erve. 1985. *Applied Anthropology: A Practical Guide.* Englewood Cliffs, N.J.: Prentice-Hall.

Rich, Robert F., and Gerald Zaltman. 1978. Toward a Theory of Planned Social Change: Alternative Perspectives and Ideas. *Evaluation* (Special Issue), 41–47.

Van Willigen, John. 1986. *Applied Anthropology.* South Hadley, Mass.: Bergin and Garvey.

PART 1
INFORMATION PRODUCTION:
DEFINING THE PROBLEM

1 / The Planning of Health Education Strategies in Swaziland

Edward C. Green

Problem and Client

In March 1981, I was hired by the Academy for Educational Development to assist in the implementation of the Rural Water-Borne Disease Control Project funded by AID (Agency for International Development) in Swaziland. The project called for a KAP (knowledge, attitudes, and practices) study on water and sanitation in Swaziland. The primary purpose of the study was to provide baseline data for the design of a national health education strategy aimed at reducing the incidence of waterborne diseases. The project paper (the main planning document for the project) called for further anthropological contributions: the identification of potential human resources for the delivery of health education, the designation of traditional opinion leaders and informal communications networks, the identification of patterns of visual literacy and perception, and the acquisition of knowledge about Swazi ethnomedical theory and practice.

One of the project's attractions for me was that it seemed to be designed with unusual sensitivity to the importance of sociocultural factors. Instead of limiting anthropological input to the later stages of project design—which was often characteristic of AID projects until the early 1980s—this project specifically called for a medical anthropologist who would spend two years conducting firsthand research and assisting in project implementation. The research findings were to guide not only

This is a shorter, revised version of a chapter that appeared in E. Green, ed., *Practicing Development Anthropology* (Boulder, Colo.: Westview Press, 1986). Reprinted by permission.

health education, the main project component, but also two other components, namely, public health engineering and environmental sanitation.

I represented and was answerable to three clients: the Academy for Educational Development, which hired me, paid my salary, and managed the project; the Ministry of Health, to which I was assigned and where my office was located; and AID, which funded the project and managed the project contract. Although all three clients were working toward the same general goals, sometimes they had differing interests and agendas. Thus my project colleagues and I not only had to be circumspect and diplomatic at all times, but we also had to mediate and negotiate between the client groups.

Process and Players

The project's technical team consisted of five advisers: a health educator (who was also chief of party), a public health engineer, an environmental sanitarian, an epidemiologist, and an anthropologist. The epidemiologist and I were essentially researchers; the other three were to work closely with Swazi counterparts to promote measures intended to reduce the incidence of diseases related to inadequate water supplies and sanitation. A certain amount of direct counterpart training was also expected of the latter three. Central to all our efforts was the development of an effective, viable Health Education Unit (HEU) within the Ministry of Health.

Prior to our project, health education activities had been carried out by a few public health nurses in the Public Health Unit, under the supervision of an expatriate health educator provided by the World Health Organization (WHO). In April 1981, a few weeks after my arrival in Swaziland, the new headquarters for an autonomous Health Education Unit were opened. The Swazi staff (all women) consisted of three health educators, one nutritionist, and a graphic artist. The expatriate staff (all men) consisted of the WHO supervisory health educator, the project health educator, and myself.

Foreign technical advisers usually advise and leave administration to host country officials. However, two of our project team members were supposed to fill supervisory administrative roles for the duration of the project. One of these, the health educator, was to act as the head of the HEU, according to the terms of the Swaziland-USAID contract. However, as an outsider he found it difficult to move right into a position of supervising local staff. The experienced WHO health educator was still on staff, leading to ambiguities and conflicts in leadership during the project's initial months.

My role as researcher/planner had far less potential for conflict. I was in the Ministry of Health to learn and only later to advise; I was therefore not in the awkward position of trying to teach Africans what to do in their own country. As an ethnomedical researcher, I naturally took an active interest in traditional beliefs and customs. I spent a good deal of time asking questions, an activity that fortunately was interpreted by my Swazi colleagues as showing respect for their culture.

The Ministry of Health had never before had an anthropologist or sociologist on staff. Even before I conducted my KAP survey, ministry officials found unanticipated uses for their new resource. My first extra assignment was a "quick and dirty" survey to determine the social feasibility of placing drinking-water tanks in areas that had inadequate water resources and were at high risk for cholera. The ministry wanted to know if people would actually use the tanks rather than the traditional sources of drinking water. Within two weeks of the initial request (five days of fieldwork and five days for tabulation, interpretation, and writing), I submitted a useful report to the ministry.

However, the KAP study was my main contractual obligation. The project paper budgeted for a sample-survey design and methodology for the KAP study. Yet I had some doubts about the appropriateness of such an approach. In addition to the general problem of obtaining valid data through survey methods in rural Africa (see, for example, Cohen 1973), the information I wanted related to sensitive areas such as toilet behavior, personal hygiene, and health beliefs. The impersonal, precoded questionnaire typical of survey research is notoriously deficient in eliciting information of this kind, even if it has value in measuring well-established patterns.

After considerable discussion, review of previous surveys in Swaziland, and preliminary ethnographic fieldwork, I presented a modified research plan to the AID mission in Swaziland. I proposed that an informal study of health beliefs and behavior, focusing on traditional healers and their patients, be carried out before considering a sample survey. I hoped the study would provide qualitative data valuable for the design and interpretation of surveys as well as supply information that surveys could never discover. I planned to rely on the traditional methods of key-informant interviewing and participant-observation, at least in the early stages of research.

I also proposed a study of health behavior, beliefs, and attitudes that would rely on rural health motivators (RHMs) as informants. RHMs are individuals, usually women, chosen by their communities to receive about eight weeks of training in preventive health care at a regional clinic. After training, RHMs work among their neighbors, promoting homestead sanitation, the purification of drinking water, proper infant nutrition, and other practices related to disease prevention.

I felt that RHMs would make good culture brokers because they are insiders in their communities yet they understand and promote public health goals. I expected that they would be more likely than their neighbors to give candid and truthful replies to sensitive and even embarrassing questions about what their neighbors thought and did. Furthermore, by querying a smaller sample of respondents than required by the KAP survey, we could use a flexible, open-ended interview schedule. My previous ethnographic research experience in Suriname had left me with an abiding preference for this type of interview instrument.

In both the ethnomedical and RHM studies I wanted to personally conduct interviews and make direct observations in order to have maximum quality control over the incoming data. My anthropological training and orientation would have made it difficult for me to sit in my office in the capital city, with no feel for Swazi culture, while hired interviewers conducted the actual fieldwork and then presented me with data that I would have had difficulty interpreting or evaluating. I felt strongly that the two proposed studies were a necessary adjunct to a sample survey; they might even eliminate the need for a survey and could thereby save the project considerable money.

The revised research proposal was written, submitted to AID and the ministry, and accepted with minimal delay. Over the next six months I interviewed a nonrandom sample of forty-two RHMs in eight regional clinics. A Swazi woman who had spent her senior high school year in the United States assisted me as a translator in most interviews. She also helped me develop effective probing techniques that were used when RHMs gave stereotyped and self-serving answers such as, "The people around here boil their drinking water because we have been teaching them how important this is."

Because each RHM visited approximately forty homesteads, the interviews provided information based on nearly 1,680 homesteads, representing some 3 percent of the estimated 50,000 homesteads in Swaziland. We regarded our RHM-visited homesteads as reasonably representative of those in Swaziland as a whole because they were situated throughout the country's four major topographic zones. I felt that the quality of information collected in this study was quite good. We found we even had quantifiable data on such factors as the number of pit latrines built or under construction—information the RHMs had no trouble remembering because they were required to report monthly on latrine progress. On the whole, the study was a good piece of research for under $300; the only direct costs to the project were the translator's hourly wage. Of course, a full accounting of costs would have included my salary, vehicles and fuel provided by the Swazi government, and salaries of support staff.

During the same period, I conducted a number of in-depth interviews with traditional healers, and I observed some of their practices—both of these gave me an excellent introduction to Swazi culture. I spent considerable time in rural homesteads, getting a feel for the culture as a whole. The healers thought it perfectly natural for a white foreigner to be interested in their curing methods. Because I did not inquire about the one thing they were secretive about, actual formulas for medicines, they seemed unthreatened by my presence and were free with information.

Within six months of my arrival, I was able to provide general sociocultural information and specific health-related findings to guide other components of the project. But several questions arose in my mind. Was my approach going to be adequate? How reliable were my research methods, and could they be replicated in a future evaluation of the project? (A follow-up KAP survey was in fact called for in the contract as part of the project's summative evaluation during its last year of AID funding.)

After some thought and discussion with colleagues, I reconsidered the value of a KAP survey. I realized that a homestead survey yielding quantitative data would serve as a useful baseline for any future studies or evaluations. And if I decided to conduct the survey, the data and methodological experience from the two preliminary studies would help me develop a better survey instrument, serve as a validity check on the incoming survey data, and improve data interpretation. In short, I felt a lot better about attempting a national survey. A KAP survey would also contribute to a more general project objective, namely, institution-building, or strengthening local capacity to carry out various technical activities on a continuing basis. Specifically, it would involve the training and participation of various nationals, thereby strengthening social science research capabilities in the Swazi government and in collaborating institutions like the University of Swaziland.

During the next month, I recruited interviewers and wrote the questionnaire. With help from the newly formed Social Science Research Unit of the University of Swaziland, I chose eighteen student interviewers, three supervisor-interviewers, and one faculty assistant. I also hired ten interviewers who worked seasonally for the government's Central Statistics Office. Although only a few of these were high school graduates, all had some interviewing experience. Five drivers and two additional supervisors were hired, bringing the fieldwork team to thirty-nine, including myself.

Although based primarily on the needs of the project, questionnaire content and wording followed to some extent that used in previous water and sanitation studies conducted in Africa and elsewhere so that our results would be comparable to those of other surveys. Four successive drafts of the questionnaire were pretested by the three graduate assistants with forty-five rural respondents living outside the survey areas. The first three pretested versions were in English so that I could evaluate the responses and guide any revisions; the last version was in siSwati. The final questionnaire included sixty-nine questions of which sixty-five were precoded and four were openended. Of the precoded questions, twenty-three allowed write-in options. Interviewers were also free to write in answers that did not conform to the available categories. I knew these concessions to data validity would add considerable time and effort when we tabulated responses, but we could not be certain in advance about the range of responses to any question.

Next we derived a stratified cluster sample based on data from the most recent census. In the first stage, a sample of eighty-nine census enumeration areas (EAs) representative of Swaziland as a whole was chosen with help from the Central Statistics Office. In the second sampling stage, specific homesteads were selected from recently derived Central Statistics Office lists of homesteads covering the selected enumeration areas. Using a table of random numbers, we chose five homesteads from each selected enumeration area, resulting in a sample of 455 homesteads that represented just under 1 percent of the estimated 50,000 homesteads in Swaziland. Given the cultural homogeneity of this area, the subject matter of the survey, and the results from the two earlier studies, this sample size was adequate.

Because of the cohesive kin-group structure and relative lack of specialized roles in Swazi society, we regarded the homestead (*umuti*) as the basic response unit for this type of survey (see Drake 1973:63–66). The head of homestead or another adult family member standing in for the head (frequently a woman) was considered a representative spokesperson. In some questions, it was desirable to ask what the individual thought or did. In this way, associations with predictor variables related to individual characteristics could later be analyzed.

I conducted some ten hours of training for the interviewers before beginning fieldwork. Because most of the interviewers were students, the fieldwork period was chosen to coincide with the university's three-week Christmas vacation. Local chiefs and their assistants had been notified of the survey by letters from their district commissioners and by public radio broadcasts. As it turned out, chiefs were often absent from their areas during the early period of fieldwork to participate in the annual "first fruits" (Incwala) ceremonies. As a result, we could often dispense with the visit to the local chief demanded by protocol, saving us considerable time.

Almost without exception, respondents and local authorities were cooperative, partly because Swaziland was in the middle of its first outbreak of cholera and people were concerned about the disease. We introduced ourselves as government workers researching the causes of cholera—which was a truthful way of putting it—and so we were welcome. As a further inducement to cooperation, each respondent was offered a cholera information packet that included potentially life-saving oral rehydration salts.

The most time-consuming and therefore expensive aspect of the survey was locating the preselected homesteads. This search often required long drives or walks and frequent requests for directions; sometimes families had moved or no one was home. Adding to this problem was the practice of earlier census takers who had recorded only the "European" first name of the homestead head; but often the person could only be located by his or her traditional given name.

Interviews usually took between thirty to forty-five minutes to complete; yet because of time spent locating homesteads, an interviewer could complete an average of only two and one-half interviews per day. In retrospect, if I weighed the various costs incurred against the marginal benefits of using a probability sample, I would think twice before repeating our sampling procedure. Although we could calculate sampling error with a fair degree of presumed accuracy (7 to 8 percent in this case), sampling error is probably not as important as the inaccuracies introduced during interviewing, translation, questionnaire construction, coding, tabulation, editing, or analysis. For a survey of this sort, designed to guide health policies and educational strategies, a systematic sample in the final sampling stage would be adequate. That would mean, for example, choosing every tenth or twentieth homestead in randomly preselected enumeration areas. Some of the time and money thereby saved could go into efforts to reduce various types of response error.

Fieldwork was complicated by logistical problems such as vehicles breaking down, and by supervisory problems over issues like overtime pay. In fact, such problems made it difficult to carefully monitor incoming questionnaires and discuss interviewing experiences with fieldworkers on a daily basis. If I were to conduct another survey of this type, I would use fewer interviewers, supervise them more closely, and allow more time for fieldwork.

Results and Evaluation

Over the next few months, I spent part of my time interpreting the analyzed data and writing the survey report and part on new research projects. The survey report also presented information from the traditional healer and the rural health motivator studies, which added considerable qualitative flesh to the quantitative bones of the sample survey. Several hundred copies of the combined report were distributed locally and to interested agencies abroad. I made several verbal presentations to the Swazi government, AID, the Academy for Educational Development, and other groups and agencies. I also revised and later published some of the KAP survey data in health-related journals (Green 1985, 1987).

I was mindful of the observation, attributed to Alexander Leighton, that "the administrator uses social sciences the way a drunk uses a lamp post: for support rather than illumination." Therefore, I had no great expectations about the immediate impact of our study. However, several of the KAP report recommendations did contribute to changes in national health policies and procedures. For example, previous ministry policy had been to promote construction of pit latrines made with concrete slabs. The survey showed that at least two-thirds of the latrine floors in our sample were made of wood or other locally available materials. Survey data further suggested that reliance on the construction of concrete slabs, which usually required the direct assistance of one of the twenty-odd health assistants for the entire country, actually constrained latrine building in rural areas. Indeed, latrines built from local materials stood up well over time, contrary to a pervasive belief among government officials and foreign advisers that wooden latrines are quickly destroyed by termites.

By October 1982, the Ministry of Health was developing a new radio campaign aimed at improving homestead sanitation. Departing from previous policy, the ministry encouraged people to build latrines from local materials if a health assistant was not available to help with the construction on a concrete slab. Technical details for the building of wooden and other local-material latrines were provided in the radio broadcasts.

Because the survey showed that 82.6 percent of respondents had a working radio in their homestead, I suggested in my report that the radio was an underutilized medium for health education. Meanwhile, interest in radio was developing in other quarters. By early 1983, two development communications consultants from the Academy for Educational Development had completed a series of in-country workshops during which seventeen radio programs were developed with the assistance of the Swaziland Broadcasting Service. The programs were intended to raise health awareness, present information, and promote behavioral change through use of true-to-life dramas about rural people and their problems. In addition to vernacular, believable dialogue, programs featured music, humor, and realistic sound effects in order to create a familiar rural setting in the listener's mind. Messages were often phrased in ways compatible with traditional beliefs, an approach that seems obvious but that is often difficult to implement in developing countries.

We were under no illusion that we had found the great panacea in health education. We recognized that radio campaigns would only be effective if they were reinforced by printed materials and face-to-face contacts with extension workers and perhaps trained local leaders. Yet health campaigns using carefully designed radio dramas were a new and promising approach for the Swazi government.

After pretesting the programs on cassettes with representative rural listeners, the first of the radio dramas was aired in April 1983. I later helped design and conduct evaluation research to monitor listeners' response to the campaigns and to assess program impact. Approximately a year later, the Academy for Educational Development signed a contract with AID to establish a development communications capability within Swaziland Broadcasting Services in order to disseminate a broad range of development topics by radio.

Another recommendation in the KAP report, based largely on information from the ethnomedical research, was that more could be done to present health messages in the familiar idiom of traditional beliefs. Even though Swazis may not understand biomedical germ theory, many traditional concepts of health and disease can be built upon to influence their attitudes and behavior. For example, Swazis believe that unseen agents can cause disease. Some diseases are thought to be "in the air" (*tifo temoya*) and highly contagious; people are infected by breathing unseen agents into their bodies. Swazis believe in other environmental dangers as well: Poisons and spells may make certain places unsafe, and some diseases may be contracted by simply walking past a location where traditional medicines have been mixed if the area has not been purified.

Practices relating to disease prevention were also found to be widespread. For example, certain medicines (*tinyamatane*) are routinely given to children through inhalation or traditional vaccination (*kugata*) to protect them from various supernatural dangers, and entire homesteads are protected from sorcerers' attacks by driving ritually prepared pegs into the ground around the perimeter of the homestead.

I recommended in the KAP report that health education messages be designed to accommodate certain traditional health beliefs without compromising public health objectives. For example, mothers might be more receptive to having their children vaccinated against childhood diseases if the practice were presented as a *tinyamatane* that protects against diseases locally acknowledged as within the medical doctor's sphere of competence. I pointed out that if we ignore traditional health beliefs we avoid reality; by challenging or confronting them directly we create stress, confusion, and resentment among the people the ministry is trying to influence.

The Anthropological Difference

The anthropological contribution to the Rural Water-Borne Disease Control Project was considerable. Indeed when an external organization evaluated the project's five technical/disciplinary components during the third project year, it judged social science (that is, anthropology) to be the most successful in achieving its objectives (Hornik and Sankar 1985). Given the nature of my assignment and of the type project, the anthropological contribution was primarily methodological. I found that time-honored, qualitative anthropological methods were essential in obtaining certain types of important information. Informal participant-observation and in-depth, open-ended interviews with traditional healers gave me a feel for the beliefs of rural Swazis and their behavior in regard to illness and health. This preliminary and quintessentially anthropological fieldwork, combined with the open-ended interviewing of RHMs, enabled me to design and interpret a culturally sensitive and culturally appropriate survey instrument, the KAP questionnaire. However, some of my most important findings, which were translated into concrete policy recommendations and into actual ministry policies, were not from the KAP survey but from the ethnomedical research that I did more or less on my own. Had I not been an anthropologist, I probably would have limited my research activities to surveys, many of my more important findings and insights would have remained undiscovered, and my policy and program recommendations would have been relatively facile, superficial, and unconvincing to the Swazis.

As an anthropologist, my training and orientation have been to look at things from the perspective of tribal, or peasant, or marginal groups— or in the AID argot, through the eyes of the poorest of the poor. This perspective was precisely what was needed to design health education approaches and messages for rural Swazis. Gaining a project-beneficiary perspective seems so obvious that it is scarcely worth mentioning. But of all the disciplines represented in overseas development work, anthropologists tend to be the most inclined and able—through a combination of training, field experience, and perhaps certain personality traits—to sympathize and empathize with the rural poor of developing countries (Green 1986).

References

Cohen, Ronald. 1973. Warning Epistemologies: Quality and Quantity in African Research. In W. O'Barr et al., eds., *Survey Research in Africa: Its Implications and Limitations.* Evanston, Ill.: Northwestern Press, pp. 36–47.

Drake, Max. 1973. Research Method of Culture-bound Technique? Pitfalls of Survey Research in Africa. In W. O'Barr et al., eds., *Survey Research in Africa: Its Implications and Limitations.* Evanston, Ill.: Northwestern Press, pp. 63–66.

Green, Edward. 1985. Factors Relating to the Presence and Use of Sanitary Facilities in Rural Swaziland. *Tropical and Geographical Medicine* 37 (1):81–85.

———. 1986. Themes in the Practice of Development Anthropology. In E. Green, ed., *Practicing Development Anthropology.* Boulder, Colo.: Westview Press.

———. 1987. Beliefs and Practices Related to Water Usage in Swaziland. *International Journal of Water Resources Development* 2 (3):29–42.

Hornik, Robert, and Pamela Sankar. 1985. A Preliminary Evaluation of the Swaziland MMHP. Philadelphia: Annenberg School of Communications.

2 / Measuring the Unmeasurable: A Microregional Study of an Undocumented Population

Joseph Nalven

Problem and Client

Major changes in U.S. immigration policy were made in the mid-1960s: The bracero program and national origin quotas were eliminated, and numerical limits were placed on immigrants from the Western hemisphere for the first time (SCIRP 1981:205–210, 457–558; Keely 1983:33–41). These changes have proved inadequate, and further major revisions to immigration policy have continued to be debated from the mid-1970s to the mid-1980s. Particularly important has been the debate over undocumented persons ("illegal aliens"). Should the status of these individuals be legalized or should they be given amnesty? Should the United States continue the status quo and tolerate the sub-rosa existence of an estimated two to six million undocumented persons living in the country? Even as national debate continues, major questions remain for local governments. County and city governments have been troubled by questions about fiscal impacts: Who will pick up the costs attributable to these individuals?

Beginning in 1974, the San Diego County Board of Supervisors wanted to know more about the numbers and impacts of undocumented immigrants. Despite two in-house studies (1975, 1977) and a resolution calling for legislative action, the board of supervisors had been unable to convince the federal government to provide special impact funds to deal with the costs incurred by the county as a result of undocumented immigrants. In July 1979, the supervisors decided to file a lawsuit against the federal government. The lawsuit not only sought monetary reimbursement for providing medical care to undocumented individuals but

26

also sought "an injunction against the government from failing to take into custody and provide medical care for illegal aliens for whom the county incurs health care costs." The lawsuit approach, however, failed.

With the impending visit of the Select Commission on Immigration and Refugee Policy to the West Coast in June 1980, the supervisors decided to have another impact study conducted—one that they could present to the select commission along with, and in support of, their own policy recommendations. This time the supervisors wanted an outside group to conduct the study: Their goal was to have an academically defensible study with which to advocate the local community perspective. Our firm bid on the proposal and eventually won the county contract.

Process and Players

The competition for the contract was tied to a debate about whether valid measures of the undocumented population could be made. On one side were the purists who believed that since no random sample could be drawn, any results would be invalid. On the other side were the pragmatic researchers, myself and other anthropologists, who believed that reasonable proxy measures could be developed that would give policymakers a plausible framework to view undocumented immigration.

The request for proposals called for a study of the number of undocumented workers in San Diego's labor force by type of industry; job displacement of individuals legally entitled to work in the United States; their economic impact (including tax contributions); the fiscal impact of undocumented immigrants on health care, welfare, education, and law enforcement agencies; and the extent of economic interdependence between San Diego and Tijuana.

The group impaneled to evaluate the proposals consisted of four analysts from the county's Office of Management and Budget (OMB), one representative from two supervisorial offices, and two outside members, a Chicano activist and an assistant in the U.S. Attorney's office. The final vote of panel was split four for the purists and four for the pragmatists. The four OMB analysts voted for the purists, whereas the more policy-sensitive panelists voted for the pragmatists.

The purist proposal came from a university research center that had already obtained a quarter-million-dollar grant from the Department of Housing and Urban Development to study cross-border trade flows; the group was also in the process of linking its efforts to a new center for U.S.-Mexican studies at another local university. In this group's view, the county's expectations were too grandiose for the time and moneys available. Instead, it proposed that the county support the research center's longer-term effort to get better data on trade flows. The center's agenda meshed well with the long-term plans of county land use planners in the development of improved industrial linkages in the border area. However, this approach missed the point of the elected officials' request: A study in hand was needed to present the county's case to the select commission some nine months down the road. A long-term study would miss the crisis dynamic that motivated the need for information about undocumented immigrants.

Our consulting group was composed of anthropologists and community-based planners. Both senior anthropologists leaned toward applied research, evaluations, need assessments, and program development (such as starting up a child care center); neither was a full-time college employee and both taught only sporadically. The categories of purist and pragmatist reflected a division between both groups: university-based versus community-based and economist-led versus anthropologist-led. Both groups recognized the importance of having a multidisciplinary approach to the study of undocumented persons. However, the university-based economists had no anthropologists on their team; they merely recognized the role that ethnography would have in describing this population. Because they proposed a retargeting of the county's research agenda to trade flows, they had no immediate need for anthropologists. In contrast, our group of community-based anthropologists started with the premise that the county's research agenda was actually possible to accomplish. We proposed as a first step to establish rapport with, gain access to, and collect data about the undocumented population. Our second major step would be to work with economists to determine the data's significance about local tax revenues and the degree of job displacement and job creation attributable to undocumented workers.

Because we anticipated the need for collaboration with economists, our proposal to the county included a joint-venture component with a private economics firm—one that specialized in conducting regional economic impact studies. The demographic and economic forecasting model (DEFM) employed by this firm was also used by the county and other state and local agencies. The results derived from this econometric model would be more compatible with those from the county's own planning model than those from the model used by the university-based economists. Thus, if one assumed that the study of undocumented immigrants was feasible, then the package we presented was more attractive: We, as anthropologists, had ties to the Mexican-origin community (legal and undocumented) and could gain access and conduct a survey; the data would be "massaged" by the anthropologists and economists so that the impacts of this population could be modeled over a twenty-year period; and the econometric model used would coincide with what the county had previously judged to be an acceptable forecasting approach.

We were very discouraged when the OMB project manager recommended to the supervisors that the university-based economists should be awarded the contract. The bottom line for the supervisors, however, was to have a product to take to the select commission. The university-based economists would not give them that product. After the supervisors had another staff person from a different department review the economic soundness of each proposal and were assured that our proposal would result in a plausible framework for measuring the impacts of undocumented immigrants, they voted unanimously to overturn the OMB project manager's recommendation and awarded the contract to us. Their decision to spend $60,000 was a high-risk tactic, given the nationwide failure of researchers to measure the numbers and impacts of undocumented immigrants. The select commission would not be swayed by a study that lacked a solid and persuasive foundation. Unfortunately, an extra month was spent in deciding who should be awarded the contract, shortening the research process to four and a half months. What could not be changed was the May 1980 due date.

Results and Evaluation

The economists who worked with us stated that the impacts of the undocumented population on the San Diego economy could be modeled much like other regional transformations. In this case, the undocumented population would be hypothetically removed from the regional population base. This "shock" to the economy could then be projected over a twenty-year time frame. This approach required (1) a simulation of the undocumented population, (2) data on the types of jobs held by undocumented workers, the numbers employed in each job type and at each wage level, and (3) the degree to which local unemployed citizens and legal residents would take the jobs held by undocumented workers and at what wage level. The comparison of the undocumented work force with the unemployed domestic (citizen and permanent resident) work force would provide a measure of job displacement.

The task of constructing the population pyramid belonged to us as anthropologists. From the outset, it was clear that we could not undertake a random household survey, especially because the supervisors had cut one month from the research period to meet the deadline for the select commission's West Coast meeting.

The proposed method for simulating (or constructing) a hypothetical universe was to merge a delphi-estimating procedure with the demographic profile of different segments of the undocumented population.

If, for example, 38 percent to 66 percent of general farm labor was estimated to be undocumented and if, in a separate survey of apprehended undocumented farm workers, the average family size for these workers was 1.06 (the majority remaining at home in Mexico), then the number of undocumented persons in farm work could be multiplied out to obtain an estimate of undocumented workers plus associated family members. Similarly, if undocumented workers in non-agricultural work have a family size of 2.6 (with the majority living in the United States), then the number of workers in different urban industries can also be multiplied out to estimate an additional number of undocumented workers and associated family members.

The estimation procedure is further complicated by the presence of U.S.-born children in undocumented families. These children cannot be counted as undocumented because the U.S. Constitution grants automatic citizenship to persons born in the United States. These children must be discounted in the estimation of undocumented family members. Furthermore, many families have more than one wage earner. To avoid inflating the associated family component, the multiplier factor must be further discounted for families with more than one wage earner.

Two elements of the estimation procedure require further specification: (1) the total magnitude of the undocumented work force and (2) the population segments used to determine the demographic composition of associated family members. Regarding element (1), staff simply accepted Immigration and Naturalization Service (INS) regional estimates, which had lumped San Diego and Imperial Counties together. On the assumption that the agricultural sector in Imperial County was about equally strong in attracting undocumented workers as the more diversified economic base in San Diego, county staff allocated 92,137 undocumented workers to each county. As a result, the county analysts gave Imperial County more undocumented workers than the actual number of people officially recognized in Imperial County through census extrapolations. Part of the problem of accepting INS estimates, especially during 1977 when this earlier study was conducted, was that the figures were inflated by a hysterical fear of a "brown-tide" invading the United States at its southern border. Current estimates are about half those promulgated by the INS at that time. Of course, no one really knows the size of this population; thus the method of estimation becomes critical in evaluating the reasonableness of the numbers used for describing the undocumented population.

As mentioned earlier, a delphi-estimation technique was used to infer the size of undocumented labor force by Standard Industrial Classification (SIC). The delphi-estimation procedure averages the best guesses of experts. In our study, a stratified survey of employers in five industrial classifications in which undocumented workers were concentrated (agriculture, construction, manufacturing, retail, and services) were asked to give high and low percentage-estimates of undocumented workers in their specific industry. These percentages were averaged and combined with estimates given by key informant employers and immigration authorities. The use of percentages precludes having actual numerical estimates that exceed actual work force size by SIC. Equally important, the use of high and low estimates forces the consumer of these data to realize that the analysis is oriented toward a plausible range and not to a single hard number.

Our approach was unique for microregional studies: It combined an economic forecasting model with a detailed methodological sequence (to infer an upper and lower limit to the numbers and impacts of undocumented persons) to better ground as well as constrain the scope of the policy debate on this subject. On a national level, the General Accounting Office study represented the only other effort that attempted to model the impacts of the undocumented population for the policy debate (General Accounting Office 1980). (Each study was conducted in ignorance of the other.)

The estimating process also required a sensitivity to the variation within the undocumented population as well as to the variation linked to the nature of the data source. We developed different ways of constructing a profile for agricultural versus non-agricultural undocumented workers. For example, apprehended undocumented workers were interviewed at the Border Patrol detaining station. As long as one recognized that the Border Patrol focused its raids on farms, then a cross section of these workers is useful for describing undocumented farmworkers. For nonfarmworkers, Border Patrol detainees are a totally inappropriate group. For the nonfarmworker and urban employment sector, we used three other data sources: non-apprehended individuals living in San Diego (whom we contacted through community members and sampled by convenience); those arrested by local police and whose files were referred to INS; and a unique and serendipitous group—Silva-Bell applicants. This last group was used to develop a stratified sample (by family size). It represented individuals who might have had the opportunity to apply for legal residence in the United States, but who, because of a precipitous action by the Department of State, were deprived of that possibility. The Department of State had awarded 144,999 visas to Cuban refugees between 1968 and 1976 that would have gone to other visa applicants in the Western hemisphere. Many of these potential visa awardees were Mexican applicants. A court decision forced the Department of State to consider many of the undocumented immigrants in the United States as possible visa awardees.

Until the decision was reached and the administrative process completed, there were some 2,000 "legals-illegals"—individuals who had an undocumented status in the United States but who were given a letter from INS stating that they could stay here as quasi-legal residents until their cases were decided. This group probably represented high-assimilation–oriented individuals in that they hoped to become permanent settlers in the United States. All three sources were combined to model the demographic structure of the urban undocumented in San Diego.

The major question we confronted was the economic impact of undocumented immigrants. The question turned in large part on the degree of job displacement of legal workers by undocumented workers. The economists that planned to model this shock to the economy could proceed easily under a zero and 100 percent substitution assumption. The forecasting model could run if no job held by an undocumented worker was taken by a domestic worker or if all of these jobs were taken by legally available workers. However, reality is normally neither black nor white, but gray. The economists required a consensus estimate: How many jobs would be taken by domestic workers, at what wage level, and in which industries? To obtain this model, we conducted an additional survey of unemployed, legally available workers, asking them if they would take jobs typically held by undocumented workers and at what wage level. Of the five industries studied, low- and middle-status jobs were used as proxies. For example, busboy and waiter/waitress represented the retail sector, dominated by the large numbers of undocumented workers employed in restaurants. Based on the available (unemployed) labor supply, the economists calculated how many jobs would be taken and how many would be permanently lost. In agriculture, more so than in any other employment sector, the jobs would not be taken by legally available workers under the prevailing wage structure. This would presumably result in a massive disruption of the local agriculture industry.

With respect to job displacement, the economists forecasted that a short-term impact of a 0.6 percent to 1.5 percent increase in the unemployment rate would result from the removal of undocumented workers from the regional economy. This increase in the unemployment rate can be explained by the loss of undocumented workers' consumer expenditures in the San Diego economy, which would outweigh the new job opportunities created for local workers, as well as by the total job loss not being replaced with the removal of undocumented workers. The long-term impact (beyond ten years) showed a net decrease in the unemployment rate of 0.4 percent to 0.5 percent. The various segments of the economy would, after ten years, be expected to recover from the removal of undocumented workers by new employment opportunities.

Table 2.1   Results of 1979 San Diego County Impact Study

	Figures for Undocumented Persons	Figures for Total County
Number of persons	24,000 to 48,000	1.8 million
Number of workers	13,000 to 25,000	259,000
Total earnings (annual)	$77.4 to 150.6 million	
Total job-related taxes	$15.5 to 31.4 million	
Sales tax from local purchases		
to California	$3.1 to 6 million	
Returned to cities and county	$.6 to 1.2 million	
Fiscal impact on school system	$10.9 to 21 million	$564 million
Fiscal impact on hospitals	$2.2 to 4.1 million	$398 million

Source: Community Research Associates, <u>Undocumented Immigrants: Their Impact on the County of San Diego</u> (San Diego: County of San Diego, 1980).

Clearly, the immediate removal of undocumented workers would shock the local economy and have a counterproductive effect.

In May 1980, the board of supervisors was satisfied with the results of the undocumented-immigrant impact study. At a news conference the county staff heralded the results of this study and the policy recommendations of a citizens' task force (which operated concurrently and independent of each other). The supervisors developed a package of recommendations and research findings that they presented at the select commission's San Francisco meeting. Several of the research findings for San Diego County for 1979 are presented in Table 2.1 (Community Research Associates 1980).

Judged by the acceptability of the findings, our impact study was a success. No media representative, policy analyst, or other researcher challenged the study. The lack of criticism can be explained by the lengths to which we went to qualify our findings and by our detailed discussion of the technical assumptions and modeling process.

To be sure, the policy track is a fast one. The difficulty of truly knowing the actual dimensions of the undocumented population may forestall any major criticisms. A former executive of the select commission stated in a personal conversation with me that he had been favorably impressed with the findings of this study: "This is what we were looking for." However, he also pointed out that he had decided not to spend any of the select commission moneys on conducting impact studies. Not only did he consider eighteen months too short a span to give the commission meaningful results, but he worked with the commission to develop its policy recommendation based on principles of constitutional rights. In this view, the current number of undocumented immigrants could be tolerated and absorbed through amnesty—so actual measures of this vaguely known reality were not critical to the decision-making process. The direction taken by the select commission not only deflates the effort that we and the county made; it also points up the difficulties local-level jurisdictions have in influencing federal policies.

The Anthropological Difference

During the process of building the job-displacement consensus model, our economist observed that what we felt (subjective factors) would weigh heavily in determining boundaries and cut-off points in modeling job displacement. Despite the hard numbers generated in such economic impact studies, the findings are sometimes constructed with contestable assumptions. The economist was acutely aware that this econometric exercise would require several judgment calls. He pointed out that because we had worked with the various study populations the anthropologists would know best where and how to make judgment calls.

Could any of the knowledge we possessed be described as explicitly anthropological knowledge? One essential component of the anthropologist's work is the translation of one culture/society into terms comprehensible by another—generally into the language of the dominant society with an interest in understanding its subcultures. The study of undocumented immigrants and the impacts of this sub-rosa culture (the county staff's term) on San Diego's mainstream society falls easily into this model of an anthropologist's work.

The study of the undocumented population required the ability to gain access to it. Such access had several facets: obtaining contacts among the undocumented population and establishing rapport and *confianza* (trust) to ensure reliable responses. The step of gaining access to a community—a major element of the first stage of an anthropological study—is generally missing from other disciplines conducting one-shot surveys. In our study, we worked through previously known individuals in building a "snowball" sample (sampling from the social networks generated from individual starting points) and through the offices of community agencies that made contacts on our behalf. This process was facilitated by our community-based contacts. We were known individuals in the community—known to have worked in socially beneficial projects. This social action attribute is sometimes eschewed by academic purists— both anthropologists and those from other disciplines. Nevertheless, our prior histories allowed us to short-circuit the access process for the project.

Access also required an ability to speak fluent Spanish and have an easy familiarity with popular Latino culture, a bilingual and bicultural fluency. The ability to communicate with undocumented persons—both those apprehended by the Border Patrol and interviewed in the context of a detention center and those interviewed in the context of their home—required a language facility and a willingness to communicate at the individual level. This ability meant not speaking across class boundaries and recognizing the tragic-comedic aspects of their situation. The essential aspect of this access element is, of course, establishing rapport with the respondent. Without it, the interviewee would be less helpful in instructing the interviewer about where the questionnaire required amplification.

The anthropological knowledge important to the success of this study included conceptual as well as methodological elements. First, the study was designed as a number-crunching exercise. It lacked a qualitative dimension, something of the human tapestry of this sub-rosa culture. Fortunately, one of the members of the anthropologist team had interviewed several families in the California segment of the U.S.-Mexican border region. We were able to incorporate her previous work in a bonus chapter to illustrate how families used the border in different ways. One family, for example, had one sibling and family move into the United States on a fairly permanent basis as undocumenteds; another sibling had found a niche in Mexico and did not intend to come to the United States as a migrant or an immigrant; a third sibling moved back and forth in a dual-residence pattern. The differential use of the informal, transnational border culture differs from the interior-of-Mexico to the interior-of-the-United States rotational migratory pattern. These patterns are important because policy founded on a border reality versus one founded on the interior-to-interior migratory reality would be quite distinct: The former would be more oriented to microregional issues affecting neighboring communities (such as San Diego and Tijuana), whereas the latter would be oriented to satisfying the needs of certain industries (such as agriculture). Thus, the qualitative description of this border networking provided an important conceptual handle to the readers of the study who were seeking to assess the impacts of un-documented immigrants. This added material, we assumed, would require the county to consider the linkages tying neighboring border cities together rather than simply the impacts that one of these border com-munities was having upon the economy of the other. Looking back, we now see that the county staff was mesmerized by the economic impact data, which, given their original agenda to influence the select commission about local-level fiscal impacts, was an understandable policy reflex.

The additional information on transborder networking proved to be merely interesting, without actionable elements.

A second element of anthropological knowledge, namely holism, entered into the structuring of the data sets and the simulation of a population pyramid. Here, however, the goal did not emphasize a comprehensive set of culture domains but rather of societal segments. (To be sure, figuring out how the undocumented are integrated into wider society requires consideration of specific cultural domains, such as "bottom-rung worker" as it applies to the use of undocumented workers, nuances in the definition of lawful immigration status, and so forth.) How these segments of undocumented persons are integrated into the wider society provides demographic clues for simulating their presence within the total population.

Let us consider this demographic simulation with respect to disciplinary focus. Narrow definitions might well limit this activity to demographers, but anthropologists do demography and demographers study different subcultural groups. Anthropology is, in many ways, an eclectic social science; however, it contributes to generic social science activities by ensuring its application in rough terrain. A demographer could, in principle, have constructed the same population pyramid—even a better one. However, the pyramid required an organic integration of different population segments and data sets. This approach meant gaining access to these populations (methodological level) and understanding how their different lifestyle realities made them important, though less visible, segments of a total population (conceptual level). The anthropologist's tool kit—field training, ability to use the "native's" language, and sense of conceptual completeness or holism—made this simulation possible. The holistic awareness also led us to add the bonus chapter on informal social networks crisscrossing the border and to include an extended caveat on the possible effect of not interviewing employers of undocumented workers. The anthropological gestalt led us to better define the limitations of the number-crunching approach as well as to set the stage for a wider study of the interactions of the transnational border community, both legal and undocumented.

It is sometimes unclear where anthropological sensitivity, developed out of a particular way of researching society, goes beyond the application of good social science. One of our decisions, in particular, proved difficult and represents the tight wire we walked between advocacy, rapport, and policy research. The question is whether being anthropologists influenced the way in which we walked that tight wire or at least led us to recognize that there was a tight wire to walk. The troublesome decision affected the analysis of job displacement. The economists were in the process of applying our estimated work force percentages to their regional employment data. We had built our estimates on official, State of California (Employment Development Department) employment data. The economists stated that they had a better set, acknowledged even by state employment analysts. However, we insisted that the economists use the same data base upon which we developed the estimates of the undocumented work force. Perhaps this was the wrong decision and it may not have made all that much difference. At the back of our insistence was the fear of the unknown: the econometric blackbox. Once the numbers went in, we would no longer have control and the chips would fall. At least with the state's existing data base for San Diego we had an idea of relative work force sizes; we did not know what the substitution of a new and "better" employment base would mean. Time had nearly run out for the project; there could be no delays. Rather than trust the economists' "better" data, we decided to go with the official data.

As a community-based group, we were concerned with the values brought to the research project. A potential existed for information abuse that could affect the Chicano and/or undocumented population—both of which were of Mexican origin. As principal investigators, we found ourselves wrestling with the problem of objectivity: Was it better for researchers to ignore the consequences of the research or not? If researchers acknowledged their bias (a concern for the welfare of the undocumented population) could they still conduct objective research? We realized that the bias question had no easy answer. The commitment to professionalism demanded that the top priority was "to let the chips fall the way they fall." Yet, in this poorly defined area, the research methodology would depend on assumptions about the population and how it would be modeled. In this area, we, as community-based anthropologists, felt we could ensure that our study was sensitive to the reality of the undocumented population. What such sensitivity actually meant could not be specified beforehand and was left as a vague commitment to ourselves. Not until the end of the study did we confront choices of consequence, such as to accede to the economists' request to use a "better than official" data set with which to forecast the impact of removing undocumented workers on the regional unemployment rate.

Anthropological knowledge in its most elemental sense is experiential. The anthropologist's quest to learn the culture of a given group often extends into an identification with it. In this particular study, the anthropologists were able to trade on their previous research as well as on their advocacy work within the Chicano community. The relative ease of access into various study populations (not only among the undocumented, but also among bureaucrats) helped them obtain the best possible data within the constraints of studying an undocumented population. Here was the strength of the methodological underpinnings of anthropological knowledge; at the same time, though, that strength became a potential weakness. Depending on one's perspective about social science objectivity, the organic relation that the anthropologist develops with a community in order to gain access to its culture can undermine a thoroughly disinterested analysis. I am not considering the outright distortion of the data. (There is the equivalent "sin" among academic anthropologists who distort data to protect their theoretical models. Data distortion is not limited to applied researchers.) In the more difficult case, and in the one we encountered, the arbitrary choice of rules to achieve mathematical elegance can have adverse impacts upon real people. The easy solution would be to take the position for numbers or for people. The more difficult road, and the challenge we faced in our role as professional anthropologists, is to evaluate these problems on a case basis, recognizing who is paying for research, how the information may be used and abused, what are the limitations of social research in capturing the ongoing transformations of contemporary society, and what is the ability to negotiate equitable boundaries between models and people, the funding source and the target of the research, as well as between disciplines. The challenge is to do all of these on the fast track of crisis-oriented, policy research.

References

Community Research Associates. 1980. *Undocumented Immigrants: Their Impact on the County of San Diego.* San Diego, Calif.: County of San Diego.
General Accounting Office. 1980. Illegal Aliens: Estimating Their Impact on the United States, PAD-80-22, Washington, D.C.
Keely, Charles B. 1983. The Failure of United States Immigration Policy. In Wayne A. Cornelius and Ricardo Anzaldua Montoya, eds., *America's New Immigration Law: Origins, Rationales, and Potential Consequences,* Monograph Series, 11. La Jolla, Calif.: Center for U.S.-Mexican Studies.
Select Commission on Immigration and Refugee Policy (SCIRP) (Staff Report). 1981. U.S. Immigration Policy and the National Interest, Washington, D.C.

3 / Issue-Centered Social Impact Assessment

Kevin Preister

Problem and Client

Since 1962 Eagle County, Colorado, has been shifting from an economy based on agriculture, timber, and railroad transportation to one of recreation. In that year, a sheep pasture in Upper Eagle Valley was converted into the Vail Ski Area. The dramatic success of Vail coincided with the decline of the traditional economy. Although the previous century had been characterized by very slow population growth, relative economic stability, and local self-sufficiency, the recreation economy fostered rapid population growth and a number of important social changes.

By the late 1970s, development and growth were affecting the entire county. Beaver Creek Ski Area, approved in 1976, was under construction. Interstate 70 had been completed through the county and with the Eisenhower Tunnel under the Continental Divide substantially increased the number of winter visitors and local commercial activity. A smaller, private ski area, Arrowhead, had also been approved. Subdivision and five- to ten-acre lot development, accompanied by commercial development along major thoroughfares, was occurring throughout the county, affecting land use in significant ways (Gallegos and Preister 1980a).

The proposal to develop Adam's Rib Recreational Area was made in this context of important physical and economic changes that were already having profound social consequences. The project proponent, Hospital Builders Equipment (HBE), Inc., of St. Louis, early in 1980 commissioned my employer, the Foundation for Urban and Neighborhood Development (FUND), to perform the social impact assessment (SIA) and to integrate it with economic data being generated by another firm.

The project plan calls for a major year-round resort centered around downhill skiing. The proposed site is near Eagle, Colorado, 130 miles west of Denver. The cost of the project is estimated to be $480 million (1981). It will require a build-out period of fifteen years and employ up to 6,600 people during construction and nearly 5,000 during operation. The site is presently pristine and isolated—elk calving areas, critical wetlands sites, and watersheds will be affected by its substantial infrastructural and operational requirements. The size of the project and its location in the western, relatively undeveloped portion of the Eagle County would offer a relative balance in the economic activity of the region (Gallegos and Preister 1981).

The project was first proposed in 1972. For a number of reasons it became controversial. The decision-making process became polarized between people supporting and those opposed; businesses were boycotted; feelings ran high. The review of the project coincided with the decision by the governor and the voters of the state of Colorado to refuse to host the 1976 Winter Olympics. When the governor also withdrew support for Adam's Rib, the first review ended without a decision.

HBE re-activated the proposal in late 1979. The developer and the responsible agencies agreed that the project would be reviewed under the auspices of the Colorado Joint Review Process. This process was developed by the state to coordinate the review of major development projects among the various responsible agencies and government levels; its purpose is to avoid the duplication of efforts and the delays characteristic of development decisions. It has since been used to review major mining and oil shale projects. Participation in the review process is voluntary, and the existing legal authority of each entity is not superseded.

Process and Players

The Joint Review Committee, composed in this case of the U.S. Forest Service, state and county governments, and the developer, determined that an updated environmental impact statement (EIS) was required because of both the outdated nature of previous work and the degree of controversy produced by the first review. The coordination and review of the EIS were the responsibilities of the committee, even though the developer was responsible for financing the study. The FUND team was thus paid by the developer but responsible to the Joint Review Committee.

The National Environmental Policy Act (NEPA), enacted in 1969, requires federal agencies to prepare an EIS for any "major federal action." The impact statement must include a discussion of the baseline environmental conditions, a range of alternatives under consideration including "no action," a forecast of the environmental effects of alternatives, the alternative chosen, and possible mitigation measures to reduce negative impacts or enhance positive ones. In the regulations promulgated by the Council on Environmental Quality (CEQ), in regulations of various agencies, and in court decisions, the importance of social impact assessment (SIA) in the overall assessment process has been clearly determined (McEvoy and Dietz 1977).

Within this existing legal framework and given the level of controversy surrounding the project, FUND management decided to utilize an "issue-centered" approach to the SIA. It has three objectives: (1) to reflect accurately the social reality of people affected by the decision; (2) to use public issues as the driving force for the collection of social, economic, and environmental information; (3) to facilitate the resolution of as many public issues as possible through the planning, design, review, and implementation of a project. The SIA then is used as a tool in promoting the long-term management of a development effort from a social perspective.

I was hired in December 1979 to lead and coordinate field operations on a full-time basis. I reported to FUND's project director who was assigned one-third time to this project, and I worked with two part-time field researchers for the first three months. We all lived in the town of Eagle during that time, and I continued living there until August 1981. The responsibilities of my teammates and myself were to

1. Perform a baseline social assessment of the area including current changes and existing trends.
2. Identify the full range of issues people believed existed in relation to the project.
3. Collect social and economic data on the basis of public issues and analyze the social and economic effects of project alternatives using baseline information, public issues, and the social and economic data.
4. Promote good communication and information flow between various individuals and publics.
5. Promote the resolution of public issues with the developer and responsible agencies.

Results and Evaluation

Baseline Social Assessment. The field team analyzed the existing social and economic situation in Lower Eagle Valley. It discovered that the area was rapidly changing; because of the growth of recreation in the upper valley, the lower valley was experiencing steady population growth, subdivision, and commercial development and the displacement of senior citizens and other vulnerable groups. Because of the influx of new and different kinds of people, lifestyles have changed. Transiency, now commonly reported in local communities, results from the seasonal nature of skiing and the concomitant seasonal employment base. The stability of personal relationships that characterized earlier times is no longer present. Relationships are now more anonymous and less permanent, and informal caretaking has given way to reliance on formal government and commercial services. Recreation is shifting from informal and dispersed (hunting, hiking, fishing) to organized and commercial (skiing, hunting clubs) (Gallegos and Preister 1980a).

Public Issues. The concept of the public issue has become useful in anthropological fieldwork and social impact assessment related to development projects (Preister and Kent 1984). A public issue is defined as a subject of deep interest to an individual or group that can be acted upon, if people so decide, to protect and maintain control of changes in their environment. This definition suggests two notions. The first is that an issue is a statement that can be acted upon. For someone to say, "I'm against growth," reveals little except an attitude. It is too general to allow responsive management action by project personnel. FUND refers to such general attitudes as themes. On the other hand, statements such as, "I'm against growth because the high rises add so many kids to the parks that my kids have no place to go," or, "I'm against growth because the recreation economy is forcing old people out of our community," are issues because they form the nucleus of opinion around which action could form. Their content is specific enough for them to be acted upon (that is, park space could be provided, the senior citizen population could be stabilized).

The second notion is that people move from a passive to an active position regarding a project, and to a position of support or opposition, when their interests are directly affected, and at that time they act upon issues. A social scientist who probes beyond initial, often emotional, statements (themes) about a project to obtain a refined, deeper, "thicker" description of concerns (issues) can aid a project review process immensely. The identification of issues is important because they

1. Provide direction for the collection of specific social and economic data, rather than assessing all possible effects.
2. Ensure that the analysis is responsive to affected people.
3. Form the basis for determining whether identified effects are favorable or unfavorable from the perspective of the people affected.

4. Provide the context for the development of mitigation measures that are practical and responsive to the people affected.

In addition, as called for by Council of Environmental Quality (CEQ) regulations, my role was to "scope" issues by measuring their accuracy, distribution in the community, intensity, and duration. In conversations with local residents, I asked who else shared their concerns or if they shared the issues others had reported. In this way, I could show that some issues concerned only individuals or small groups, whereas others, like population growth rates, affected nearly everyone.

Over 130 specific issues were identified through the course of fieldwork, and those selected for illustration in this chapter include the following (Gallegos and Preister 1980a and 1980b).

Economic

We can't hold out much longer. We have maybe one good year in four and if cost of living keeps going up, we're going to have to move. (Logger)

All the firewood cutters are making it hard for us to use the forest. They park their vehicles where they get in the way and sometimes they are wrecked. (Logger)

Logging can't work with skiing. It happened in Vail and Aspen. Now people don't want to see logging trucks on their roads. Vail is raising a big stink about the lime quarry. (Logger)

We pay for fuel in a month now what used to last us for a season. Higher prices in every category of expense have not been matched by rises in cattle prices. (Rancher)

We just can't get anyone to work for us anymore. (Rancher)

A couple of times a year, we drive cattle through Eagle to get them across the Interstate. With new people, they won't be used to cattle and so we probably won't be able to do that much longer. (Rancher)

The cost of living is making it hard to stay here. Everything is expensive and most jobs don't pay that well. If we both didn't work, we couldn't make it. (Homemaker)

Quality of Life

Adam's Rib will accelerate the negative changes already occurring. We've already become more like Vail; shops are looking similar, people coming in have lots of money and are professionals who can afford to buy the land and housing. Transients are increasing. House and land prices are out of reach for normal people. (Public employee)

The family is in real trouble. Both parents work. There is no extended family to help. Even grandparents like me often work. Kids are ignored and turn to drugs or get pregnant to get out of the home. (Long-time resident)

Teacher turnover is a real morale problem. I think at least 30 out of 150 quit last year. They stay for a year or two, look around for other jobs because of the housing problems, and then quit mid-summer, leaving the District in the lurch for September. (School district employee)

Young families just don't realize how expensive it is to live here—and end up not staying long. Out of 328 students this year in the high school, 46 are new faces and 25 of them left within six months. (Teacher)

The house across the street sold four times in the last few years. How long are newcomers going to stick around? This is becoming a transient community. (Senior citizen)

Adam's Rib will bring changes at a faster rate and bigger scale. Too many people would come in. The rural atmosphere of Eagle would be lost. (Storekeeper)

Services

The town has not done their homework on water. I've been told that if all proposed water taps are hooked up, the town will be at 98 percent capacity. (Newer resident)

We're going to be drinking Adam's Rib sewage water because Eagle's drinking water source is downstream from Adam's Rib effluent release point. (Long-time resident)

The big problem is housing. If you can find it, you can't afford it. (Construction worker)

We can't afford housing anywhere else in the valley. It's getting worse and neither the county nor the businesses are looking at it. (Rural renters)

Social and Economic Analysis. The issues were used to structure the collection of social and economic data. As indicated by the examples, community members have serious questions about the economic viability of timber and agricultural activity, as well as about the effects of living factors and growth rates on people. People were concerned about how Adam's Rib would affect the type and rate of growth and the kinds of jobs generated. Moreover, residents wanted to know how the quality of life would be affected by Adam's Rib—whether transiency would become worse and whether their shops and housing would become like Vail's.

The issues were structured into assessment questions for which social and economic data were collected. For example, the concern that the project might adversely affect ranching in the area was strongly held within some social networks. Curiously, these issues were expressed not by ranchers but by recent newcomers who wanted to protect the lifestyles that had attracted them to the area. The assessment, however, revealed that the project would have minimal effects on ranching activity. Not only was the project site of limited use for ranching, but agriculture—as well as timber and logging—had already become marginal activities within the local economy and thus minimally affected the economy.

Transiency, one of the more widespread issues in the local communities, was consequently analyzed. Two types were identified. Resort transiency refers to singles and young couples who move to resort areas for the short term to take advantage of seasonal jobs, skiing, and mountain living. Although they are needed to fill resort area jobs, they cause problems for the communities by competing for scarce housing, causing a higher degree of drug involvement, and lacking commitment to community problems. Resort transiency had not been a significant factor in Lower Eagle Valley at the time of the study. The second type, displacement transiency, includes people who are forced out of the community by the high cost of living. These people may be existing residents made vulnerable by changing economic conditions, such as senior citizens, or they may be incoming residents, such as school teachers or county employees, who are valuable community members unable to stay because of the higher cost of living. The degree of transiency that could be expected for each alternative was projected in the assessment.

The remaining public issues were analyzed in a similar fashion as were the management concerns of the Joint Review Committee. These factors included the type and rate of growth, effects on jobs and business, diversity and stability in the local economy, taxes, housing, community services, education, and recreation.

Communication and Information Flow. One of the more critical roles for FUND fieldworkers was the facilitation of good information flow between individuals and groups regarding the assessment process and their own issues. For example, while working with local loggers for several weeks, I explored with them the prospects for buying out the last local mill when it closed. I communicated to the developer the loggers' interest in placing a small, portable mill on site during construction of the project. Direct communication between the two parties resulted. Although neither of these efforts resulted in formal agreements by the end of the assessment, one outcome was better relations and less hostility toward the developer. Adam's Rib was no longer blamed in logging networks for the depressed timber industry.

Similarly, many people feared that the project would further contribute to the demise of ranching in the local area. As already indicated, the assessment failed to substantiate this concern. Rather than relying on interested individuals reading the assessment, however, I actively sought out these people and informed them of the assessment results. This issue, which had threatened to become disruptive and which people had used in public meetings in past reviews, was thereby diffused.

In addition, I communicated continually with people who were strongly for or against the project, clarifying with them their issues, informing them of assessment results, and discussing possible mitigation measures. I informed these individuals about the positions of others, thus countering many stereotypes and incorrect information. The people very much in favor of the project, many of whom were members of the local Chamber of Commerce, told me, for example, that an individual from the opposition group was opposed to everything "in principle," and I countered by saying that I talked recently with that person and she was really saying something very different. I believe this constant communication flow helped reduce the emotional level of people's interactions and led to more issue-centered discussion. I think it also resulted in less polarization. Business-oriented, pro-growth people, for example, early on supported the project regardless of impacts. When informed of significant assessment results and the widespread issues of others, they were convinced that their unquestioning support of the project was not a tenable position. At the hearings, these people reiterated their support but called for mitigation measures to reduce the level of some impacts. Similarly, project opponents worked directly with our team to understand the laws that applied to the decision and used the assessment documents directly to substantiate their concerns. Although they did not give up their position, many individuals softened their language and stressed the importance of addressing negative impacts if the project was approved. Officials at the county hearings commended them for their thoroughness and well-developed positions.

Team members were careful to be sensitive to rumors and repeated phrases. The Chamber of Commerce members, for example, relied on one person for cues on their own position. This man had such a characteristic way of phrasing words that it was clear when members had been talking with him. When I spent a lot of time with him, going over the assessment, stressing the nature of certain impacts, and pointing out the importance of mitigation measures, this new language was later picked up in his social networks. It was getting "institutionalized," however temporarily, in the language of others who trusted this man. In a similar manner, the strident quality of some issues was reduced through good information and ongoing communication. People opposed to the project softened their language and acquired wording and in-formation from the assessment. Terms such as "impacts," "growth rates," "quality of life," and "mitigation measures" were heard more frequently among local residents.

Issue Resolution. The final role of the field team was issue resolution. Some issues were determined through the assessment not to be impacts of the project, such as local perceptions that the project would negatively affect ranching and logging; these issues were resolved by providing information from the assessment to the issue holders. Other issues were revealed to have substantial impacts indeed, and as these effects were documented in the assessment and people informed about the results, efforts were undertaken to resolve them through the assessment process.

Both legal and political pressures exist for mitigation efforts to reduce the level of negative impact or enhance the level of positive impact. NEPA states that mitigation measures must at least be identified, even if decisionmakers choose to ignore them. In addition, however, political pressure for mitigations varies from site to site and depends also on the specific impact.

In the case of Adam's Rib, the developer made substantial efforts to build public support for the project through voluntarily offering certain mitigation measures for issues related to water, lost recreation opportunities, road requirements, and housing. The developer offered to construct a water treatment facility jointly with the town, saving it thousands of dollars and protecting water quality. The developer also offered to deed over 800 acres that the developer owned in a drainage neighboring the project site to the U.S. Forest Service to compensate for lost recreation opportunities at the site; this move was a response to the preference of a sizable number of local residents who participated in dispersed recreation activities like hunting, hiking, backpacking, and fishing. An offer was made to the County to upgrade the present secondary road from the town of Eagle to the project site into a two-lane highway over a distance of 16 miles. The developer also agreed to construct employee housing for nearly all of the expected 5,000 person work force, although the late timing proposed for the construction would still have had significant housing impacts.

The developer did not address other more complex issues, particularly cost-of-living problems. The rate of growth accompanying the project would be high, nearly 18 percent for fifteen years for the Eagle area, and it was of wide-spread concern. Such growth would strain and very likely exceed the ability of local government to provide services as well as the ability of the existing social system to absorb newcomers. Nevertheless, the developer did not feel that it could afford to expand its fifteen-year construction schedule to slow those rates, nor was there sufficient political support in the county to force it to do so. Similarly, the problems with transiency, such as worker and teacher turnover, the presence of "ski bums," and the displacement of senior citizens and young families because of cost-of-living factors, were not addressed. Substantial housing requirements, some of which existed before the project and some of which were created beyond what the developer agreed to provide, were not brought into the decision-making.

FUND maintained a field presence from January 1980 until the decision in September 1981. During that time, the Joint Review Committee coordinated and reviewed assessment findings, reported to decision-makers about the progress of the assessment, and facilitated early discussion and agreements regarding impacts and mitigations. It also held occasional public forums. FUND personnel served as technical assistants for this effort, providing and clarifying information and promoting mitigation measures supported in the community. Each entity, however, maintained its own decision-making authority. The Forest Service, for example, had the legal requirement for the EIS; the state issued air and water quality permits; and the county had its requirements for planned unit developments (PUDs) but relied heavily on the assessment. The Forest Service, in its draft EIS (which drew directly on the SIA), approved a scaled-down version of the original proposal. Eagle County, however, rejected the proposal, citing the inconsistencies with its master plan because the developer refused to provide a four-lane highway to the site. Furthermore, agreement could not be reached with the county on the location of employee housing—on-site housing would have created another substantial urban center in the county, whereas housing in the Eagle area would significantly swell its population and service demands.

By way of postscript, HBE resubmitted its proposal late in 1982 and was granted approval by the county. This approval was given after HBE agreed to provide a four-lane highway to the site and it had purchased land next to Eagle for the construction of employee housing. Local sources contend that construction of the project is awaiting better economic conditions.

Results and Evaluation

The issue-centered approach to SIA in the Adam's Rib case had a number of advantages. As a nonprofit institution, FUND is committed to accurate ethnography. Many people commented to the field team on the quality of the reporting in the assessment documents. "I really saw my town in your report" and "It was interesting reading" were typical comments. In describing informal caretaking, we had reported on a woman who was well-known for giving senior citizens birthday gifts. This woman, whom we had never met, approached us to comment with surprise on "my own little story" in the assessment. In data analysis and in the communication process, we had a commitment not only to the developer and other members of the Joint Review Committee but also to the people actually affected by the decision. We believe that advantages to all parties result from such commitment.

Our interest in issue-centered documents led naturally to the close integration of social and economic data, an integration not often achieved in other impact assessments. In addition, citizens and affected parties were able to track their issues throughout the decision-making process both in the documents and in the ongoing communication maintained by the field team. Moreover, by acquiring good information about their interests and through reflection, individuals and social networks became prepared to cope with their changing situations, with or without the project. People acting in their own self-interest, on the basis of good information and grounded through the support of others, expedite the political process.

Shortcomings were also associated with the issue-centered approach. For such a process to be fully successful, understanding and commitment are necessary from the developer, government officials, and citizens. The differing perceptions by each of these three groups about the process employed by FUND confused the outcome to a degree.

The project developer gained noticeably from an issue-centered process by having advance information about the issues of local residents and the opportunities available to resolve them. The developer was not surprised at any point in the process by unknown issues. This allowed it lead time to prepare for responsive management. The developer might consider its interests negatively affected by the work of the field team with project opponents, but not necessarily. To begin with, the project was highly controversial, and it would have been impractical to ignore the opposition. Moreover, the listening and facilitating functions of the field team, in helping to reduce the emotional aspects of the issues, were probably helpful. Further, helping the opposition to understand the legal considerations promoted predictability in the review process so that everyone was "playing by the same rules." Public support for the project and credibility for the developer also resulted from the assistance to the developer in resolving issues prior to formal hearings. Even so, several critical issues remained unaddressed because of financial and other reasons and eroded project support among community residents and officials.

Government officials, while supporting the documents produced through this process, were threatened at times by the degree and nature of citizen contact by field team members. They seemed to feel that the only proper role of the field team was analysis and not the processual aspects such as public involvement or mediation. Inferences about "stirring things up" made it clear that some officials felt issues were being created rather than simply identified. Continuing communication with elected county officials was problematic; because information was expected to be channeled through their representative on the Joint Review Committee, communication became unwieldy and too removed for the amount and sensitive nature of the information we possessed.

Citizens were generally very supportive of the issue-centered process, especially because many felt ignored in the first review. As is typical of many development settings, however, those people in favor of the project had very little incentive to stay involved. Though contact with people in favor of the project was maintained, the people against the project were most interested in the SIA process as a vehicle for addressing their issues. As a result, we found it difficult at times to counter the perception of taking sides or of supporting a few malcontents. Nevertheless, both groups moderated their positions through this process, and both advocated mitigation measures to reduce negative impacts.

Without question, "business as usual" was changed in the process of making this decision. Those typically uninvolved became involved; impacts ignored in the previous assessment were identified and assessed; and involvement became more focused and issue centered, less characterized by emotion, personality conflicts, and politics. In general, those groups with vested interests in maintaining status quo decision-making were most threatened by the issue-centered approach.

The Anthropological Difference

The outstanding anthropological contribution to social impact assessment is the manner in which fieldworkers enter into a community, understand cultural dynamics, and translate cultural understanding to decisionmakers. Clearly an issue-centered approach to SIA is not only product oriented but process oriented. In addition to the rigor of analysis and the benefits of a scientific approach that characterize other social science approaches, it can be argued that the manner of relating is at least as important. The way in which citizen contacts are handled and the ways in which their input structures the assessment process are absolutely critical. The gathering of quantitative data then becomes technical assistance directed by citizen contact rather than the primary force in the assessment.

Other writers have noted the importance of the insider/outsider perspective in the social sciences and the value of both a qualitative and a quantitative approach in social research (Geertz 1975; Gold 1977). Some years ago, Marvin Harris (1979) distinguished between conceptual categories of information generated in social science. *Emic* categories are those people use themselves to describe their environment, whereas *etic* categories are those that describe relationships more easily discerned by objective criteria, such as by a stranger to the culture, particularly one with scientific training. In the issue-centered SIA process, both categories of data become critical for a scientifically as well as politically sound assessment. Issues in this context are the emic categories that sensitize the field team to the values, concerns, and social meanings of affected people. Quantitative data gathering, by contrast, reveals etic categories that can be verified by objective, statistical methods.

Anthropology is unique in its commitment to the emic, or insider's, point of view. This objective is accomplished by participant observation in which fieldworkers immerse themselves in the local setting, engage in local routines, and attempt to experience events as a local resident would. Participant observation adds a critical and much needed dimension to social impact assessment and mitigation. The tendency has been to use a "number crunching" or "boiler plate" approach to SIA in which a predetermined checklist of social variables is inventoried to assess impacts of specific development alternatives. Strong evidence indicates that this approach is inadequate primarily because it fails to consider the unique social conditions of each study area. Officials of local jurisdictions and federal agencies are insisting on SIAs that are practical and understandable to lay people and that provide management direction. Citizens are insisting that they participate in decisions, and they have successfully demanded SIAs that identify effects on specific individuals, groups, and communities and that do not gloss over significant impacts with statistical generalizations (Francis 1975, Kinney 1982).

An example in the Adam's Rib case is transiency. Local residents were angry that the first assessment did not include an analysis of this factor because they felt that its effects on local lifestyles were critical. The turnover in the local population was increasing because of the resort nature of the economy—higher prices, the lack of housing, and the seasonal nature of employment. High costs were forcing old people from the community; teacher turnover in schools was very high; informal caretaking was disappearing because people knew each other less— people began to rely increasingly on formal services for support such as child care and welfare; and an unstable work force increased the time and cost of worker training. People were concerned that their rural lifestyle of personal relationships and informal caretaking was being threatened by the urbanization of the county brought about by resort development. Participant observation revealed this dynamic in the community and people's concern with it long before it would have shown up statistically. This early information shaped and directed the assessment in socially responsive ways.

The concept of social network is a valuable contribution of social science and a central methodological principle in issue-centered SIA. A network is defined as an arrangement of individuals who support each other in predictable ways because of their commitment to a common purpose, their shared activities, or their similar values. Networks are the vehicle by which issues are expressed and communicated in the community.

Routine contact with informal networks of people who make up neighborhoods and communities reveals the full range of interests and concerns people have in relation to a development project. The network approach is a way to get accurate information about a project into the community and to facilitate participation of citizens in the decision-making process. Each network has gathering places for routine contact such as a home, school, cafe, or feed store. Relating with people in natural and comfortable settings improves the quality of the information received. Because it is unobtrusive, the network approach also helps reduce the emotional aspects of issues and helps people focus on their substance.

By including the question, "Who else should I talk to about this issue?" networks can be mapped out in lines (or circles) of increasing inclusiveness. Remarkable convergence occurs in a short time about respected informal leaders and the boundaries between networks. Network contact thus reveals key informal leaders in the community, appropriate communication channels for each network, and opportune times for continued contact.

Network analysis is an extension of anthropological work in small-scale societies. After Radcliffe-Brown's early and initially unheeded suggestion (1952) that social networks constitute the focus of anthropological studies, Barnes (1954) and Bott (1955) published seminal works on the subject that have stimulated a generation of research (Rogers and Kincaid 1981). This chapter shows the practical and operational utility of that research.

The final anthropological contribution is the value, if not always the practice, of citizen advocacy which has been the hallmark of anthropological tradition since its inception. The issue-centered approach outlined here has become a means to institutionalize citizen interests more effectively into public decision-making.

The issue-centered assessment process has been used in numerous development settings in the last several years. In addition to Adam's Rib, which resulted in a "no" decision during our involvement but ultimately in a "yes," two other examples are noteworthy and ended in "yes" decisions. One was the Beaver Creek Ski Area, an expansion of Vail, Colorado, in 1972 (Kent and Bailey 1973). The first social mitigations in the nation tied to a Forest Service special use permit were included in the approval of Beaver Creek. They called for the construction of employee housing and a career conversion program that helped local residents manage changes created by the rapid growth of the recreation industry. The second assessment is the Kahuku Windfarms development in Hawaii in 1982, which won the Citation Award from the American Association of Human Geographers for outstanding contribution (Casino et al. 1981). In a development setting characterized by disruption and controversy, the Kahuku Windfarms project was the first major development approved on Oahu in nearly eight years with citizen support.

Trends in the SIA field indicate a continued demand for practically oriented documents, broad-based citizen involvement, and decisions responsive to public issues. The demand for professionals capable of serving as a resource to citizens as well as to government and industry officials is growing. The approach to SIA outlined here is an effective way to respond to the growing importance of SIA in the overall EIS decision-making process.

This case study has shown that the application of anthropology in the field of social impact assessment, and in economic development generally, has processual as well as analytic aspects. Analytic components of social science contributions may include implementing a random sample survey or analyzing how economic changes will affect lifestyles or how various alternatives may affect demographic variables. Processual aspects may include a broad-based assessment of public issues, the facilitation of communication between conflicting parties, mediation regarding particular mitigation measures, or the training of corporate and agency personnel in methods of direct contact with citizens as part of an ongoing management system.

The current application of anthropology in development settings far exceeds the legal mandate for social impact assessment and includes a range of activities affecting development decisions. Corporations and government agencies are utilizing strategic planning and social trend analysis as well as social and political risk analysis. Many corporations are now developing social policy, and some have whole divisions devoted to it. FUND has implemented numerous management training programs to promote social responsiveness; these have lasted from three days to five years, they have included corporations as well as agencies and city governments, and they utilize participant observation as a central data-gathering method.

The processual demands of applied work should encourage anthropologists not to abdicate the strong qualitative and holistic tradition in favor of the quantitative priority in anthropological training advocated by some (for example, van Willigen 1982). Such an abdication will preclude our greatest contribution. The present era is characterized by greater diversity, increasing decentralization, and stronger values for self-sufficiency. Anthropologists capable of building cultural bridges between groups with differing perceptions and interests (such as corporations, governments, and citizens) will be in high demand and offer capabilities unduplicated in the social sciences.

This chapter has presented an argument for the "native's point of view," a sound position not only from an ethical standpoint but also from a practical one. Sensitivity to local interests and a professional means to accomplish it can save money, improve project design, and lead to greater long-term stability. A greater goal of applied social science could not be wished for.

References

Barnes, J. A. 1954. Class and Committees in a Norwegian Island Parish. *Human Relations* 7:39–58.

Bott, Elizabeth. 1955. Urban Families: Conjugal Roles and Social Networks. *Human Relations* 8 (4):345–84.

Casino, Eric S., Myongsum Shin, and James E. Freeman. 1981. *Kahuku Windfarm Project: Social-Economic Impact Assessment and Mitigation Measures*. Honolulu: FUND Pacific Associates.

Francis, M. 1975. Urban Impact Assessment and Community Involvement: The Case of the JFK Library. *Environment and Behavior*, September, 373–404.

Gallegos, Robert M., Jr., and Kevin Preister. 1980a. *Social Impact Assessment Adam's Rib Recreational Area Report No. 1: The Current Situation* (with James Kent and Kathi Cannan). Denver: Foundation for Urban and Neighborhood Development (FUND) Inc., March.

————. 1980b. *Impact Questions Regarding the Lower Eagle Valley: A Summary of Issues, Concerns and Opportunities to be Used in the Review of Adam's Rib Recreational Area*. Denver: Foundation for Urban and Neighborhood Development (FUND) Inc. (with the Joint Review Committee), October.

————. 1981. *A Future in Motion: Social Impact Assessment for Adam's Rib Recreational Area*. Denver: Foundation for Urban and Neighborhood Development (FUND) Inc.

Geertz, Clifford. 1975. On the Nature of Anthropological Understanding. *Amer. Scientist* 63:47–53.

Gold, Raymond M. 1977. Combining Ethnographic and Survey Research. In Kurt Finsterbusch and C. P. Wolf, eds., *Methodology of Social Impact Assessment*. Stroudsburg, Pa.: Dowden, Hutchinson and Ross.

Harris, Marvin. 1979. *Cultural Materialism: The Struggle for a Science of Culture.* New York: Vintage.

Kent, James A., and Jean Bailey. 1973. *Major Recommendations Based on Phase 1 of the FUND Descriptive Study of Redcliff, Gilman and Minturn Areas.* Denver: Foundation for Urban and Neighborhood Development (FUND) Inc.

Kinney, Everett. 1982. *Assessment of Geothermal Development Impacts on Aboriginal Hawaiians.* Hawaii: Puna Hui Ohana Organization. U.S. Department of Energy Contract No.: DE-FC03-79ET 27133.

McEvoy, James III, and Thomas Dietz. 1977. *Handbook for Environmental Planning: The Social Consequences of Environmental Change.* New York: John Wiley and Sons.

Preister, Kevin, and James A. Kent. 1984. Clinical Sociological Perspectives on Social Impacts: From Assessment to Management. *Clinical Sociology Review,* vol. 2. Also in *Social Impact Assessment Newsletter,* no. 71/72, November-December 1981.

Radcliffe-Brown, A. R. 1952. *Structure and Function in Primitive Society.* London: Oxford University Press.

Rogers, Everett M. and D. L. Kincaid. 1981. *Communication Networks: Toward a New Paradigm for Research.* New York: Free Press.

van Willigen, John. 1982. The Great Transformation? Applied Training and Disciplinary Change. *Practicing Anthropology* 4, no. 3 and 4, summer.

4 / Practicing Sociomedicine: Redefining the Problem of Infant Mortality in Washington, D.C.

Margaret S. Boone

Problem and Client

The problem was death—the highest infant death rate in the United States. In Washington, D.C., babies were dying in their first years of life at the highest rate for any large American city, and nobody could figure out why. In 1979, Washington's high infant mortality rate became a political issue in the campaign of Marion Barry, who promised to appoint a special blue ribbon committee to search for possible solutions. He won his first race and continues to head the city government— although infant mortality has proved to be a more stubborn problem than anticipated.

This chapter describes an unusual research and public policy project in effect from 1979 to 1980 that remains important in today's efforts to reduce teen pregnancy. During these years the Mayor's Blue Ribbon Committee on Infant Mortality actively reviewed the city's policies and programs for pregnant women. My work on the infant mortality problem was funded separately by the National Science Foundation (NSF), so it was first and foremost a scientific research project. However, it also included a strong effort to make research results known to political

Dr. Boone pursued the activities reported in this chapter from 1979 to 1980 while at the District of Columbia General Hospital, with support from a public service science residency grant from the National Science Foundation, OSS-791726. The views expressed in this chapter are those of the author and do not necessarily reflect those of NSF. Boone conducted a follow-up survey on the same samples of inner-city residents for the U.S. Census Bureau in 1983–1984.

participants. The result was a shift in the definition of the infant mortality problem away from a strictly medical model and toward a broader framework that included a better understanding of social and cultural behavior.

Infant mortality was a good issue for a Black mayor because Washington has one of the largest, most concentrated Black urban populations in the country. Not only was it the first U.S. city to have a population that was 50 percent Black, but it also was the first big city encountered by north-bound Black migrants from the Carolinas and Virginia during the first sixty years of the twentieth century. Washington has a strong Black middle class that thrives, as do whites, in a city that is almost recession-proof because of the federal bureaucracy. Although in many ways it is a model Black city, the indicators for its Black health problems are consistently bad.

Infant mortality in the United States is mainly a Black health problem because of the large and increasing number of disadvantaged Black women—initially Southern and rural but now more often Northern and urban—whose infants are born too soon and weigh too little to have a good chance of survival. The low-birthweight rate for Blacks is the highest of any U.S. racial or ethnic group: Black infants die at almost twice the rate of White infants. Infant mortality is a minority health issue that joins medicine, politics, demography, and health in a powerful, complex web of causation. It has been a subject for research by epidemiologists, clinicians, and sociologists but rarely by anthropologists.

Even during the year of intense effort by the mayor's blue ribbon committee to understand Washington's infant mortality problem, there was a growing conviction that the city's crisis was essentially unsolvable. This belief was founded on the premise that the problem involved large numbers of disadvantaged Black women whose health status was connected to their socioeconomic condition. No one saw their health behavior as also being culturally based and therefore able to be changed. The question for Washington, D.C., was this: If culture played a role, then what was it?

Who wanted that question answered and why? Who would sponsor complicated and controversial research to discover the possible cultural causes and solutions for infant mortality when it was much easier to continue after-the-fact medical care or social welfare as solutions? The problem was more than money; it was behavior. Who would champion policy and program change directed at behavior? As it turned out, many people favored that kind of change, but they needed solid evidence from a scientist who specialized in cultural behavior. The client who originally sponsored the sociomedical project on infant mortality in Washington, D.C., did so less because of specific concerns about infant mortality and more because of general concerns about the role of science in government decision-making in the mid-1970s.

In February 1979, I called a reporter at the *Washington Post* because I thought that I had found an issue that involved the public understanding of science in an article he had written on the city's infant mortality problem. At that time I was teaching full-time at a university, having graduated two years before with a PhD in cultural anthropology and an emphasis on urban studies and women. I wanted to direct my career into two areas: health and statistics. I reasoned that there would be money in health for at least the rest of this century and plenty of it as the baby-boom generation aged. And, I had found a funding program at the National Science Foundation (NSF) that intrigued me. It gave postdoctoral fellowships to different kinds of scientists to serve in public interest or action groups: for example, a physician in a migrant farm-workers organization in California, a chemist in an environmental group in the Midwest, and an anthropologist in an inner-city hospital.[1] The purpose of the grants was to increase public understanding of issues involving complex scientific information. NSF funded scientists in organizations in which they were not usually found and then encouraged them to make what they knew (or could find out) available to everyone involved in a particular public policy issue. The obligation was to "disseminate results widely." It was not the usual scientific research project; it required outreach.

The *Washington Post* reporter sent me to the new medical director at the city's only public hospital. It had a largely poor, Black service population and was the only acute-care facility required to provide medical care regardless of a patient's ability to pay. On the telephone to the medical director I began, "Now I know I'm calling you clear out of the blue. . . ." But he listened. Later I met with him and we developed a proposal, which was funded that spring by NSF. I spent a year and a half at the hospital trying to understand the sociocultural basis of poor maternal and infant health among inner-city Blacks and brokering that understanding to people in Washington who could change it. I completed a research project that combined a medical record review, statistical analysis (with computer facilities at Georgetown University), interviews with women whose infants had died, and, above all, daily working experience at one of the most important "community centers" for inner-city Black Washingtonians. Toward the end of my residency, the medical director and I testified together before the District Committee of the U.S. House of Representatives on the infant mortality problem in Washington, D.C., and the reporter I had talked to originally covered that hearing. This presentation began for me a long series of public speeches, meetings, reports, and public policy work on the infant mortality problem that continues at this writing. Three years after the residency, I was back at the same hospital in a follow-up study for the U.S. Census Bureau on another public policy issue involving inner-city Blacks: the undercount in the decennial census.[2]

The National Science Foundation funded my research and public service residency at the hospital. However, in the following years the clients, broadly speaking, came to include many units of federal and local government, as well as private groups like the Children's Defense Fund and the National Academy of Sciences. They and many others sought me out as part of their own work to bring down the country's embarrassingly high infant mortality rate—not only among urban Blacks but also among rural Blacks, Mexican-Americans, American Indians, and other minority and refugee groups. Ultimately, the clients for all my activities were inner-city Black women and other minority women at high risk of poor pregnancy outcome, as well as the health care providers who deliver services to them and who are themselves at high risk of chronic burnout, and finally the American taxpayers who shoulder most of the burden for poor minority health.

Process and Players

What did I do every day at an inner-city hospital that served disadvantaged Blacks? I had written a proposal broad enough to support a wide range of activities, with the overall goal of investigating the sociocultural basis of poor maternal and infant health. As I look back, I see that my role as a medical anthropologist was defined more by the requirements of other people than by myself and more by real health policy needs than by any preconceived advocacy stand of my own. Some individuals in city health and at the hospital knew what an anthropologist was; many knew what a social scientist was; and nearly everyone could relate to a college teacher. Many people in the District of Columbia were glad to see the social science perspective represented in the policy review in 1979–1980. Many felt that a sociological examination of Washington's infant mortality problem was needed. However, at that time most people still believed that medical care for newborns was about as good as anyone could do. Social and health programs were considered too expensive to be feasible for more than a handful of women. Yet, they were glad to see that the social science perspective was represented. In a positive sense, I was willingly "co-opted," and my skills were used to the maximum, especially at the hospital. For example:

1. I designed a case/control study[3] and collected all the data for it on women in two equivalent samples. I then statistically examined social, health, and medical care variables familiar to physicians and

epidemiologists. I planned interviews with women and conducted them. I supervised the research assistants who helped me. I conducted an in-depth medical record review and scoured charts for quantitative and qualitative information that would give me clues about the origins of poor maternal and infant health.

2. I served on the hospital's Internal Review Board (that year and for four more years), reviewing social and psychological research proposals submitted to the hospital, as well as medical research projects on maternal and infant care.

3. I went on rounds and to case presentations with staff psychiatrists and saw some of the effects of chronic alcoholism, poor social support, and mental illness in an inner-city Black community.

4. I spent long hours working in the Obstetrics Service, defining my sample, collecting data, talking to patients, nurses, social workers, and physicians—especially those who worked in the intensive-care nursery.

5. I became a familiar face in the medical records department and worked to maintain good relations with the staff there and with all the other support staff—secretaries, clerks, custodians, and administrative staff.

6. I almost always ate lunch in the hospital's staff cafeteria and usually sat with the physicians and administrators. I learned their problems and attitudes. I enjoyed the mixture of cultures and styles they represented. The medical officers came from all over the world, and they were eager to talk about their own reactions to the inner-city Black community they confronted.

7. Away from the hospital, I met with members of the Mayor's Blue Ribbon Committee on Infant Mortality, its representatives from the Centers for Disease Control, representatives from other hospitals, and other public and private health policy organizations, reporters, and staff at the District of Columbia health commissioner's office and at other city health programs for pregnant women. When my research results began coming in, I gave presentations on my project at the District of Columbia's health commission and the Medical Society and to academic colleagues.

The people who worked at the hospital and the people in city government and health services that I met during that time insisted on placing me within their own familiar frames of reference. In response, I constructed a set of roles—colleague, friend, investigator, teacher, mentor, and information source—that intersected with my own research needs and with my own determination to participate in the policy debate as an expert rather than as a political activist or health advocate. Above all, I remained an anthropologist—a teacher, a researcher, a writer—a scientist like the many other scientists in the hospital. That stance paid good dividends, but the entries in my log still sound like the field notes of any anthropologist going through initial culture shock. In the first month, I wrote:

> I do not find the hospital a special world because it is "Black," but because it is a hospital. I am beginning to feel like I am visiting a special village whenever I go over there. But I am beginning to feel comfortable walking down the halls. I got my hair cut. I look different, but do not don the white coat of the physician. I should try that some time just to see what difference it makes. . . .

I also had an office at Georgetown University's Center for Population Research that year, so I was constantly running back and forth between the computer and my research assistants at one end of town and data collection and fieldwork at the other end. Each day I confronted the jarring difference between rich and poor. Less than a week after I wrote the previous comment, I wrote this:

> I am finding it a relief to be over here at school for the day. Every day at the hospital is a strain. I feel a stranger, on "my best behavior," and more than anything, pushing to get the data I need. . . . Above all, I am tired. I feel overwhelmed on several fronts. I feel overwhelmed by the research angle to the project, and I feel overwhelmed by the multiplicity of roles at the hospital. . . .

But only through that working experience did I come to understand better the world that disadvantaged Black women face: the frustration, the image of limited good, the good humor and good will in the face of insurmountable obstacles, the importance of friendships with other women, and a certain laissez-faire attitude that was unavoidable sometimes when they just got too tired. These insights gave an invaluable background to the long interviews I had with women whose infants had died.

Results and Evaluation

Some of my results were expected; some were not. Some were controversial and some were not. In many cases, no one had ever thought of asking the questions I asked in the interviews.[4]

As expected, measures of previous poor pregnancy outcome (infant deaths, miscarriages), absence of prenatal care, smoking, and alcoholism characterized the women who bore low-weight infants or infants who died. However, drug abuse did not because it was high in both samples of women—those with normal-weight infants and those with low-weight infants. Previous abortions did—a controversial finding in light of the high rate of abortion in Washington, D.C. (higher than the live-birth rate in the years of my study) and the widely—if covertly—acknowledged need to provide abortion as back-up contraception.

Qualitative factors also set apart the women with small infants: psychological distress during pregnancy and hospitalization, evidence of violence (beatings and accidents) in their personal lives, ineffective contraception, and very rapidly paced child-bearing beginning in the teens. Case histories documented a "multiple-abuse syndrome" in which several harmful drugs were used together. Three-quarters of the women in all samples were unmarried at the time of delivery, and the average age for first pregnancy in all samples was eighteen years. The reproductive population was young—thus the later importance of the results in discussions of teen pregnancy.

The results of interviews were disturbing, especially the histories of chronic difficulties in the use of all forms of contraception and the number of times women had been pregnant and failed to deliver because of either miscarriage or abortion. There were no indications of planned pregnancies, although on the surface it seemed that many, many attempts were made in that direction. Attitudes toward men ranged from suspicion and manipulation to outright hostility; yet women remained romantically convinced of the desirability of the conjugal union. Men were very important in their lives for the meager emotional and financial support they managed to give. Surprisingly, mothers of women did not provide the emotional support expected, but girlfriends did. The predominant emotion toward the remembered infant death was disappointment rather than open grief. Women usually became pregnant again soon after an infant death. The attitudes toward physicians and nurses were also disturbing: The women were afraid of doctors and resented nurses who left them alone and handled them roughly.

The result that caused the greatest stir was the strong statistical relationship between alcoholism and prematurity. This finding was headlined in the *Washington Post* the day after the hearing on infant mortality in May 1980. There were many subtle, negative feelings expressed toward this finding by the hospital staff, although nothing overt. To this day, most people are convinced that heroin abuse is far more important in the District of Columbia's infant mortality picture, even though a special alcohol program began at one of the clinics (and has since closed) and public service announcements starting in the early 1980s always mention the dangers of alcohol abuse for pregnant women.

Evaluation of the results of research and public service activities is always difficult when the goals are broadly defined and the definition of achievement is abstract. To determine whether a research project has achieved a practical impact depends on the definition and measurement of "impact." I have previously noted that

> Measuring the results of an individual's or a group's involvement in a health policy issue is extremely difficult because it requires assessment of public sentiment and political trends whose origins are complex. It is easier to trace bureaucratic efforts, such as a decision to change a regulation or fund a program. To a degree, the impact of my participation in the infant-mortality debate in Washington, D.C. can be determined by asking some questions:
>
> Do public health policy makers show any interest in research results? Were congressional testimony and scientific papers picked up by the national and local press? Have any research results sparked public debate and strong reaction? Do privately funded policy reviews quote and publish the results? Do health planning agencies request detailed information for their use in policy recommendations? Is the definition of the problem, as gauged by newspaper coverage and private contacts, changing from a strictly medical model? . . . The answer to all . . . is yes. (Boone 1985:120)

More specifically, the change toward a sociomedical redefinition of the infant mortality problem is evident from the comments returned to me on evaluation forms that I sent to major policy participants right after my residency at the hospital in 1981. A physician from the Centers for Disease Control observed that

> The infant mortality problem in the District is well known yet little concerted action has been undertaken. Dr. Boone's work is of high quality and has helped to focus much of the recent discussion concerning possible approaches. She has used the innovative position of an anthropologist on a hospital staff well, both in the quality and impact of her work and in her choice of issues, i.e., one with social, medical and anthropological facets.

A statistician in the District of Columbia's government—who made available to me the city death certificate data so I could track the deaths of infants born at the hospital—noted the following: "Dr. Boone did a very thorough study, made excellent use of the Division's data, and contributed significantly to our understanding of the causes of infant mortality. The anthropological approach was much needed—opened new perspectives." The District of Columbia's health commissioner in 1981 wrote:

I have been aware of Dr. Boone's efforts and have been most impressed with her enthusiasm and commitment to the project. I believe that her findings will contribute greatly to the formulation of strategies designed to reduce the infant mortality rate in the District of Columbia. In particular, it has surfaced a number of misconceptions that have been widely held pertaining to the specific make-up and behavior patterns of maternity patients at greatest risk.

The chief of psychiatry at the hospital said this:

Dr. Boone's research at the hospital has been extremely useful in giving the physicians a better understanding of the social characteristics of their patients and thus allowing for a more comprehensive and holistic approach to patient care. Dr. Boone was especially helpful to the Department of Psychiatry as she contributed significantly to the development of our educational program and brought new insights into our understanding of psychopathology and patient care. Dr. Boone's understanding of the social and cultural aspects of normality, pathology, and patient care was appreciated by staff members, psychiatric residents, and medical students, alike.

Equally important was a note written at the bottom of a letter I received five years later in 1986, inviting me to a reception at one of the private programs for maternity care now in Washington, D.C. Its director wrote: "Come see! After all, you helped shape the Program! The head of NICHHD will be another speaker [along with the Mayor]." However, more significant than any of these comments was a statement sent to me by one of the women I interviewed. When asked if she had learned anything in the interview, she wrote: "I learn that Many Dr. or a wear of How uncomfortable I am after Heving 1. Abortions 1. Stillbirths 3. miscarraige one Live son Bore Blue."

The Anthropological Difference

The infant mortality project relied on a broad segment of the literature and a wide range of methods. However, from beginning to end it was based on my background in anthropology. This approach can be seen most clearly in four areas: (1) the design and analysis of the interviews with women who had infant deaths, (2) the selection of some variables and derivation of others for quantitative and qualitative analysis, (3) the reliance on my working experience at the hospital to understand better the sociocultural basis for infant mortality among inner-city Blacks, and (4) the use of information brokerage to satisfy the requirements of the original client.

The Interview Difference

A broad understanding of natality, human reproduction, population dynamics, and social structures to support pregnant women can all be gained from any good introductory coursework in cultural and physical anthropology. It is surprising that this understanding has not yet been widely applied to the sociomedical problems of inner-city Blacks— problems such as high rates of infant mortality, childhood disease, teen pregnancy, drug abuse and alcoholism, homicide, and accidents. The best work in practicing anthropology in the maternal and child health area has been carried out among Mexican-Americans in California and Texas and in developing countries. The ethnographic and theoretical work on inner-city Black culture is far from complete, but it is not insubstantial. In fact, two ethnographies are specifically devoted to Washington, D.C., Blacks, mostly males: Liebow 1967 and Hannerz 1969. Fieldwork in other cities such as Chicago has given rise to fascinating, in-depth explorations of Black male ethos (Keiser 1969). Anthropological understanding of Black females is more often restricted to rural or Southern groups, except for the excellent extensive work by Snow (1974, 1977, 1978) and the classic study by Stack (1974).

Using these works and others by sociologists Ladner (1971), Rainwater (1960, 1965, 1966), and Seeman (1959), I developed a large set of YES/ NO response items to explore the attitudes and beliefs of women who had suffered infant deaths. I pretested them on obstetric inpatients at the hospital and conducted a final set of interviews with women who had lost their infants. No one had thought of asking them about their feelings of alienation (expressed in familiar idom), their attitudes toward men and children, their feelings about the rightness or wrongness of contraception,and their abstract conceptions of birth, death, and lifecycle. I also asked them about their pregnancy histories: each time they had been pregnant, the type of contraception they used between pregnancies, and the outcome of each pregnancy. Questions on their familiarity with contraceptive forms were adapted from the World Fertility Survey, with the substitution of "partner" for "husband." The former term seemed more appropriate in a community where 75 percent of the women are not legally married at the time of delivery. Finally, I asked them about their social relationships and psychological state during pregnancy.

Interview results—in combination with the review of secondary sources and the statistical analysis—gave a historical portrait of the reproductive lives of inner-city Black women. It brought into sharper focus what the medical records had only outlined: the women's rapidly paced pregnancies and chronic difficulty in carrying an infant to term because of abortion, miscarriage, or other poor pregnancy outcome.

Taken together their stories were revealing and disturbing, but they had a certain internal consistency. They were understandable in light of the women's histories of poor interpersonal relationships, substance abuse, anxiety and depression, and some of their cultural values and conceptions. For example, the following cultural factors may well play a role in their reproductive lives: a belief in a birth for every death; a high value placed on children; a value on gestation without necessarily any causal or sequential understanding of the children it will produce; a lack of planning ability; distrust of both men and women; and a separation of men's roles from the process of family formation (Boone 1985). The integration of all aspects of their histories within the context of their attitudes and beliefs represents one important element of the anthropological difference in the infant mortality project. The resulting portraits have an ethnographic quality of compelling realism that has been useful in policy-related work.

The power of this type of material in public policy work should not be underestimated, especially if it is presented along with quantitative data and alongside statistical tests of variables that are more familiar to practitioners in the field—in this case, physicians and epidemiologists. Presentation of ethnographic material by itself is not particularly useful in policy-related work because it looks so unusual. It can confuse other practitioners or simply look foolish. Similarly, the use of terms with good, reliable meanings for anthropologists—but emotional overtones for nonscientists—can be counterproductive and "turn off" a non-anthropologist bureaucrat or policymaker. I used terms like "population regulation" and "infanticide" in my congressional testimony but would not use them again in that context. In the infant mortality project, most material—especially the case histories based on interviews, medical records, autopsy reports, and death certificates—had to be presented with a dry, scientific style or it could easily be seen as sensationalist. The right balance between scientific report styles can sometimes be achieved by clearly demarcating (with "boxes" or italicized blocks of text) which sections of writing are reporting and which are ethnographic.

A Difference in Variable Selection

The anthropological difference in the infant mortality project was also evident in more fundamental ways such as the choice of variables for transcription and analysis. A background in anthropology shifted the focus of the infant mortality project from medical care to health and social factors known to be related to health. However, I was careful to use variables that have already been proved to be related to infant mortality, as well as new and more experimental kinds of variables.

For example, I took pains to note whether each woman had any prenatal care (from a medical history form in her chart) and how many years of education she had (from the birth certificate worksheet). Both are known to affect pregnancy outcome in the general U.S. population. In this inner-city community, I found that prenatal care was indeed significantly related to pregnancy outcome but years of education were not. Use of these variables made the results appear familiar to physicians and epidemiologists. In this context they were willing to consider other variables based on anthropological and sociological theory.

For example, the concept of a woman's source of social support was operationalized from notes on the responsible person she listed on hospital admission. An analysis of stability of social support was possible by examining the responsible person for three hospital admissions (in the follow-up survey). Similarly, residential stability was analyzed by examining three consecutive addresses over a six to seven year period. The hypothesis that stability of lifestyle and social support affects pregnancy outcome comes directly from studies in the sociology and anthropology of health. The notion that disadvantaged women may receive less support from society during pregnancy comes straight from the theory of social stratification, as well as from physical anthropology, which clearly demonstrates among nonhuman primates that a female's status affects her offspring's chances of survival.

The Difference Experience Makes

No matter how sophisticated the statistical analysis or the construction of the interview instrument, my basic understanding of reproduction in an inner-city Black community comes from daily working experience at the "community center" for birth and death—the hospital. It is a large, complex institution, much like the small society pictured in other anthropological studies of hospitals. It is a symbol for inner-city Black residents, but it also represents the larger society in many of their dealings with it. It serves as a conduit for knowledge and action, connecting disadvantaged Blacks with networks at other levels of medicine and society. Thus, the hospital serves the dual function of community center and cultural broker for the larger society, much the same way that the church and priest serve as brokers for peasants in the villages of developing countries.

Because of the complexity and intensity of the inner-city hospital's functions, I was able to talk with a large number of inner-city Blacks and hospital employees about their experiences and attitudes. Every working day was an experience in classic participant observation—one of the very few sources of ethnographic information. Because of the multicultural nature and the multiple social classes of the staff, I was constantly forced to make more than Black/White and rich/poor comparisons. I saw a wide range of styles and mechanisms for coping with fatigue, burn-out, and material shortages and with people from other cultures and classes. Not all of it was attractive or flattering, but it was all comprehensible and it was all set in sharp relief by the inevitable crisis nature of much of the action at an acute-care facility. Among staff, patients, and physicians, an anthropologist in an inner-city hospital can see people at their worst and at their sterling best. My year and a half of experience at the hospital made the largest anthropological difference.

Science Brokerage

Anthropological knowledge of culture and class brokerage confers an enormous advantage in disseminating results widely—the original requirement of my NSF grant. Knowledge of sociocultural sensitivities can aid information exchange by helping an anthropologist know, for example, when to make research results known to the press or to a political leader; when to leak or suggest a result so that more information will be requested officially; when to write a thank-you letter or make a keep-in-touch call with an important information source; and above all, when to keep one's results under wraps. The type of scientific information anthropologists can offer is extremely valuable when couched in terms that are acceptable to the public and to political players. If, as an anthropologist, you become convinced that part of your obligation to society is to disseminate your research results widely, then it makes good sense to use the principles of social interaction that you know to do the best, most helpful job possible in brokering that knowledge.

The Rewards of Successful Practice

Now, seven years after the infant mortality issue emerged in Washington, D.C., medicine seems to have done about all it can. The infant mortality rate has fallen but still remains the highest in the country. The neonatal mortality rate (in the first twenty-eight days of life) has also fallen but principally because of improved care in the newborn, intensive-care nurseries of the city's hospitals. The low-birthweight and fetal death rates—which reflect maternal lifestyle—remain steady and high (Fig. 4.1). So the social scientists and the social engineers are now being listened to as never before. It has been a hard-fought battle to redefine Washington's maternal and infant health problem as sociomedical rather than strictly medical and as sociocultural rather than simply and overwhelmingly socioeconomic. Changes toward this definition of the problem began to speed up back in 1979 but should have begun much sooner.

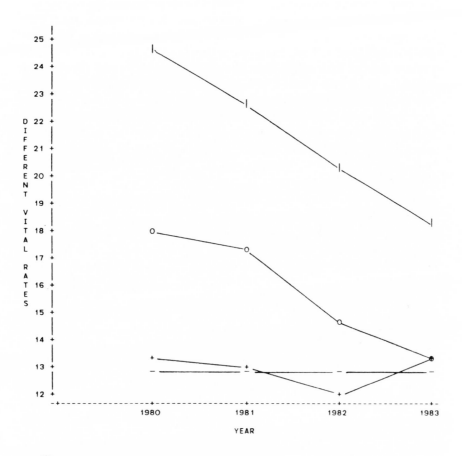

(|) Infant deaths per 1000 live births.

(0) Neonatal deaths per 1000 live births.

(+) Fetal deaths per 1000 deliveries.

(_) Low birthweight deliveries given as a percent of all live births.

FIGURE 4.1 Infant, neonatal, and fetal mortality rates, and low birthweight rate, District of Columbia, 1980–1983.

As had been evident for a long time in the lives and health behavior of disadvantaged Black women, socioeconomic status and culture have combined in ways that have hindered health progress.

The results of the project on infant mortality in Washington, D.C., have been good. Policies and programs have changed and sociomedical explanations have been adopted—if only by default after a strictly medical model was exhausted. But the option had been provided. A different, more complicated definition of the infant mortality problem was available and waiting when the overreliance on medical solutions was finally acknowledged slowly over the past seven years. After high-tech equipment had been provided and staffs trained, the infant mortality and low-birthweight rates were still high, and people were anxious to find other solutions. In Washington, D.C., we are slowly beginning to understand which social and cultural characteristics are connected to poor Black health in the inner city, and from that understanding, service delivery solutions are emerging.

Notes

1. The research and public service project described here was funded as a Public Service Science Residency from the National Science Foundation's Office of Science and Society, Grant No. OSS-7917826. The views expressed in this report are those of the author and do not necessarily reflect those of NSF. The Office of Science and Society is no longer in existence.

2. This was the "Inner-City Hospital Feasibility Study," which I directed at the U.S. Census Bureau in 1983–1984.

3. A case/control study statistically compares cases (usually of a disease, condition, or other health factor) with equivalent controls (which have an absence of the disease, condition, or factor) to determine correlative (and hypothetically causal) factors.

4. A limited number of copies of the Attitudes and Beliefs Section of the interview schedule is available from Margaret S. Boone at GAO/PEMD, Washington, D.C. 20548.

References

Boone, Margaret S. 1982. A Socio-Medical Study of Infant Mortality Among Disadvantaged Blacks. *Human Organization* 41(3):227–236.

_____ . 1985. Social and Cultural Factors in the Etiology of Low Birthweight among Disadvantaged Blacks. *Social Science and Medicine* 20(10):1001–1011.

_____ . 1985. Policy and Praxis: Anthropology and the Domestic Health Policy Arena. In Carole E. Hill, ed., *Training Manual in Medical Anthropology*. American Anthropological Association Special Publication no. 18, pp. 111–129.

Boone, Margaret S., and S. A. Roman. 1980. Statement Before the Subcommittee on Fiscal Affairs and Health of the Committee on the District of Columbia, U.S. House of Representatives, Ninety-Sixth Congress, 2nd Session, May 7, Serial No. 96-15, pp. 29–32.

Colen, B. D. 1980. Alcoholism, Premature Births, Linked in Study at D.C. General. *Washington Post*, p. B7, May 8.

Hannerz, Ulf. 1969. *Soulside*. New York: Columbia University Press.

Keiser, R. Lincoln. 1969. *The Vice Lords*. New York: Holt, Rinehart and Winston.

Ladner, Joyce A. 1971. *Tomorrow's Tomorrow*. New York: Doubleday.

Liebow, Elliot. 1967. *Tally's Corner*. Boston: Little, Brown.

Rainwater, Lee. 1960. *And the Poor Get Children*. Chicago: Quadrangle Books.

———. 1965. *Family Design*. Chicago: Aldine.

———. 1966. *The Crucible of Identity*. *Daedalus* 95(2):783–791.

Seeman, Melvin. 1959. On the Meaning of Alienation. *American Sociological Review* 24:783–791.

Snow, Loudell F. 1974. Folk Medical Beliefs and Their Implications for Care of Patients. *Annals of Internal Medicine* 81:82–96.

Snow, Loudell F., and Shirley M. Johnson. 1977. Modern Day Menstrual Folklore. *Journal of the American Medical Association* 237(25):2736–2739.

Snow, Loudell F., Shirley M. Johnson, and Harry E. Mayhew. 1978. The Behavioral Implication of Some Old Wives' Tales. *Obstetrics and Gynecology* 51(6):727–732.

Stack, Carol B. 1974. *All Our Kin*. New York: Harper and Row.

5 / The International Sorghum/Millet Research Project

Edward C. Reeves, Billie R. DeWalt, and Kathleen M. DeWalt

Problem and Client

Sorghum and millet are important food grains in many lesser developed countries (LDCs); yet the socioeconomic constraints on their production and use are poorly understood. This chapter describes the contribution of a group of economic and ecological anthropologists based at the University of Kentucky to a multilateral agricultural research project sponsored by the U.S. Agency for International Development (AID). Our special contribution has been to study the farming systems of small-scale, limited-resource agricultural producers who are highly dependent on sorghum and millet as food.

In response to the so-called New Directions Mandate passed by Congress in 1975, AID created a number of collaborative research support programs (CRSPs). These CRSPs are long-term, multidisciplinary research efforts primarily organized around staple commodities and are collaborative with LDCs. Because of the great importance of sorghum and millet as food grains in some of the poorest countries of the world, the second CRSP created was the International Sorghum/Millet Research Project, or INTSORMIL. The project involves a consortium of eight U.S. land grant universities formed to undertake the task of improving the worldwide production and utilization of sorghum and millets. The participating institutions were selected on the basis of a competitive submission of proposals in one or more of the following areas: plant breeding, agronomy, plant pathology, plant physiology, food chemistry, and socioeconomic studies. Our responsibility at the University of Kentucky was to use the field research techniques of the anthropologist to gain first-hand knowledge of the socioeconomic constraints on the production, distribution, and utilization of sorghum and millets in selected areas of the world.

The lion's share of INTSORMIL's research budget has gone to support technical agricultural research; only a small proportion of funds has been allocated to support social science research. The University of Kentucky received only minimal support for its participation in INTSORMIL at the beginning of the project (July 1979), but by 1984 its budget had grown to about $200,000 per year as respect for our input grew.

The first year or two were somewhat frustrating for INTSORMIL institutions and scientists because AID missions in LDCs were hesitant to surrender some of their turf to allow CRSP entities to establish working relationships. This problem arose because of the dual structure of AID. In the past, AID missions were accustomed to supervising projects of their own proposing, whereas the CRSPs were creatures of AID headquarters in Washington, D.C. The unprecedented nature of the CRSPs caused some confusion, therefore, and some time was required to assuage uncertainty of mission officials. The first AID mission to allow an INTSORMIL team to visit was in Sudan. In November 1980, Ed Reeves was a member of the team that established a working relationship with USAID mission Sudan, the University of Khartoum, the Western Sudan Agricultural Research Project, and the Agricultural Research Corporation of the Government of Sudan. Similarly, Bill DeWalt was a member of the team that visited Honduras in March 1981. This trip ultimately led to an agreement with the Ministry of Natural Resources and the Honduran Institute of Anthropology and History. These agreements made it possible for INTSORMIL scientists to begin research operations within LDCs. This project was extremely important because the promotion of in-country, collaborative research was the objective when the CRSP was created.

In both cases the negotiations revealed that government officials and agricultural scientists were anxious to benefit the poorer farmers in their countries but had little understanding of the goals and constraints characteristic of limited-resource farming systems. A major provision in both agreements authorized University of Kentucky anthropologists to begin field studies of farming systems in the two countries. Simply stated, the objectives of the anthropologists were (1) to obtain an understanding of the immediate and long-term constraints faced by farming families in areas of southern Honduras and the western Sudan where reliable information on this was lacking and (2) to communicate the findings to INTSORMIL as well as to scientists and government officials in the host countries in ways that would most effectively direct research and development efforts.

The perspective adopted—that of farming systems research (FSR)—is a holistic approach to determining the techniques limited-resource farmers use to cope with the social, economic, and ecological conditions under which they make a living.[1] FSR can be distinguished from conventional applied agricultural research because it does not focus on single crops or types of livestock and because it is not concerned with isolated agricultural constraints such as a type of pest or disease. Instead, FSR is a holistic view of how farm production enterprises' (different crops and livestock) are integrated and managed as a system. It also attempts to relate farm productivity to household consumption and off-farm sources of family income—issues rarely addressed in conventional production-oriented research. FSR has been hailed as a breakthrough for dealing with the problems of farmers whose marginal financial and biophysical resources have left them unable to take advantage of the many technological advances in modern agriculture. Moreover, we chose the FSR perspective because it is looked upon favorably by agricultural development agencies and because it serves to translate the anthropological perspective on human adaptation into terms familiar to agricultural scientists.

Process and Players

The anthropologists at the University of Kentucky participating in INTSORMIL include the authors, who are the principal investigators, and a number of graduate students. Collectively we identified ourselves as the Farming Systems Research (FSR) Group. The primary interest of the Kentucky FSR Group has been to conduct socioeconomic studies of the production, distribution, and nutritional systems of selected parts of the world in which sorghum and millets are important food grains for humans. The purposes of this research have been (1) to identify the principal constraints on increased production of these grains, thus identifying priorities and directions for agricultural research efforts; (2) to identify the perceived needs of farmers regarding the aspects of new technology that might be of greatest benefit to them; (3) to suggest how new varieties and/or technologies might most easily and beneficially be introduced into communities and regions; and (4) to suggest the long-term implications that changing production, distribution, and consumption patterns might have on these communities.

Two primary means that we use to accomplish our aims are cultural brokering and good ethnographic field research on the client as well as on the farmers and their setting. The most productive agricultural research efforts come about when there is constant dialogue between the farmer, who can tell what works best given the circumstances, and agricultural scientists, who produce potentially useful new solutions to old problems. For agricultural research to be effective, therefore, the lines of communication must be open between farmer and scientist, but this is often difficult to achieve because the farmer and the scientist speak different languages, literally and figuratively. A major part of the FSR Group's role has been to learn the conceptual systems and languages of both the farmers and agricultural scientist collaborators so the beginnings of a dialogue may be established between the two.

To realize these objectives the FSR Group has established close relations not only with INTSORMIL agricultural scientists and with the farmers in developing countries but also with government agencies, research organizations, international agricultural research centers, and multilateral and bilateral assistance agencies.

Projects in Sudan and Honduras

In June 1981, members of the FSR Group began research in the el-Obeid region of the western Sudan and in southern Honduras. In Sudan Ed Reeves was the field director of a team that included an American PhD student (Tim Frankenberger) and several Sudanese university students who were research assistants. This fourteen-month project was undertaken in cooperation with the Agricultural Research Corporation and the Western Sudan Agricultural Research Project. These organizations were building several agricultural experiment stations in the western region and had asked for baseline studies of current farming practices, markets, and infrastructure. To fulfill these obligations we did participant-observation and in-depth interviewing in eighteen villages prior to survey interviewing 166 limited-resource farmers and fifty-eight village merchants and middlemen. Bill DeWalt directed the field research in southern Honduras in which six anthropology graduate students and a number of Honduran research assistants worked for various periods during 1982–1984.

The goals of both field research efforts have been to understand the existing farming systems in these two regions and to determine the principal constraints that would have to be overcome to allow the farmers to be more productive and achieve a more secure livelihood. The main assumption guiding both projects was that the INTSORMIL agricultural scientists, who are generally acknowledged among the best sorghum and millet researchers in the world, would be better able to direct their research efforts if they were made aware of the numerous difficulties faced by LDC farmers. These scientists were unaware of many of the problems because they had not spent much time working on LDC problems and the unique nature of limited-resource farming; their previous efforts had been more directed to solving the problems of the relatively affluent sorghum and millet farmers in the United States.

Five technical reports were published in the years 1981 to 1984: three on Sudan (Reeves and Frankenberger 1981, 1982; Reeves 1984) and two on Honduras (DeWalt and DeWalt 1982; Thompson et al. 1983). These studies contained detailed descriptions of the agricultural, marketing, and nutritional conditions in the research areas and made recommendations for the initiation of host country programs and new thrusts for INTSORMIL research. Realizing that we were providing important, relevant information, INTSORMIL and the collaborating institutions in Sudan and Honduras started to commit additional personnel and resources to bolster the research effort with biotechnical expertise. And our role expanded somewhat from one of strictly conducting research to one of making sure that collaborating agricultural scientists understood how local farmers view their opportunities and constraints.

In early 1982, an INTSORMIL plant breeder was posted to the experiment station at La Lujosa in southern Honduras. The Ministry of Natural Resources (MRN) of the government of Honduras assigned a counterpart breeder, a breeder in training, and an agronomist to the project. Vehicles and other equipment in short supply were also committed. The experiment station has gradually been transformed from being overgrown by weeds to a productive research facility. Research goals for the scientists focus on the farmers' needs and constraints that were identified by the DeWalts and their research team. These include sorghums that can be intercropped, that have good food quality in the grain and good forage quality in the stalk, and that are resistant to damage by grain weevils when stored. The scientists have adopted as specific goals the breeding of varieties (as opposed to hybrids) because varieties fit better into the intercropping system of hillside farmers (see DeWalt and DeWalt 1982). Varieties generally have a higher tolerance than hybrids for the conditions usually associated with marginal farming. They are better adapted for intercropping (simultaneously planting more than one crop in the same hole), planting on hillsides or in low-fertility soils, midseason drought, and resisting weeds. Finally, the use of varieties does not require the establishment of a national seed supply business.

Similarly, in 1982 an INTSORMIL agronomist was assigned to the newly constructed experiment station at el-Obeid, Sudan. The Western Sudan Agricultural Research Project, the Sudan Agricultural Research Corporation, and the Kordofan Regional Extension Service assigned counterparts and collaborators to the station. Again, work focused on the factors identified as important to farmers in our reports—drought tolerance; intercropping; early maturing varieties of sorghum and pearl millet; labor-saving technologies for the operations of land preparation, planting, and weeding; control of the *senta* (a damaging insect pest about which very little is known); bird resistance; fodder quality of sorghum stover and construction quality (for houses and fences) of millet in the stalk; and the extremely limited financial resources of the area's farmers (see Reeves and Frankenberger 1981, 1982).

In both Sudan and Honduras our long-term field studies made it clear that, although INTSORMIL scientists could provide important backup work with their research on experiment stations in the United States, this style of research, which is preferred by U.S. scientists, did not take sufficient cognizance of local constraints. Real progress in addressing the needs of small farmers in the Third World called for promising innovations to be tested at village sites and on farmers' fields under conditions that closely approximated those which the farmers experience.

Our FSR group's role expanded a second time to include the negotiation of collaborative agreements and involvement in the planning and bud-geting process of INTSORMIL. INTSORMIL is required to engage in collaborative research with institutions in LDCs. As a consequence, the negotiation of agreements with collaborating institutions is a key to the success of the program.

Bill DeWalt was the principal negotiator and signed the agreements between INTSORMIL and the Ministry of Natural Resources of the Government of Honduras, the Honduran Institute of Anthropology and History, and the Interamerican Institute for Cooperation on Agriculture (Costa Rica). He was also involved in negotiations with the Tropical Agronomic Center for Research and Teaching (CATIE in Costa Rica) and the Universidad Autonoma Metropolitana in Mexico. Ed Reeves was a principal figure in negotiations for INTSORMIL's collaborations with the University of Khartoum, the Agricultural Research Corporation, the Sudan Ministry of Agriculture, the Western Sudan Agricultural Research Project, and the millet/sorghum breeding programs of the International Crop Research Institute for the Semi-Arid Tropics (ICRISAT) in Sudan.

In all the negotiations we as anthropologists shouldered the respon-sibility of representing the interests of small, limited-resource farmers. To do this effectively we had to understand and transpose between three subcultural settings: the goals and adaptive strategies of the farmers themselves, the bureaucratic setting of policymakers in the host countries, and the unique subculture of agricultural scientists with its long-standing bias toward solutions to agricultural production problems that are unsuited to the capacities of limited-resource farmers.

The FSR Group has also been involved in policy-making for INT-SORMIL since Bill DeWalt was elected a member of the Technical Committee in 1982. The six-member Technical Committee is elected by the more than fifty principal investigators of the consortium. The Technical Committee is the main policy-making and budget-making entity of INTSORMIL. In 1983, DeWalt was elected chairperson of this group. In this capacity, he represented INTSORMIL (along with the project director) in a wide variety of contexts. Despite being the only social scientist on the Technical Committee, DeWalt has received the respect of the agricultural scientists—further evidence of the good reputation which the FSR Group has achieved in INTSORMIL. As chairperson DeWalt was able to influence the selection of countries in which INTSORMIL worked, the level of funding for projects, and the creation and implementation of goals for INTSORMIL that would have the greatest benefit for the small farmer. As an example of his effective leadership, DeWalt argued for the importance of looking at the relationship between small farmers, nutrition, and sorghum production in Mexico. Mexico is considered by AID and UN experts as falling outside the category of a "poor country." Yet, DeWalt had firsthand knowledge of the impoverishment of small-scale Mexican farmers and was able to demonstrate the impact that a short-sighted sorghum policy would have not only in Mexico but elsewhere in Central America. His research indicated that sorghum production was gradually displacing the traditional food crop, maize. The problem was that sorghum was not going to be used for human food, even though malnourishment is common in the rural population; instead, it was being grown as feed for poultry and swine, in order to supply less expensive meat to urban middle-class consumers and even to the United States because of a profitable export market.

Results and Evaluation

Largely because of our studies of farming systems INTSORMIL and the Honduran and Sudanese governments have allocated more resources to projects earmarked to help limited-resource farmers. In Honduras, the DeWalts and INTSORMIL were responsible for revitalizing the sorghum program of the National Program of Agricultural Investigations (PNIA). An agricultural experiment station was essentially rebuilt, and the Honduras Ministry of Natural Resources allocated staff to it to work in collaboration with INTSORMIL investigators. The research results of the anthropologists in Honduras are guiding the breeding efforts of the INTSORMIL and Ministry of Natural Resource breeders.

In Sudan, the farming systems study provides a baseline for planning research being undertaken at the new agricultural experiment station at el-Obeid. An INTSORMIL agronomist was posted to el-Obeid because of the success of the diagnostic analysis carried out by the FSR Group. The agronomist arrived before we left the field so we were able to introduce him to local leaders and help him make arrangements for housing, a vehicle, mail service, and similar necessities. By participating in our final survey of farmers he established rapport in the villages and gained firsthand experience with local farming conditions as well as with the difficult field logistics that face agricultural research in the Western Sudan.

Increasing the productivity and welfare of limited-resource farmers is a long-term proposition. It is too soon to demonstrate gains in sorghum or millet production and utilization in either Sudan or Honduras as a result of the redirected research efforts that have been helped along by the FSR Group. Nevertheless, INTSORMIL scientists are clearly coming to accept the farming systems research goals and the value of anthropological fieldwork. The FSR Group, in publications and personal contacts with agricultural scientist collaborators, has argued that on-site research is both desirable and necessary for the problems of farmers to be correctly identified and that eventually on-farm testing of new plant varieties and technologies will be essential to ensure that farmers are going to accept them. This change in perspective should enable INTSORMIL scientists to conduct research directly relevant to the needs and capacities of small farmers in these two areas of the world.

There are several indications that the information collected by the FSR Group has been beneficial: As a result of baseline work by the University of Kentucky anthropologists, INTSORMIL (in collaboration with organizations in Sudan and Honduras) has begun funding long-term breeding and agronomic research in both countries, with the emphasis on alleviating farmer constraints. In Sudan, for example, two of the main priorities are intercropping and stand establishment (improving the successful germination and growth of the crop under adverse conditions). These considerations were determined to be highly significant from the farmers' perspective of ensuring adequate yields with the least expenditure of labor. It is anticipated in this case that agricultural research will have the greatest benefit for the farmers in developing early-maturing varieties of sorghum and pearl millet and of low-cost, labor-saving technologies adapted to the practice of intercropping. In Honduras, INTSORMIL research is centered on modifying the existing varieties of sorghum (as opposed to introducing hybrids or other exotic materials). Sorghums currently grown there have excellent food quality characteristics and fit into an intercropping system with maize that is well adapted to the bimodal rainfall pattern. Better yielding local varieties are the answer for steep-slope farmers.

The Anthropological Difference

Farming systems research is a methodology in search of a theory. We found it to be highly compatible with cultural ecology, a theoretical perspective familiar to anthropologists. Thus, to give FSR method a theoretical grounding and to reap the benefits it would provide by generating hypotheses about the nature of limited-resource farming systems, we operationalized a number of important concepts drawn from cultural ecology theory. In particular, John Bennett's concept of adaptive strategies—"specific acts with a predictable degree of success, which are selected by the individual in a decision-making process"— has been used extensively to identify variations in farm management and household decision-making as central concerns for the study of farming systems.[2] Thus, the coping mechanisms of farm families have been described as agricultural strategies (B. DeWalt), marketing strategies (Reeves), and nutritional strategies (K. DeWalt). Studying the decision-making of farmers in these respects has helped to identify some of the most significant constraints in farming systems: uncertain rainfall, low soil fertility, and limitations on farm labor and financial resources. For example, in Sudan the FSR group identified a critical trade-off confronting the poorest third of farmers. During the cropping season a poor farmer faces the choice of expending labor in weeding his or her own fields versus weeding someone else's for a wage. The first option satisfies long-term food requirements of the family but at the expense of more immediate hunger.

In addition to the decision-making of individuals, the FSR Group is also interested in the longer-term adaptation of farming systems. In both Sudan and Honduras, the decision-making of farmers appears to be at odds with the long-term sustainability of the resource base. In Sudan, the short-term adaptive strategies that farmers find necessary to follow have been shown to exacerbate desertification (Frankenberger 1983). In Honduras, the strategies followed by the larger farmers are seen to lead to a shortening of fallowing periods and deforestation (B. DeWalt 1983). In sum, the FSR Group has used the cultural ecology perspective to understand both the short-term microlevel behavior of individuals and the long-term macrolevel evolution of the farming systems under study. Our theoretical perspective allowed us to make recommendations for research and policy that were based on both considerations.

Agricultural research and policy-making typically rely upon highly quantified studies over a rather narrow range of concerns. We knew that we would have to produce quantified results for our studies to have credibility for agricultural scientists and policymakers. At the same time, being anthropologists we felt that the interests of most agricultural researchers in the strictly biotechnical and economic aspects of farm production and marketing[3] left out a lot of important determinants of human behavior and adaptation. We therefore attempted to make quantitative assessments of farmer enterprises and strategies and then went the extra step to fit these into an understanding of social and cultural conditions. To accomplish this feat our research methods entailed a mixture of traditional anthropological approaches—participant observation and in-depth interviewing of key informants to identify local features of culture—with quantitative survey techniques focused upon farming enterprises and marketing. Moreover, in both Sudan and Honduras research objectives necessitated studying heterogeneous villages in order to highlight complex regional processes and needs.

Without the input of anthropologists INTSORMIL would not have the benefit of detailed field studies of sorghum/millet farmers in Sudan and Honduras. Lacking these studies INTSORMIL agricultural scientists would not have an understanding of small farmer rationality and constraints to guide their research into needed channels. The usefulness of the anthropological studies to the agricultural scientists was enhanced by the cultural ecology perspective. This theoretical approach permits the circumstances of small farmers to be conceptualized as heterogeneous systems of human-plant-animal relationships embedded in frameworks of environmental and socioeconomic possibilities as well as constraints. Perhaps the most important lesson that a cultural ecology approach teaches is that limited-resource farmers are not all alike. Much of the failure to date of agricultural research in the LDCs can be attributed to an insensitivity to this fact. Research that has aimed at the mythical "average farmer," or, an even worse prospect, at those farmers most able to adopt costly imported technologies, has a very poor track record when the needs of the large majority of the world's farmers are considered.

Anthropologists have further contributed to the goals of INTSORMIL by insisting on the importance of fieldwork, which led to the early shifting of research operations to sites in developing countries. By laying the groundwork through establishing collaborative agreements, setting up research sites, and providing important baseline data, anthropologists were instrumental in convincing INTSORMIL of the desirability of conducting field research in Sudan, Honduras, and elsewhere.

Anthropological research in Honduras was important in convincing the Honduran government to put more resources into sorghum research. Even though national nutritional surveys have been conducted in the country, nutritionists in Honduras assured the members of the FSR Group there that sorghum was only used as an animal feed. It took an anthropological field study to show the crop's real importance and potential as an insurance food crop for human populations in average and poor agricultural years (see K. DeWalt and Thompson 1983; Thompson et al. 1983).

In Sudan, the FSR Group encountered a belief among Sudanese officials and expatriate experts alike that the small farmers of the western Sudan were poorly integrated into the market economy and that those who were integrated were being severely exploited by rural middlemen. Moreover, an assumption was prevalent that market infrastructure—transportation and storage—was primitive and inefficient. The evidence of our anthropological field study demonstrated that these ideas were largely unfounded. The production of crops for market was virtually a universal practice among farmers and highly important to their livelihood. Rural middlemen rarely were able to exert monopoly power over farmers, and transportation and storage were highly effective. This finding argued all the more strongly for the importance of technological innovations and crop improvement as means not only of increasing agricultural yields but also of enhancing the welfare of the rural population. It also pointed to the desirability of integrating village merchants and urban wholesale crop buyers into the development process. Heretofore, the Sudan government had shown a deep mistrust of private entrepreneurial talent that was assumed to be devoted entirely to selfish, antisocial ends (see Reeves 1984).

The amount of INTSORMIL resources allocated to research in Sudan and Honduras would certainly have been less without the impact of anthropological research. More important, the direction of research would have been different. In both Sudan and Honduras, as a result of better understanding of the farmers' problems and capabilities, greater emphasis is being placed on breeding varieties rather than on hybrids, on varieties that can be intercropped rather than monocropped, and on varieties that have good food quality characteristics as opposed to those that only give high yields.

Notes

1. The literature on farming systems research has grown significantly in recent years. Two essential references are Norman et al. (1982) and Shaner et al. (1982).

2. See especially Bennett (1969, 1976, 1982). For a broad overview of relevant literature, see Barlett (1980) and Orlove (1980).

3. The division of labor in agricultural research has in fact progressed to the point where agronomists and animal scientists are concerned with the biotechnical but not the economic, whereas agricultural economists deal with the latter but not the former.

References

Barlett, Peggy F. 1980. Adaptive Strategies in Peasant Agricultural Production. *Annual Review of Anthropology* 9:545–573.

Bennett, John W. 1969. *Northern Plainsmen: Adaptive Strategy and Agrarian Life.* Arlington Heights: AHM Publishing Corporation.

———. 1976. *The Ecological Transition: Cultural Anthropology and Human Adaptation.* London: Pergamon.

———. 1982. Of Time and the Enterprise: North American Family Farm Management in a Context of Resource Marginality. Minneapolis: University of Minnesota Press.

DeWalt, Billie R. 1983. The Cattle Are Eating the Forest. *Bulletin of the Atomic Scientists* 39 (1):18–23.

DeWalt, Billie R., and Kathleen M. DeWalt. 1982. Cropping Systems in Pespire, Southern Honduras: Farming Systems Research in Southern Honduras, Report no. 1. Lexington: University of Kentucky.

DeWalt, Kathleen M., and Karen S. Thompson. 1983. Sorghum and Nutritional Strategies in Southern Honduras. *Practicing Anthropology* 5(3):15–16.

Frankenberger, Timothy. 1983. Understanding Desertification Through Farming Systems Research. *Practicing Anthropology* 5(3):7,10.

Norman, David W., Emmy B. Simmons, and Henry M. Hays. 1982. *Farming Systems Research in the Nigerian Savanna: Research Strategies for Development.* Boulder: Westview.

Orlove, Benjamin S. 1980. Ecological Anthropology. In *Annual Review of Anthropology* 9:235–273.

Paul, Compton L., and Billie R. DeWalt, eds. 1985. *El Sorgo en Sistemas de Produccion en America Latina.* Mexico City: CIMMYT.

Reeves, Edward B. 1984. An Indigenous Rural Marketing System in North Kordofan, Sudan, Report no. 3. Lexington: University of Kentucky.

Reeves, Edward B., and Timothy Frankenberger. 1981. Socio-economic Constraints to the Production, Distribution and Consumption of Millet, Sorghum and Cash Crops in North Kordofan, Sudan. Farming Systems Research in North Kordofan, Sudan, Report no. 1. Lexington: University of Kentucky.

———. 1982. Aspects of Agricultural Production, the Household Economy, and Marketing. Farming Systems Research in North Kordofan, Sudan, Report no. 2. Lexington: University of Kentucky.

Shaner, W. W., P. F. Philipp, and W. R. Schmehl. 1982. *Farming Systems Research and Development: Guidelines for Developing Countries.* Boulder: Westview.

Thompson, Karen S., Kathleen M. DeWalt, and Billie R. DeWalt. 1983. Household Food Use in Three Rural Honduran Communities. Farming Systems Research in Southern Honduras, Report no. 2. Lexington: University of Kentucky.

PART 2
POLICY FORMULATION: CHOOSING AN ALTERNATIVE AND SETTING A DIRECTION

6 / The Integration of Modern and Traditional Health Sectors in Swaziland

Edward C. Green

Client and Problem

I went to Swaziland in March 1981 to serve as an anthropologist on the AID-funded Rural Water-Borne Disease Control Project. The project called for a knowledge, attitudes, and practices (KAP) survey on water and sanitation in Swaziland, and the survey was my primary responsibility as a member of a multidisciplinary project team of U.S. technical advisers. (The project and my activities are described in Chapter 1.) This chapter describes a major research and policy planning effort that developed serendipitously while I was involved in carrying out the KAP survey.

During the KAP survey I decided that getting to know and interview some traditional healers would be a good introduction to Swazi health-related beliefs and attitudes. My informal interviewing focused on diseases related to water and sanitation, but I also found myself discussing a variety of topics of interest to both healers and their patients. One finding with important implications was that most healers appeared interested in learning more about "modern medicine" (a shorthand term used here to denote Western allopathic biomedicine) and working cooperatively with doctors and nurses. Another was that healers regarded some diseases as distinctly African and therefore treatable only by African medicines and rituals, whereas they regarded others—a smaller number in fact—as new or foreign diseases more treatable by modern medicine. Swazi healers appeared to refer patients with the latter type of disease to modern clinics and hospitals. I discussed these findings with Swaziland Ministry of Health (MOH) officials in light of the World

Health Organization recommendation that poorer nations try to find ways for indigenous healers to work cooperatively with modern health sector personnel. The health planning unit of the MOH was especially interested in developing some sort of working relationship with healers. This unit was particularly aware of human resources shortages in the modern health sector, having just concluded an assessment of health personnel. After discussions among health planners, the MOH director of medical services, and myself it was decided that the MOH should take preliminary steps toward fulfilling the WHO mandate, especially because traditional healers seemed to be especially numerous and influential in Swaziland.

In August 1982, the permanent secretary of the MOH formally asked my colleague Lydia Makhubu and myself to prepare a report on Swazi traditional healers. Makhubu was vice-chancellor of the University of Swaziland and a chemist who had been studying the properties of traditional medicines. Specifically, we were asked to provide an assessment of (1) human resources in the traditional health sector; (2) the areas and extent of cooperation possible between the traditional and modern health sectors, with special reference to the prevention and treatment of diarrheal diseases; (3) the extent to which alternative systems of health care had developed for the consumer; (4) customary law, modern legislation, and government policies regarding traditional healing and healers; (5) prospects for the development of a national traditional healers association, and a possible role for the MOH in promoting, monitoring, and liaising with such an association; and (6) the potential for the paraprofessional training of certain types of traditional healers.

The report and the research required for its preparation were sponsored by AID through two of its ongoing projects, Health Planning and Management, and Rural Water-Borne Disease Control. The former project employed Makhubu as a consultant and laid important groundwork within MOH. The contribution of the latter project consisted mainly of a few months of my time and the loan of three Swazi interviewers I had trained and employed in the KAP survey and research. The MOH contributed a car and driver, and most important, it sanctioned the investigation.

Process and Players

Makhubu and I divided the tasks called for between ourselves. Makhubu reviewed her own research findings, checking on various points with her key informants, and consulted experts on Swazi law, customs, and traditions. I conducted a survey of healers to measure some of the apparent trends that had emerged through my earlier in-depth interviewing and participant-observation research. I also attempted to estimate the number of healers practicing in Swaziland. We felt that quantification was necessary because policymakers usually want statistics to back up the recommendations of researchers.

Between August 1982 and January 1983, my research assistants interviewed 144 traditional healers of all types (herbalists, diviner mediums, faith healers). No adequate sampling frame of healers existed, and thus a random or probability sample was not feasible. However, roughly equal numbers of healers were interviewed in the four major geographic regions of Swaziland. Although the healer sample could have been more randomized by selecting only those healers who lived in randomly selected census enumeration areas, time and effort were saved by allowing interviewers to work primarily in areas where they had kinship ties or where they had interviewed during previous surveys. This approach also helped minimize suspicion and mistrust among the healers. In addition, a house-to-house census was conducted in four rural and four peri-urban communities in order to estimate the number of healers in Swaziland, along with certain of their characteristics. A total of 598 residential units in three geographic regions were covered in the census.

I decided that a precoded questionnaire that limited the range of responses would not be appropriate. My earlier interviews with Swazi healers suggested that at best, they would give stilted, formal, and stereotyped answers to a fixed interview schedule. On the other hand, if healers were approached properly, they would open up and offer rich information that went far beyond specific questions asked. This approach combined a sincere, interested, respectful attitude by the interviewer with a flexible, open-ended mode of questioning assisted by subtle probing techniques. The three Swazi interviewers chosen for the survey had worked on standard surveys before, but they had never done open-ended interviewing. I trained them in appropriate interview techniques as well as in taking shorthand notes and translating these into complete, detailed accounts of interviews.

I continued my participant-observation and in-depth interviews among some twenty healers I had come to know, while the interviewers carried out the fieldwork phase of the survey. The interviewers required little supervision in the field, but I carefully monitored the incoming data and discussed findings and their implications with the interviewers. Among the more important findings was that about 5,400 healers seemed to practice outside the modern health sector; in a country the size of Swaziland this number means one traditional healer for every 110 population. This figure compares to a physician/population ratio of about 1:10,000. Some 50 percent of the total number of healers were herbalists, 40 percent were diviner-healers, and 10 percent were Christian ("Zionist") faithhealers. About half the healers were female, and the vast majority of these were diviner-healers. Diviner-healers tend to be more prestigious than herbalists because ancestor spirits are believed to work directly through them.

The survey confirmed my earlier finding that nearly all types of illness were believed to be ultimately caused by sorcery or less frequently by loss of ancestral protection. However, many healers were prepared to accept the theory that illnesses might have more immediate causes about which doctors and nurses were knowledgeable. For example, a Swazi mother might accept the idea that her child will develop diarrhea if flies walk over the child's food; but she will also want to know how and why her enemies sent flies to harm her child.

We found that patients might seek treatment from both doctors and traditional healers for the same complaint. The doctor was considered capable of eliminating symptoms or treating the immediate cause of illness, and the healer was relied upon to explain the illness in culturally meaningful terms and to treat or eliminate its ultimate source. Clearly, a basis for cooperation already existed between the traditional and the modern health sector. In fact some 90 percent of healers surveyed claimed to routinely refer some of their patients to clinics—even though very few instances of referrals from clinics to healers were encountered.

Several survey questions showed that healers believed that their own rituals and medicines were superior to modern medicine in treating most diseases and that people relied on traditional medicines to ensure the sexual fidelity of a partner and to provide luck. A majority of healers said that modern medicine could better treat cholera, tuberculosis, heart disease, venereal disease, and bilharzia. In a separate question on cholera, 76 percent of healers said that they refer patients to clinics rather than try to treat a new disease that they do not understand (cholera first appeared in Swaziland in 1980).

The survey revealed that healers admired doctors for certain technical capabilities as well as for the medicines they possess. Most commonly cited were various surgical practices, blood transfusions, and use of X-ray machines. On the other hand, diviners felt that their ability to diagnose the ultimate causes of illness (thereby anwering the "why" or "why me" questions of misfortune) and to perform the *femba* ceremony through which agents of illness are removed—both of which involve cultivated relationships with spirits—are as important skills as those that doctors possess. In fact, most of the healers interviewed either implied or explicitly stated their wish to be treated as equals by doctors.

The survey also sought to measure in some way the frequency of use of healing practices that seemed harmful. These included medicinal enemas used to prevent and treat several types of childhood diarrhea; induced vomiting to "clean out the chest" of tuberculosis patients; traditional vaccinations performed with an unclean razor; and use of powerful, mind-altering herbal medicines in treating madness. It was impossible to measure frequency of such practices with any accuracy, but all were employed. The use of enemas for children seemed sufficiently widespread that soon after the survey report was presented, the MOH asked me to conduct a study focusing specifically on beliefs and practices related to diarrheal diseases in Swaziland (Green 1985).

Since Makhubu and I were well aware of modern practitioners' strong negative bias toward traditional healers, we pointed out traditional healing practices that were probably beneficial to the patient—and perhaps to the patient's family and community as well. These included use of herbal medicines that seemed to be effective in various ways; the reduction of stress through ritual and through explanations reassuring to patient and family; and the removal of a patient from home to a therapeutic environment at the healer's homestead in which the patient can recover. We also pointed out that healers helped ease pressure on overburdened clinics by treating minor, self-limiting, psychosomatic, and certain other kinds of conditions in which traditional therapies are probably effective and appropriate.

Although it was difficult to obtain information on patient fees in the survey, I personally observed patients paying between $120 and $130 for treatment of a single condition such as *umtsebulo*, or soul loss. Healers were also earning about $140 for protecting (*kubetsela*) a homestead against mystical lightning strikes by enemies. A basic diagnostic fee of about $2 was standardized by a royal order-in-council in 1954, but healers earned an additional fee of between $10 to $20 to "open the bag" (*imvula sikhwama*) of medicines, which formalizes the beginning of any treatment.

Although Swaziland is a poor country, most people somehow find the money to pay the relatively high fees requested by traditional healers. These fees were even more remarkable because modern-sector clinic services at the time of the survey cost the equivalent of about $0.20 whatever the treatment entailed. My findings on healing fees helped explain why a recent attempt by the MOH to train healers as rural health motivators met with little success. These community health workers were being paid $20 a month. Several survey respondents were candid in remarking that healing is a lucrative and respectable profession and perhaps the best one to which women and those lacking formal education can aspire.

A system of registering healers began in Swaziland late in the British colonial period when the government recognized that doctors and nurses would not easily displace traditional healers and that the latter could not be completely ignored. Registration represented a first step toward recognition of healers and exercising a modicum of control over their activities. It also provided tax revenues. Since independence, the Swaziland government has continued to register and collect taxes from healers.

The survey showed that 82 percent of healers reported that they were currently registered, and 8 percent said that they had only recently qualified as healers and they intended to become registered. Even allowing for overreporting, the proportion of registered, tax-paying healers is higher than might be expected for a traditional African society. In addition, healers seemed to be favorably inclined toward registration. When healers were asked why they had registered, 30 percent commented that the police would support only registered healers in collecting overdue patient fees and that they would also protect healers against complaints of patients or their families. Other common remarks were that registration conferred legitimacy, respectability, and authority on healers, and it allowed them to travel and practice freely throughout Swaziland and neighboring countries.

Finally, the survey sought information on cooperation and paraprofessional training. An impressive (if slightly suspect) 98 percent of healers interviewed claimed they would like to achieve better cooperation between themselves and doctors and nurses. Ninety-one percent specifically expressed enthusiasm toward undergoing some sort of training in modern medicine. Most said that they wanted to improve their healing skills and to learn more about the treatments given in hospitals. However, several healers—most of them female—expressed concern that their lack of formal education would make communicating with doctors difficult.

In spite of the positive survey results, both Makhubu and I were aware that traditional healers were still suspicious about the motives of the MOH. And a great deal more suspicion and outright negative bias could be found in the modern health sector. Many local doctors preferred to pretend that healers did not exist, and some took the view that healers should be arrested for practicing medicine without a license. This bias resulted from a failure to understand the traditional healer's role in Swazi society, from the nature of formal (Western) medical education and professional socialization, from a certain amount of professional jealousy, from the "bad press" healers tended to receive by local, sensation-seeking media, and from the fact that healers engage in several practices deemed unacceptable by public health standards.

In view of the difficulties of developing a workable policy in an atmosphere of suspicion and mistrust, Makhubu and I recommended that the MOH proceed cautiously and not expect quick results. We suggested a policy of seeking cooperation rather than integration. Cooperation implies a better working relationship between the two health sectors by which appropriate referrals are routinely made between the sectors, certain traditional healing practices are improved or made safer, and the "cultural" or interpersonal sensitivity of modern health care workers is increased. The term "integration" implies a fundamental alteration of both healing systems and of the roles of the respective practitioners, although in reality only the traditional healer is expected to change. The danger here is that the traditional healer may become a second-rate paramedical worker and thereby cease to carry out his or her important function in the local community—a function with social, psychological, and spiritual as well as physical health dimensions. Such an outcome could be disruptive in multiple ways, including the undermining of a community's capacity to solve its own health problems.

We realized the importance of starting with an area of cooperation that would interest people in both health sectors and that was likely to succeed. We decided upon the treatment and prevention of childhood diarrheal diseases and the use of oral rehydration therapy (ORT) as an appropriate focus for an initial and experimental program of cooperation. The 1981 outbreak of cholera in southern Africa helped center attention on diarrheal diseases in both the government and the traditional sectors. By 1983 diarrheal diseases, especially those of childhood, had become a highest priority health concern of the MOH, and the widespread use of ORT was recognized as a technique that could significantly reduce morbidity and mortality from these diseases.

We believed that a program focused on diarrheal diseases and ORT would be of interest to traditional healers for several reasons: (1) Research indicated that healers would like to have a means by which they could prevent deaths from diarrheal diseases; (2) cholera had become a disease of high concern among healers as well as the general public, and most healers surveyed admitted they did not understand or try to treat cholera; (3) ORT is compatible with traditional treatments for diarrhea, i.e., herbal decoctions taken orally over a period of time; and (4) distribution of ORT packets to traditional healers would constitute an important gesture of trust and cooperation on the part of the government.

We recommended that the health education unit of the MOH be given the main responsibility for organizing and implementing a series of workshops designed to upgrade healers' skills in a few priority areas, most notably diarrheal diseases of childhood, and to sensitize modern health sector personnel to work more cooperatively with healers. Packets of oral rehydration salts (ORS) should be given to healers on a pilot basis, and subsequent evaluations would indicate if healers were mixing and administering the salts properly. If they were, then ORS distribution to healers could become a national program and other areas of potential cooperation could be explored.

Results and Evaluation

As a result of the survey report, the MOH officially adopted a policy of seeking cooperation with traditional healers. Within a few months of receiving the health policy report, the MOH, through the health education unit, conducted three preliminary workshops designed to establish a dialogue between healers and modern health sector personnel. Topics focused on diarrheal diseases and administration of ORT, as well as on secondary topics such as immunization against childhood diseases, maternal/child health, breastfeeding, and nutrition.

The first regional workshop for healers, held in Motjane on June 1, 1983, was disappointing because only twelve healers turned up. The turnout was poor partly because of the failure to contact most healers in the area and partly because of the healers' mistrust regarding MOH motives. No diviner-healer wore the characteristic red-ochre hairstyle, the brightly colored cloths, the empowering medicine bags, or the beads that symbolize special relationships with certain spirits, indicating that the healers expected disapproval or even ridicule to be directed at them.

However, those who attended were well treated, and all present shared in an interesting exchange of views. Healers were treated as peers and colleagues. The nurses who attended the first workshop were health educators or public health nurses, and all were personally in favor of the new MOH policy. Their positive attitude toward the experiment in cooperation did not go unnoticed by the healers. The second and third regional workshops attracted more than 100 healers each, and the healers came in full traditional regalia. Part of the high turnout was due to the active support of an influential healer, Nhlavana Maseko, who had personally attended the late king of Swaziland. During 1983 Maseko was active in organizing a national association of traditional healers. Since the Green-Makhubu report had recommended that the MOH support the formation of such an association, the workshop organizers were happy to work with the emerging association leaders, especially because they offered a ready-made network for the dissemination of information about the workshops.

These first workshops in mid-1983 served the intended purpose of establishing a dialogue between healers and MOH personnel. Although critics of intersectoral cooperation could be found on both sides, good will and trust began to develop between those who attended the workshops. I witnessed genuine changes in the attitude of several MOH officials after they attended a workshop. Some of these had shared the view of many expatriate physicians in Swaziland that traditional healers are unprincipled charlatans. Others in the modern health sector seemed to drop their pose of contempt toward healers once the new MOH policy made it respectable to deal with healers.

My employment in the MOH ended in September 1983 when my already extended contract expired. I returned to the United States but returned to Swaziland from January 1984 to March 1985 as a personal services contractor for the AID mission. Although I primarily worked on other research and planning topics, I kept abreast of developments with traditional healers. One of these was the rapid growth of the Swaziland Traditional Healers Society (STHS) at both the national and district levels. Another was the continuation and growth of the MOH-sponsored training workshops for traditional healers. A U.S. health educator who joined the Rural Water-Borne Disease Control Project in 1983 became very active in promoting and implementing these workshops—probably too active in fact. There was a danger that the Swazi staff of the health education unit would feel that healer training was a U.S. project and not their own. However, as of late 1986, nearly two years after the departure of the last American from the health education unit, the unit was actively implementing workshops for traditional healers in all districts of Swaziland.

The Anthropological Difference

In retrospect I can assess the contribution of anthropology in the overall effort of formulating and implementing a new policy toward traditional healers. First, a body of anthropological literature on traditional healers helped me understand the complex belief systems and behavioral patterns of healers, the role and function of healers in their communities, the significance of ritual in curing, the sociological dimension of recruitment and membership in healing cults, and a host of other aspects of traditional healing.

John Janzen's recent comparative historical work (unpublished) on *ngoma* therapeutic cults in Africa helped me develop a wider and deeper perspective in my understanding of Swazi therapeutic cults. Likewise, I. M. Lewis's theoretical contributions on cults of affliction and the upward mobility of oppressed or marginal members of society (Lewis 1969, 1971) stimulated my insights into the cult of Swazi diviner-healers, even though the Swazi situation did not always fit Lewis's model. Lewis's ideas were especially useful in understanding the appeal of the diviner cult to Swazi women. Membership in this cult is the only traditional means by which Swazi women can achieve power and wealth (even though women can be born to this position) in a male-dominated society.

Three other anthropologists, W. D. Hammond-Tooke, Harriet Ngubane, and Martin West, all with research experience among groups closely related to the Swazi, provided theoretical perspectives that guided my research and thinking: Hammond-Tooke on the sociology of witchcraft accusations, Ngubane on the support networks among Zulu diviner-healers, and West on Christian-Zionist faithhealers in Soweto.

It must be admitted, however, that the contribution of anthropological theory was indirect in my practical, policy-oriented work with traditional healers. The contribution of anthropological methods was more direct. I would not have been able to either advocate or undertake a survey of healers had I not gained in-depth information about traditional healing through standard anthropological methods. Furthermore, the healer survey design followed recognized anthropological procedures: a preliminary phase of in-depth interviewing and participant observation research, followed by a survey based on flexible, open-ended interviewing. And anthropology provided a framework for interpreting the resulting qualitative data, some of which were rather abstruse and arcane by the standards of other disciplines. Another direct contribution to my work came from the anthropologist D. M. Warren who has published about his experience in designing workshops for traditional healers in Ghana (Warren et al. 1981).

The contribution of an anthropological perspective and orientation cannot be overlooked. It was natural for me to regard traditional healers as fonts of wisdom and culture brokers par excellence and as respected health opinion leaders (rather than as quacks or charlatans) in their own communities. Yet the same cannot be said for those for other disciplines; otherwise someone would have begun mediating cooperation between the traditional and modern health sectors before I arrived in Swaziland.

References

Kuper, H. 1947. *An African Aristocracy, Rank Among the Swazi.* Oxford: Oxford University Press.

Green, E. 1985. Traditional Healers, Mothers and Childhood Diarrheal Disease in Swaziland: The Interface of Anthropology and Health Education. *Social Science and Medicine* 19(3):277–285.

Green, E. C., and L. Makhubu. 1984. Traditional Healers in Swaziland: Toward Improved Cooperation Between the Traditional and Modern Health Sectors. *Social Science and Medicine* 18(12):1071–1079.

Lewis, I. M. 1971. *Ecstatic Religion. An Anthropological Study of Spirit Possession and Shamanism.* Middlesex: Penguin Books.

Lewis, I. M. 1969. Spirit Possession in Northern Somaliland. In J. Beattie and J. Middleton, eds., *Spirit Mediumship in Africa.* New York: Praeger, pp. 188–210.

Marwick, B. A. 1940. *The Swazi.* London: Frank Cass.
Warren, D. M., G. S. Bova, M. A. Tregoning, and M. Kliewer. 1981. Ghanaian National Policy Toward Indigenous Healers: The Case of the Primary Health Training for the Indigenous Healers (PRHETIH) Programs. Paper presented at the annual meeting of the Society for Applied Anthropology, Edinburgh.

7 / Customary Law Development in Papua New Guinea

Richard Scaglion

Problem and Client

After a long colonial history dating back to the nineteenth century, Papua New Guinea became an independent nation on September 16, 1975. For most of its history, the territories of Papua and New Guinea, which together constitute the eastern half of the island of New Guinea in the southwest Pacific, had been administered by Australia. Upon independence, national leaders adopted the Australian legal system then in force as an interim national legal system. This Western legal system often clashed with the customary law of tribal peoples within the new nation. National leaders, therefore, wanted to develop a self-reliant national legal system based on their own customs and traditions rather than on those of their former colonial administrators. In 1979, I was hired by the government of the new nation to help bring about this development.

National leaders knew that this task would be prolonged and difficult. Papua New Guinea is well known for its cultural diversity. In a country of some three and one-half million people, there are at least 750 mutually unintelligible languages and probably about a thousand different customary legal systems. Amid such diversity, would it be possible to uncover basic legal principles common to all these Melanesian societies? If so, could the essence of Melanesian customary law, which functions smoothly in small-scale tribal societies, be reconciled with the requirements of a modern nation-state?

To investigate these issues on a long-term basis, the Papua New Guinea government established a Law Reform Commission as a constitutional body whose special responsibility was to "investigate and report to the Parliament and to the National Executive on the development, and on the adaptation to the circumstances of the country, of the underlying law, and on the appropriateness of the rules and principles of the underlying law to the circumstances of the country." Recognizing that customary law was essential in creating an underlying law appropriate for Papua New Guinea, the Law Reform Commission designed a basic framework for a Customary Law Project to conduct research on the nature of customary law and the extent to which it could form the basis for a unique national legal system. The commission hoped that some of the problems with the interim legal system could be resolved through this project.

In 1978 I was a relatively new assistant professor of anthropology at the University of Pittsburgh. My PhD research had been a study of customary law and legal change among the Abelam people of Papua New Guinea (Scaglion 1976). During that study, I became aware of many of the problems faced by the Abelam in reconciling their customs and traditions with imposed Australian law (Scaglion 1985). Knowing of my interest in legal development in Papua New Guinea, officers of the Law Reform Commission asked me to direct their Customary Law Project for a few years. I was expected to design an ongoing research strategy to gather data on customary law patterns of different tribes, analyze the data, identify problem areas, and help create draft legislation designed to alleviate such problems. Officials also hoped that I could train other people to carry on the work after I left. In other words, I would help design and initiate a broad policy direction for legal development in Papua New Guinea. I found this prospect very exciting.

While I was gathering data for my PhD research on the early period of contact with the government, an Abelam man told me that he had been jailed for burying his deceased mother inside her house. Under Abelam custom, corpses were laid to rest in the houses in which the people had slept and worked. The corpses were covered with only a thin layer of soil, and the houses were allowed to fall into disrepair and eventually collapse. Australian patrol officers wanted this practice discontinued because of potential health problems. My informant was not really aware of the "new" rules or the reasons behind them. Furthermore, to bury his mother's body outside the house, somewhere in the jungle, would be disrespectful. By following customary law, he broke national law.

I also remembered a discussion with another informant, an elderly man who had two wives to whom he had been married for many years. Although many Abelam marriages are monogamous, polygyny is also customary. I explained that in my own country, the United States, men were permitted only one wife under the law of most areas, and he asked me if this were also true of the Australians. I explained that it was and that technically it was also true in Papua New Guinea. I felt bad when he became upset that he might be arrested, but he declared that he could never choose between his wives, both of whom he loved.

I was greatly interested in the prospect of working on problems like these. I had heard of Bernard Narakobi, the chairman of the Law Reform Commission, when I was first contacted about this work. Although he was an indigenous lawyer, he had a social science background, and I expected him to be receptive to an anthropological approach. After working out the scheduling, I began a fifteen-month period of initial research in May 1979 under a leave of absence from the University of Pittsburgh.

Process and Players

The Customary Law Project staff consisted of myself as project director, supervising a full-time Papua New Guinea project officer (Bospidik Pilokos). Secretarial and support functions were performed by Law Reform Commission staff. The project was designed to be fairly auton-omous but was under the supervision of the secretary of the Law Reform Commission (Samson Kaipu for most of the project) and ultimately under the chairman of the Law Reform Commission, the secretary for justice, and the minister for justice. A separate fund was available for the project director on behalf of the project, subject to normal financial approval.

I spent the first several months of the project organizing activities. Initially, I conducted extensive bibliographical research and identified hundreds of sources on customary law in Papua New Guinea. The project officer catalogued these references according to subject matter and geographical area. My examination of these bibliographic sources underlined the need for more detailed and more complete research on the subject of customary law in specific Papua New Guinea societies.

Many if not most of the materials on customary law unearthed in the bibliographic search had been gathered by anthropologists working in relatively unacculturated parts of the country. What was missing was a corpus of case studies from rural areas that had had a longer history of contact with the government and had begun the process of reconciling customary law with a national legal system. Several alternative strategies for gathering this primary data were investigated, including the use of magistrates, foreign anthropologists, lawyers, and student researchers. To make the best use of available resources I hired students from the University of Papua New Guinea to work in their home areas during their long year-end break. These students already spoke the local language and were familiar with their own cultures. I also felt that their descriptions of their own customary legal systems would be more likely to reflect indigenous categories than if, say, Australian lawyers had done the research.

To develop a comparative methodology for the project, I tested several research strategies in the Maprik area of the East Sepik Province, where the Abelam live, and did preliminary analyses of the data collected. To make these results available to interested parties, and also to publicize the project, I published articles in both the *Melanesian Law Journal* (Scaglion 1979) for the legal community and *Oceania* (Scaglion 1981a) for applied anthropologists working in legal development in the Pacific. Based on this preliminary research, we decided that the overall data-gathering strategy should focus on the collection of original conflict case studies from which principles of customary law in particular societies could be extracted. These cases could then be analyzed as a homogeneous data base to investigate possibilities for cross-cultural national unification of customary law.

After selecting twenty university students to form the first research group, I designed a format and minicourse for training and conducted training sessions at the university. Bospidik Pilokos, the project officer, later used the minicourse training format to train the next group of ten student researchers. We tried to supervise researchers in the field as much as possible; however, many of the research locations were relatively remote and required considerable time and travel to visit. Transportation proved to be a problem for our researchers as well.

Despite these problems, our student researchers gathered a corpus of roughly 600 extended case studies from all parts of the country. We then coded these cases according to such variables as type of case, geographical area, remedy agents used, and decision reached. I wrote a computer retrieval system to allow legal researchers to scan various types of cases and to receive a print-out of summary information about the cases, together with individual case numbers. These case identification numbers can now be used to retrieve the original cases from Law Reform Commission files for further study. In this way, a basic corpus of customary law cases has been created for use in developing the underlying law of Papua New Guinea.

We also initiated a Law Reform Commission monograph series to disseminate certain materials from our research. The first volume in this series (Scaglion 1981b), which contains anthropologists' reactions to certain provisions of a draft bill on customary compensation, is described in the next section. The second volume (Scaglion 1983) contains background materials related to the case materials. The student researchers have described their fieldsites, including the conditions under which the cases were gathered and, where possible, have provided broad summaries of principles of customary law in their areas.

Toward the end of my active involvement in the project, I experienced scheduling problems. I had initially agreed to a two-year commitment for this research, consisting of a fifteen-month initial period of residence in Papua New Guinea to get the project under way, followed by a return to Pittsburgh to resume my teaching duties and to analyze preliminary data, and ending with another nine-month period of residence in Papua New Guinea. Although officials of the Law Reform Commission had agreed to this schedule, it subsequently turned out to violate certain Public Service Commission guidelines. Consequently, we could only negotiate a brief three-month return. As a result, much of the editing of monographs had to be done from abroad, and the writing of some of the results of the study has been delayed or abandoned.

Results and Evaluation

Despite problems in completing the research, I feel that the original goals set for the early stages of the project were accomplished. These goals were (1) to create a data base on Papua New Guinea case law and legal principles that would be useful to legal practitioners and (2) to begin to identify and investigate problem areas and facilitate the preparation of draft legislation to alleviate such problems.

The first goal was accomplished through the preparation of the computer retrieval system allowing legal researchers and practitioners to identify cases relevant to their problems. The actual extended cases can be researched at the Law Reform Commission. During my residence in Papua New Guinea, I helped a number of lawyers find customary precedent cases related to issues they were arguing in court. For example, one attorney asked me to help her find cases that might provide information about customary divorce practices in a particular region. Several such cases were in our files, and she referred to these in preparing her case. Thus our data have helped facilitate legal development through the use of customary law cases in court.

These data have also been useful in exploring a variety of problems in legal development. For example, the Institute for National Affairs and the Institute for Applied Social and Economic Research (INA 1984:209–226) used our case study data in examining law and order problems in the country. A colleague and I used these case studies to address problems of domestic violence and women's access to justice in rural Papua New Guinea (Scaglion and Wittingham 1985).

The second goal, the identification and alleviation of legislative problems, is an ongoing, long-range effort involving the Law Reform

Commission, the Justice Department, and the National Parliament. A three-part structure consisting of research, preparation of sample legislation circulated for comments, and preparation of final draft legislation is being followed. During my involvement with the Customary Law Project, a number of problem areas were identified.

For example, my Abelam friend who was concerned about the possible legal consequences of his bigamy turned out to have a lot of company. The project identified family law as an area in which customary principles were often at variance with statute law. A wide range of customary arrangements were technically illegal. A draft family law bill has been prepared that would formally recognize customary marriages as legal marriages and would provide for polygamous customary marriages under certain conditions. I am happy to say these conditions would include my old informant and his wives.

Customary compensation, particularly homicide compensation, was identified as another specific problem area. Compensation is a form of conflict management, common in Melanesian societies, in which an aggrieved party demands payment of some sort from another party. The payment demanded is generally thought to be proportionate to the severity of the act that precipitated the dispute and is usually proportionate to the magnitude of the dispute as well. Payment of compensation generally implies acceptance of responsibility by the donors and willingness to terminate the dispute by the recipients. However, such arrangements are not generally recognized under the law.

Unfortunately, it was not a simple matter of just recognizing the legality of these arrangements. A series of cases, recently popularized by the local news media, showed the complexity of the problem. These cases involved huge groups of people and "excessive" compensation demands. In one case a man from one province had been driving a vehicle that struck and killed a man from another province. Representatives from the clan of the victim were demanding hundreds of thousands of kina (Papua New Guinea currency roughly equivalent to the Australian dollar) from the whole of the driver's province.

Thus, homicide compensation appeared to be an area in which social development had outstripped the ability of small-scale customary legal systems to adapt. Inflationary compensation demands had created law and order problems and diverted cash away from development in large sections of the country. Although the basic customary law patterns were worth preserving, how could they be adapted to modern conditions?

A draft bill (Law Reform Commission 1980) was prepared that provided for the formal recognition of customary compensation as an institution for dispute resolution. Exchanges of wealth and services as a means for settling compensation claims for deaths, injuries, and property damage were recognized, and appropriate tribunals modeled on customary conflict management were provided. The bill tried to control and regulate claims and payments by specifying circumstances and amounts for such payments. I solicited further anthropological input by asking anthropologists to prepare papers commenting on the draft bill from the viewpoint of their fieldsites. Papers were collected, edited, and published as a monograph (Scaglion 1981b). Anthropologists identified particular geographical areas where such legislation might cause problems, as well as possible unintended consequences of stipulating maximum payments. For example, anthropologist Andrew Strathern (1981) showed that in Hagen society compensation was part of a system of escalating competitive exchange called *moka* and cautioned against setting limits on *moka* or confusing it with the compensation payments related to it. As a result, a revised version recommending regional legislation and revised conflict management strategies is currently being prepared.

Domestic violence was another problem area in parts of the country that had experienced culture change. Traditional cultures often practice patrilocal residence, in which newly married couples live near the husband's family. However, in customary situations, the bride is rarely far from her own family and can usually return home easily if her husband becomes physically abusive. However, as couples take up residence in new locations to pursue opportunities in the cash labor sector, wives cannot easily return home to avoid beatings. The same situation can occur when a man and a woman from widely different locations meet in a town, marry, and go to live with the husband's family. Again, the woman is far from her supportive kinship group. This broad problem, which formed the basis for the third monograph in our series (Toft 1985), was researched by my successor at the Law Reform Commission.

The Anthropological Difference

The Customary Law Project applied anthropological knowledge by making use of theory, concepts, and methods derived from anthropology. These are described in the following section.

Theory

Legal anthropologists often distinguish between substantive law (rules for normative behavior, infractions of which are negatively sanctioned) and procedural law (mechanisms through which legal issues are handled). Lawyers tend to stress the substantive aspects of the legal process. They often see "law" as the relatively rigid application of rules to a given fact situation. Individuals are considered equal before the law, and rules should be impartially applied. In Papua New Guinea, however, customary law is a system of ensuring a just solution through compromise. Customary law recognizes the social uniqueness of each individual, and each case is considered separately without regard to precedents. Thus Melanesian customary law lends itself to analysis as procedural law, and anthropological theory is particularly useful in this endeavor.

Legal anthropologists tend to study interpersonal conflict in a processual sense. They are less concerned with substantive rules of law than with strategies for conflict management. Anthropological theories of law suggest that we study techniques rather than rules and that customary law is flexible and responsive to changing social situations—an important factor in contemporary Papua New Guinea. Consequently the customary law project did not undertake to prepare formal and detailed restatements of customary law as was done in certain African nations. It was thought that in Papua New Guinea, where social change continues to be rapid, this approach would freeze customary law at a single and quickly out-dated point in time. Thus the anthropological theory of law was used in broad project planning.

Concepts

Anthropological concepts consonant with the anthropological view of law were used throughout the project. The research focused on extended cases as a basis for extrapolating legal principles—an attempt to elicit real rather than ideal principles. Because Melanesians do not seem to think in terms of abstract rules for behavior in the legal sense, when pressed to describe rules they often give ideal moral precepts or religious obligations that Westerners do not consider strictly legal rules. This problem was noticed by Malinowski in his classic studies of the Trobriand Islands area of Papua New Guinea in 1914–1918.

Pospisil (1971:2) has frequently pointed out that the English term "law" really consists of two separate concepts that are distinguished in many other languages. One, which in Latin is called *ius*, means law in terms of the underlying principles implied in legal precedents, whereas *lex* means an abstract rule usually made explicit in a legal code. Lawyers often are preoccupied with *leges* (plural of *lex*: the statutory rules); anthropologists tend to uncover the *ius* or the underlying law. The Customary Law Project made use of such anthropological distinctions. Also, a wide variety of concepts from legal anthropology were used to provide direction for the project. Examples of such concepts are "moot courts" (informal meetings for conflict management; see Gibbs 1963) or "negotiation," "mediation," "arbitration," and "adjudication" (procedures for settling conflicts which involve varying involvements of a third party; see Koch 1974:29–30).

Methods

In addition to standard anthropological techniques such as participant-observation, the Customary Law Project used the case method of legal anthropology as a primary data-gathering technique. First popularized by Llewellyn and Hoebel (1941) in their classic work *The Cheyenne Way,* and refined by Laura Nader and her students (see Nader and Todd 1978:5–8), the methodology involves gathering detailed data on all aspects of conflict cases according to a carefully prepared schedule. The four basic types of cases collected are observed cases, cases taken from recorded materials, memory cases, and hypothetical cases. Elicitation of all types of cases provides a corpus of information from which "law" (*ius*) can be abstracted. The Customary Law Project employed this methodology throughout the research phase of the project.

The anthropological difference, or the effects of anthropological theory, concepts, and methods on the Customary Law Project was quite significant and derived mainly from taking an anthropological attitude toward law. Virtually all the senior legal officers and research officers in the Justice Department in Papua New Guinea are lawyers rather than social scientists. Most are from Commonwealth countries. By providing an anthropological view of law, and one flavored with American jurisprudence, the Customary Law Project succeeded in presenting an alternative point of view for consideration.

Initially many of the officers of the Justice Department assumed that the project could or would provide them with discrete compendiums of principles of customary law in various societies. However, the results of the Customary Law Project indicate that a Papua New Guinean common law must be developed as the underlying law of the nation and that this objective would best be accomplished by reference to customary case law. Throughout the duration of the project, informal conflict management forums such as the village court system, designed to provide an interface between customary and introduced law, have been supported. Village courts give traditional leaders magisterial powers and permit them to arbitrate according to custom. Decisions or consensus solutions then have the weight of law. Research from the project indicated that such forums were much more successful than had been previously assumed. The village courts secretariat has received increased support, perhaps in part because of the Customary Law Project. It is felt that a legal approach stressing legal norms would have impeded the development of Papua New Guinea case law.

Research into customary law is ongoing. The anthropologist set up a basic structure for data collection and organization that could continue into the future. Thus, although the implementation phase has been completed, the anthropological input continues. In this way, anthropological concepts, theory, and methods have helped to develop a structure for ongoing legal change in Papua New Guinea.

References

Gibbs, James L., Jr. 1963. The Kpelle Moot: A Therapeutic Model for the Informal Settlement of Disputes. *Africa* 33:1–11.

INA. 1984. *Law and Order in Papua New Guinea*, vol. 2. Port Moresby: Institute for National Affairs.

Koch, K. F. 1974. *War and Peace in Jalemo: The Management of Conflict in Highland New Guinea.* Cambridge: Harvard University Press.

Law Reform Commission of Papua New Guinea. 1980. Customary Compensation. Report no. 11. Port Moresby: PNG Government Printers.

Llewellyn, K., and E. A. Hoebel. 1941. *The Cheyenne Way: Conflict and Case Law in Primitive Jurisprudence.* Norman: University of Oklahoma Press.

Nader, L., and H. F. Todd, Jr. 1978. *The Disputing Process: Law in Ten Societies.* New York: Columbia University Press.

Pospisil, L. 1971. *Anthropology of Law: A Comparative Theory.* New York: Harper and Row.

Scaglion, R. 1976. Seasonal Patterns in Western Abelam Conflict Management Practices. Ph.D. thesis, University of Pittsburgh.

————. 1979. Formal and Informal Operations of a Village Court in Maprik. *Melanesian Law Journal* 7:116–1291.

————. 1981a. Samukundi Abelam Conflict Management: Implications for Legal Planning in Papua New Guinea. *Oceania* 52:28–38.

————. 1985. *Kiaps as Kings: Abelam Legal Change in Historical Perspective.* In D. Gewertz and E. Schieffelin, eds., *History and Ethnohistory in Papua New Guinea*, Oceania Monograph no. 28, Sydney, pp. 77–99.

————, and R. Whittingham. 1985. Female Plaintiffs and Sex-Related Disputes in Rural Papua New Guinea. In S. Toft, ed., *Domestic Violence in Papua New Guinea*, Law Reform Commission of Papua New Guinea, Monograph no. 3, Port Moresby, pp. 120–133.

Scaglion, R., ed. 1981b. Homicide Compensation in Papua New Guinea: Problems and Prospects. Law Reform Commission of Papua New Guinea, Monograph no. 1, Port Moresby.

————, ed. 1983. Customary Law in Papua New Guinea: A Melanesian View. Law Reform Commission of Papua New Guinea, Monograph no. 2, Port Moresby.

Strathern, A. 1981. Compensation: Should There be a New Law. In R. Scaglion, ed., *Homicide Compensation in Papua New Guinea: Problems and Prospects.* Law Reform Commission of Papua New Guinea, Monograph no. 1, Port Moresby, pp. 5–24.

Toft. S., ed. 1985. *Domestic Violence in Papua New Guinea.* Law Reform Commission of Papua New Guinea, Monograph no. 3, Port Moresby.

8 / Redesigning Social Service Delivery Policy: The Anthropologist as Mediator

Stanley Hyland, Bridget Ciaramitaro, Charles Williams, and Rosalind Cottrell

Problem and Client

An extensive network of applied anthropologists in the Memphis area have redesigned the delivery of a housing weatherization program to more effectively meet the needs of over 300,000 low- to moderate-income customers. Although the actual project began in 1983, the groundwork was laid much earlier. In 1977 faculty and students from the local university began building a data base on the activities and needs of neighborhood groups. Simultaneously, anthropologists examined the role of local agencies in the delivery of social services and established an active internship program in the community. By 1979 ample data had been collected and analyzed to document a gigantic communication chasm between local urban agencies and neighborhood groups. Some local agencies had even adopted a policy of nonparticipation in their social programs. Within this context a team of three applied anthropologists (the Center for Voluntary Action Research at Memphis State University) in 1982 approached one agency that was open to discussion about a collaborative effort in energy conservation through weatherization.

The client, Memphis Light, Gas and Water (MLG&W) Division of the City of Memphis, serves more than 900,000 customers with electricity from the Tennessee Valley Authority (TVA), natural gas from a transmission company, and water from deep artesian wells. As a municipally owned utility company, MLG&W has a mandate to market programs throughout the Memphis community.

In response to public criticism of increasing utility bills, MLG&W, like many utility companies, increased its effort in energy conservation programs in 1977. Through mass media advertising, middle- and upper-income residents in the MLG&W service area were informed about the energy conservation programs. However, MLG&W failed to communicate its programs to its low-income customers—the group in most need of utility assistance. Instead of responding to new programs, low-income customers became increasingly alienated and hostile toward the utility company because of rising utility bills and the complexities of dealing with a large-scale impersonal bureaucracy. The mission of the Center for Voluntary Action Research (CVAR) was to develop an effective communication system between MLG&W and low-income residents, increasing their awareness and participation in energy conservation programs. Specifically, MLG&W desired increased participation in a no-interest, long-term loan program for residential customers to weatherize their homes and reduce energy consumption.

Process and Players

Our initial team included three applied anthropologists and one graduate student from CVAR and two managers from MLG&W's Communication and Weatherization Departments. Over a two-year period the initial team activated managers from eight other public agencies and numerous grassroots networks. Our approach in solving the client's problem involved research at the agency (studying up) and neighborhood (studying down) levels, translation of that research to agencies and neighborhood residents, and mediation between the agencies and the neighborhood as they moved toward a working relationship.

The mediation of a working relationship involved the reallocation and pooling of resources by the agencies and neighborhood groups. Staff members from each agency were assigned to the neighborhood to personally interact with residents. The agencies utilized neighborhood networks in disseminating information about these resources. The mediation enabled residents to have direct impact in the redesign of the delivery system.

The two-year pilot project unfolded in five stages. Stage one was studying up. CVAR spent nine months researching MLG&W's weatherization delivery program and determining its overall effectiveness. From the research we agreed to target one low-income, inner-city, Black neighborhood with a low level of participation in the energy program.

In stage two we identified communication barriers. CVAR spent four months in extensive participant observation and conducting unstructured interviews in the target neighborhood. Through ethnographic research we uncovered the prevalent grassroots beliefs concerning the utility company and identified active communication networks, including churches, street corner groups, senior citizen clubs, community center youth groups, home owners, renters, and extended families. This information pinpointed the major issues that residents faced including rising utility costs. The information was divided into seven broad categories of belief: (1) fatalism, (2) racism, (3) big government, (4) folk notions concerning conservation, (5) individualism and self-reliance, (6) distrust, and (7) holding on. Although many of the beliefs could be viewed as structural (race and class generated), their expressions were integrated into a unique set of folk beliefs and myths. This crucial finding indicated that weatherization and utility issues were embedded in other issues such as employment, crime, health, and housing.

In stage three we developed an agency-action team. Based upon the ethnographic research, CVAR next spent three months establishing a coalition of public agencies that had an identifiable interest in the neighborhood. It paid particular attention to identifying anthropologists within the agencies.

Four anthropologists from four agencies participated: the director of the county's Office of Neighborhoods, Housing and Economic Development; the director of the Community Action Agency; the director of media relations for the public library system; and the director of outreach for the city's neighborhood program. These anthropologists were graduates of the Memphis State University applied anthropology master's program and had been involved as students in building the neighborhood data base at the university.

During stage four we presented our research results. In developing the agency-action team, CVAR made numerous presentations to participating agencies as well as to numerous neighborhood groups to clarify research findings and to establish a translation list of these findings.

The first list was an agency translation of ethnographic research into action that included the following:

1. Personalization of weatherization delivery and agency outreach.
2. Allocation (targeting) of actual fiscal resources to the neighborhood, i.e., real savings, real services, and real jobs in the neighborhood.
3. Neighborhood participation in program development and delivery.
4. Recognition of multiple-interest groups and networks in delivery.
5. Sensitivity that weatherization delivery is embedded in other issues such as jobs, health, crime, vacant lots, and transportation.

The second list was a neighborhood translation of ethnographic research into action.

1. Resurrection of a neighborhoodwide organization that would include somewhat active, but fragmented groups.
2. Involvement of the neighborhood to obtain what was lost (school and clinic).
3. Recognition that despite past participation and poor organization, it was possible to begin anew.

The translation lists became the basis for the development of an action agenda.

Stage five, which lasted six months, reallocated resources and redirected activities. In view of the translation of the research, the coalition of local agencies reallocated existing dollars as well as reassigned office staff to a neighborhood field effort. This resulted in a series of workshops held in the neighborhoods that led to agency cross-referrals and demonstration projects (see Table 8.1). Voluntary sectors within the neighborhood also contributed valuable resources necessary to the success of the project (see Table 8.2).

Results and Evaluation

In the first six months of 1984, the coalition, through the mediation role of the anthropologists, was able to bring about a dramatic turnaround in conservation in the targeted low-income neighborhood. From 1977 to 1983, 387 energy survey requests had been made from the neighborhood and 175 dwelling units were weatherized. During the first half of 1984, 140 survey requests were submitted, and, combined with earlier requests, 278 units were weatherized so that the number of weatherized units jumped from one-half unit per week before the project to 10 per week as the project progressed. The overall participation rate moved from a six-year total of 9.0 percent at the end of 1983 to 15622.0 percent by the middle of 1984. In effect the team effort produced a twentyfold increase in the number of weatherized units—representing in six months a total increase greater than the number weatherized during the previous seven years. Although spillover into adjacent neighborhoods was not measured, it must have occurred.

In addition to the rapid increase in weatherization, there were some positive secondary effects at the neighborhood level. A neighborhood association was formed that worked with different public agencies to reopen a neighborhood school that had been closed for three years (a first for Memphis). The neighborhood asked the local Jobs Training Partnership Act (JTPA) agency to assign neighborhood youth hired for the summer in neighborhood work. As a result the summer youth employment drawn from the neighborhood was directed toward neigh-

Table 8.1   Weatherization Resources by Agency and Neighborhood
            Organization

Agency/Neighborhood Organization	Contribution	Personnel	Technical Assistance
MLG&W	$28,000	4	12 workshops
Tennessee Valley Authority	$292,800 (loan program)	7	7 workshops, installation of solar heater
CVAR	$20,000	4	7 workshops, community organizing
Community Service Agency	$20,000	1	Client intakes, volunteer training sessions
County's NHED Community Div.	$70,000 (through state funds)	1	9 workshops, job training
Mayor's Action Center		1	Referrals concerning daily problems
OPD Planning Department		1	8 workshops, provided all statistical data
Library		1	Directory
Center for Neighborhoods	$100	1	3 workshops, newsletter assistance
City Beautiful		1	

borhood house painting and weatherization and consumer energy education. Finally, the neighborhood association signed a contract with the National Association of Neighborhoods and the local county government to initiate a small business that is currently contracting with county government to deliver weatherization services to the neighborhood.

The Anthropological Difference

Current solutions to increasing participation in weatherization delivery programs in the United States have ignored the literature on innovation in developing regions, such as the introduction of irrigation systems,

Table 8.2 Volunteer Sector Resources by Group

Group	Contribution	Volunteer Hours	Volunteer Efforts
Neighborhood association	$2,000 (nongrant) Dues to association funds from fund-raising efforts	1,000	Dissemination of information Organize workshops Work with agencies on policy changes
Newsletter committee		500	Dissemination of information
Senior citizens groups			Previously organized audiences for workshops Dissemination of information
Churches	Xerox machine for client intake $200	400	Meeting space Dissemination of information Previously organized audiences for workshops
Youth group		100	Dissemination of information Distribution of newsletter
Community center			Meeting space Dissemination of information

improved livestock, high-yielding seed varieties (Cochrane 1979), and even the shopping cart (Stern 1984). Social scientists in general and anthropologists in particular have established that word-of-mouth communication about a new product or practice, direct experience using it, and testimony of users have proved to be much more effective than less personal mass media advertising in developing regions.

Equally important to the knowledge of word-of-mouth communication systems is an understanding of the dynamics of how social network systems function in a particular locale. Urban ethnographers involved in network analysis in inner-city neighborhoods have yielded significant insights into the areas of job relationships, family support systems, landlord-tenant relations, and community space considerations (Suttles

1971, 1972; Stack 1974; Hannerz 1969; Liebow 1967; M. Williams 1981). In light of this ethnographic research on social networks and community organization, our action research methodology adapted the ethnographic approach to the demands of time and the production of results.

Our ethnographic research clearly established that the neighborhood-level networks and groups had deep-seated beliefs about government agencies and the utility company. The residents did not separate energy conservation issues from health, housing, and employment issues. This view was in marked contrast to the value orientation of most public agencies—that they must operate in carefully defined programmatic areas. We recognized this basic contradiction in beliefs as the key to building cooperative efforts. As a result we stressed the need to include a coalition of different agencies in the weatherization effort as well as a reallocation of existing funds and their office staff to field efforts (see Table 8.1).

We intended that staff operating in the field would personalize and individualize delivery efforts. In fact personalization of field efforts reaffirmed our research findings by disclosing neighborhood frustrations with school system policy (closing of their neighborhood school) and city planning policy (refusing to hire neighborhood youth for work in the neighborhood). The feedback from field staff to the public agency managers (coupled with our research) led to joint efforts to reverse local agency policy decisions and to create alternate delivery systems. The promotion of the neighborhood's agenda in conjunction with more personalized agency efforts (a new communication system) advanced the weatherization program in this pilot neighborhood.

As anthropologists we assisted in setting up a new communication system. In this instance communication represented a source of power for a low-income neighborhood and also served the public agencies' agenda of increasing participation rates and hence implementing a more effective delivery system. The overall effort was to advance both agendas cooperatively. Although such a communication mode is fragile, it has obvious appeal in revitalizing citizens' roles through the activation of traditional structures in a public life characterized by impersonal and large-scale programs.

Although it is difficult to generalize, individual programs within a public agency are usually marketed through the mass media. The agency assumes that the needy will respond. In reality, a sizable number of the needy will remain outside the agency's delivery system. The agency often simply chooses the easiest mechanism by which to market its services: mass media with defined costs, ratings, and market segments. Social scientists have recently questioned the utility of such a media-oriented approach by public agencies. For example, in a national review of the energy conservation delivery systems, Stern (1984:23) notes that even though U.S. utility companies now spend millions on mass media advertising campaigns to promote energy efficiency, they have little effect.

In this context, our work with the municipally owned utility company demonstrates the effectiveness of the development of a communication system (marketing system) through the activation of a network of public agencies and grassroots groups. In the communication system the anthropologist serves initially as researcher of agency and grassroots belief systems, then presenter of the research for the development of translation lists, and finally mediator of action between agencies and grassroots networks. The joint advance of the agendas of agencies and neighborhoods through continual feedback leads in this instance to the reallocation of human and fiscal resources at both levels—thus representing a critical step in the redesign of this service delivery system. In our effort the initial success of such a communication model led to the inclusion of other public agencies such as health groups and health programs in the target neighborhood as well as to the expansion of the energy conservation program into another low-income neighborhood.

As applied anthropologists we urge that successful communication models (agency-grassroots partnerships) enter into competition with mass media corporations for public marketing dollars. We hope that a continual shift of public marketing dollars will become an indicator of change in regional policy implementation, an indirect measure of neighborhood participation and a more effective means of program delivery.

References

Ciaramitaro, Bridget, and Stanley Hyland. 1983. 1982 Memphis Neighborhood Association Survey Report. Memphis, Tenn.: Center for Voluntary Action Research, Memphis State University.

Ciaramitaro, Bridget, Rosalind Cottrell, Stanley Hyland, and Charles Williams. 1983. Binghampton Pilot Project: Phase 1 Neighborhood Study Final Report. Memphis, Tenn.: Center for Voluntary Action Research, Memphis State University.

Cochrane, Glynn. 1979. *The Cultural Appraisal of Development Projects.* New York: Praeger.

Goodenough, Ward. 1966. *Cooperation in Change: An Anthropological Approach to Community Development.* New York: John Wiley and Sons.

Hannerz, Ulf. 1969. *Soulside.* New York: Columbia University Press.

Hyland, Stanley. 1979. Multiple Urban Power Structures: The Impact of Neighborhood Associations in Memphis. In Billye Fogelman, ed., *Urban Anthropology in Tennessee*, pp. 26–38. Knoxville, Tenn.: Tennessee Anthropologist.

Liebow, Elliot. 1967. *Tally's Corner.* Boston: Little, Brown.

Rogers, Everett, and F. Floyd Shoemaker. 1971. *Communication of Innovations.* New York: Free Press.

Schwartz, Norman B. 1981. Anthropological Views of Community and Community Development. *Human Organization* 40(4):313–322.

Stack, Carol B. 1974. *All Our Kin.* New York: Harper and Row.

Stern, Paul. 1984. Saving Energy: The Human Dimension. *Technology Review* 87:16–22.

Suttles, Gerald D. 1971. *The Social Order of the Slum.* Chicago: University of Chicago Press.

———. 1972. *The Social Construction of Communities.* Chicago: University of Chicago Press.

Williams, Charles. 1982. *Two Black Communities in Memphis, Tennessee: A Study in Urban Socio-political Structure.* PhD dissertation, University of Illinois, Urbana, Ill.

Williams, Melvin. 1981. *On the Street Where I Lived.* New York: Holt, Rinehart and Winston.

9 / Activating Community Participation in a Southern Paiute Reservation Development Program

Allen C. Turner

Problem and Client

In this chapter I describe how an anthropological methodology was applied to problems of community development on the Kaibab Paiute Indian Reservation in northern Arizona. The basic objective of the project was to restore the long dormant communal decision-making process to prominence in tribal affairs. Once that had been accomplished, significant physical improvements were made in the delivery of much needed water resources and in the reconstruction of reservation housing to bring it up to community standards. The principal beneficiaries—the real "clients" of the project—were the members of the Kaibab Paiute community. The planning and development program was sponsored by the Kaibab Band of Paiute Indians, the United States Department of Housing and Urban Development, and Southern Utah State College. A postproject evaluation study was sponsored by Idaho State University.

The Community Setting

The 200-square-mile Kaibab Paiute Indian Reservation lies on the Arizona Strip, a segment of the canyonlands physiographic subprovince just north of the Grand Canyon. Ranging in elevation from 4,000 to 7,000 feet, it is transected by the 1,000-foot-high Vermilion Cliffs. Below the cliffs grows the cold desert vegetation of the Upper Sonoran Life Zone—sagebrush, juniper, and pinyon pine. Above the cliffs, the Ponderosa pine of the Transition Zone is dominant.

Annual temperatures range from below zero to over 100 degrees Fahrenheit. Diurnal variation is about 30 degrees. Water resources are limited to rainfall of about 10 inches per year, six wells tapping the Sevier Aquifer, and four springs. Two of the springs, Moccasin and Pipe, lie within non-Indian enclaves established in the late nineteenth century by Mormon settlers whose descendants remain there.

In 1974, the reservation was a scene of stark contradictions. Despite a flood of well-funded and well-intentioned Federal economic development programs, there was little apparent benefit coming to the residents. The Kaibab people seemed to have given up hope of improving the quality of their lives by their own initiative and to have surrendered to the benevolent paternalism of Washington.

Water from the spring at Moccasin, contaminated by cattle there, trickled through to several houses with plumbing. Water hauled from stock tanks supplied those without. Yet a camper-trailer park with forty-eight well-watered sites was under construction to accommodate expected tourists.

Winter winds blew through the walls of many peoples' homes. Fuel costs exceeded average income, and jobs were few. Yet a million dollar multipurpose building housing a gymnasium and offices was soon to be completed.

Springtime planters relied on neighbors, usually non-Indian, for plows and timely good will. Sometimes their quiet patience was in vain. Summer sun dried out gardens when irrigation ponds broke through their worn-out dikes. Without heavy equipment, effective repairs could not be made. Yet, several electric-powered wells had been sunk and 200 acres of sagebrush had been cleared making room for commercial hayfields to supply hoped for demands.

In 1974, this was home base for 132 Southern Paiute Indians in twenty-three crowded households.

Decision-making

The reservation had become less a home than a refuge. The composition of the population fluctuated on a seasonal if not daily basis. About one-half of the residents had married into the Kaibab tribe and were enrolled in other tribes. Nonmember residents were essentially barred from participating in the formal political process by which decisionmakers were elected. The general population could take part only in the election of the tribal council, a process reminiscent of the election of boarding school class officers. Only tribal enrollees, at least twenty-one years of age, attending the tribe's annual meeting could cast votes. This practice effectively disenfranchized the majority. Absentee voices were not heard and absentee ballots were uncommon; nonmember residents of the reservation and the underage majority could not participate. Because of such limitations on eligibility a member of the council was typically elected by a plurality of only two or three votes, and many people felt unrepresented by their elected tribal officials.

Tribal council meetings were seldom attended by anyone other than council members and petitioners before it. With the focus on responding to federal rather than local program guidelines, requirements of the bureau or agency sponsoring a program, or details of budgets, little in the proceedings touched on the immediate needs of the local community. In truth, the council meetings were often tedious and ambiguous in outcome. Few on the reservation understood the complex language of the federal rules and regulations. Few had any experience in participation in long-range planning. Only a remnant remained of the more traditional decision process and that had no viability at the level of the community or tribe.

A final example of the lack in participatory decision-making was shown in the responses to the tribal planner's attempts to elicit community attitudes toward choices offered by his sponsoring agency, the Economic Development Administration (EDA). (EDA is a federal agency that makes development grants to local, including tribal, governments.) His efforts were not productive. In his words: "I try to go to different families on the Reservation and ask them what they think about this or that program. Usually I don't get much response. They either say, 'I don't know,' 'I don't care,' or 'anything you do is OK.'"

A member of the community commented, "The Council never asks us what we want. The Council never tells us what they are planning." A council member responded, "The people never come to Council meetings; all they do is complain. We don't want them to get their hopes up only to have a program fail so we don't tell them what we are planning."

Both the elected tribal council and its constituency perceived this situation to be unsatisfactory. All wanted to have a more participatory decision-making process, but none seemed able to establish it. There was a deadlock.

The Intervention

In 1974, the Southern Utah State College economic development specialist, David Conine, and I approached the tribal chairperson with an inquiry and a request: "Do you have community problems that might be effectively resolved using an anthropological approach?" "May we provide our services in exchange for learning opportunity for ourselves and our students?" After some discussion the chairperson responded, "We don't have enough housing and jobs for our people and we are afraid that they will move away and the community will not survive."

We offered to contribute technical and analytical expertise in community research and development in exchange for an opportunity for our students and faculty to learn through participation in tribal community affairs. We drafted an informal prospectus outlining an extension role for the faculty, student involvement, and tribal participation in a comprehensive community research and development program. In exchange for my assurance that students would be involved in the program, the college allowed me to schedule Fridays for work on the reservation, some ninety miles away. The proposal was approved by the college administration and by the tribal council, and work began.

The tribal planner (a member of the tribe) with technical assistance from the Indian Development District of Arizona used the prospectus as a basis for drafting a more detailed request for funding for a planning assistance grant from the U.S. Department of Housing and Urban Development (HUD).

In fall 1976, the tribe was awarded a HUD 701 Planning Assistance Grant. The grant called for specific applied research in (1) designing a planning process involving citizen input, (2) developing specific information on community needs in housing, land use, employment, economic development, and health care, (3) establishing priorities, and (4) implementing beneficial programs. The problem of participation was brought into focus by the specific requirements of the HUD grant: "Each recipient of assistance . . . shall carry out an ongoing comprehensive planning process which shall make provision for citizen participation pursuant to the regulations of the Secretary where major plans, policies, priorities, or objectives are being determined" (Pub. L. No. 90-383, Sec. 701).

This act of Congress called for the devolution of power from the administrative level of the tribal council to that of the citizen or community member. Given the current situation on the reservation, such devolution would not be easy to achieve. Neither the council nor the reservation community possessed the requisite expertise to design and implement participatory planning as mandated by HUD.

The focus of the anthropological research and development program became the HUD 701 planning process. The key problem was to design and implement a planning process involving citizen participation in a community that was not accustomed to having a significant voice in tribal affairs. The principal objective was to improve the quality of life on the reservation.

Process and Players

When I learned that the tribe had received its grant, I met with the newly elected tribal chairman to talk about the possible contributions that an outsider's perspective on community life could provide. The chairman gave me permission to enter the reservation and to take a series of baseline photographs of landscapes and structures.

To announce the HUD 701 Planning Assistance Grant, the tribal council called a general meeting of the community for September 3, 1976. About thirty people attended, including about ten children. The tribal chairman noted the need for land use planning and the identification of unspoken community values. She spoke quietly to the group, asking, "What is it that you value about how you live? What do you want the reservation to look like? These are the things that we must think about." The tribal planner explained the value of the program in placing limits on development. "How far do you want to go in economic development? The agencies always want to know if a proposal is in your comprehensive plan. We need a plan. We are not the ones that will be here to benefit by what we do. It's for the children who will be grown up in twenty years."

In response to a request from a member of the audience the planner and the chairman explained the program in the Paiute language "so the older people [could] understand," and a bilingual discussion of the program followed.

I was introduced by the chairman as "someone with an outsider's perspective" who could interpret the community and help the community to see itself. My designated position was "planning consultant," and my role was to assist the community in organizing and analyzing information.

Slide photographs that I had taken were then showed to the group. For most, these were the first pictures they had seen of their homes. The program focused attention on the physical appearance of the reservation. Pleasant scenes of the landscape, the ponds, the gardens, the houses, and the people were shown as well as unattractive features—dilapidated shacks, abandoned junk cars, public areas overgrown with weeds. The slide program was well received and stimulated considerable discussion about the reservation and what could be done to improve it. A perceptive member of the group asked a challenging question: "What do *you* get out of doing this?" My somewhat hesitant response was that I had been trained to do such work, that I was expected by my colleagues to do it, and that the project might assist me in my career. Although a salary was allocated for the position, because I was already employed by the College I suggested that we use that money to fund some positions in the program for members of the community.

In the course of the meeting the fact was brought up that the tribe had attempted to incorporate a system of community committees to monitor needs in the areas of health, education, natural resources, housing, and other areas. The tribal secretary read a list of these committees and their assigned membership. Typical responses indicated that the committee system had not been effective.

We should get a new Housing Authority. The old one never meets and we never know what they are doing. We need some Indians on the Housing Authority. . . .

I didn't even know there was a Natural Resource Committee and now I hear that I have been a member of it. . . .

I am on three committees but they never meet so I don't go. . . .

[LB] is on the Education Committee but she hasn't lived here for years.

A participant offered another challenge: "We have had enough planning. We need results. Our houses are cold in the winter and the water from the spring doesn't come for us."

Obviously, the application of anthropological insights could not wait for formal analysis; the situation called for immediate, if tentative, applications of anthropological facts and theory. For the project to be successful it would have to use existing social resources and show some early beneficial results.

The findings of our earlier ethnohistoric and historic ethnographic studies combined with preliminary observations of community life suggested that no aspect of the Southern Paiute tradition supported formal committee organization or formal systems of cooperative planning.

Whether through hypothesis or on-the-spot hunch, I thought the participation would increase if the planning system were reorganized in ways more harmonious with precedent and present patterns of social organization. An operable proposition, I thought, was that in this small-scale community with fluctuating population composition, a flexible membership planning advisory committee homologous with traditional patterns of ephemeral task-specific hunting and gathering parties would be a productive way to maximize citizen participation. Such an approach had sustained the Southern Paiutes for centuries, and, though the object of "the hunt" had changed, the hunters had not.

I suggested that the council abandon the fixed membership committees and decision style and that I meet weekly with whomever chose to participate in an ad hoc planning committee. The group discussed this proposition at length in the Paiute language and decided that I should return the following Friday.

We defined the beneficiaries of the planning program as the extended Kaibab Paiute Indian community comprising all reservation residents, both enrolled members and their in-marrying spouses, and Kaibab enrollees living elsewhere. This definition of the community was more inclusive and more realistic than the federal administrative definitions that excluded nonmember reservation residents and off-reservation tribal members.

During the following week, the woman designated to coordinate the meetings circulated written announcements of the forthcoming meeting of the "A. D. Hock Planning Committee." On September 10, 1976, the first meeting was held and was attended by sixteen participants. The main order of business was to select a program staff. By a process of discussion-to-consensus, two cochairmen, a paid program coordinator, and two paid data collectors were selected. One of the cochairmen was an elder statesman respected for his wisdom. He had assumed a traditional *niav* (leadership) role in the earlier meeting and was instrumental in securing the assent of the assembled community members. The other, a younger businesswoman, was selected for her familiarity and comfort with formal programmatic details. The program coordinator and data collectors were to be paid from program funds.

For the next year we held weekly all-day meetings. I usually brought sufficient fresh fruit, cheese, and cold meat to share at lunch with the ten or so participants. This inducement kept people from leaving and failing to return. Not everyone stayed for the whole day; people came and went as other obligations and interests intervened. These meetings served as a setting for innovation as we accumulated ideas and concentrated on issues. Early meetings were group interviews in which I elicited emic or cognitive categories of program objectives, problems, and solutions. Rather than following the formal categories of the planning grant, we used Paiute concepts. Thus, the terms of the grant, "Information Gathering," "Decision-making," and "Implementation," were replaced by "Ne we Kai va ne" (What we people must do to continue), "Tu ntu gwa" (Planning ahead), and "A hu nka va ru" (What we will do).

Two principles were identified as basic to the success of the program: (1) Developmental change should be based on existing Paiute cultural and behavioral patterns rather than on federal goals and procedures, and (2) specific change programs should be broadly beneficial to the community and not just to a few people with special needs.

Most of the fieldwork was carried out by the members of the community in a guided self-study approach patterned after that of Kimball and Pearsall (1954) in their study of the health care system in Talledega,

Alabama. This approach had at least two advantages. First, it allowed the people themselves to discover their own problems and to design solutions. Second, it was time effective for me because I was unable to spend full time at this job (although I did spend three full-time summers on the reservation in addition to two years of weekly meetings).

We purchased several inexpensive cameras and issued them to the participants to take pictures of places, people, and activities. This provided both a photographic record of physical developmental change and a source of immediate feedback to the community in subsequent community development slide shows.

During the early meetings the participants and I established a small set of high priority concerns: (1) Adequate water should be provided to the community gardens and to every household on the reservation and (2) every house should be insulated and supplied with woodstoves. Based on these concerns we designed survey questionnaires. Two paid Paiute fieldworkers conducted a house-to-house census, compiling information about occupancy, income, housing conditions, food consumption patterns, traditional and modern skills available, and attitudes about change.

My role as applied anthropologist was enacted along a continuum suggested by Gallaher and Santopolo (1967) as appropriate for extension agents. As a participant analyst, I designed research, elicited and articulated ideas and plans from the Paiute planning committee, and assessed the social impact of, for example, proposed housing locations, water supply routes, and commercial development schemes. As participant adviser, I outlined various developmental alternatives based on the foregoing analyses and presented them for the community to the tribal council and to the various federal agents. As participant advocate, I developed a collegial relationship with HUD officials in the San Francisco Regional Office. In this role, I actively promoted Kaibab as a community that deserved attention despite its small size.

Penetrating the anonymity of the Office of Indian Programs was beneficial. The program director accepted our invitation to visit the reservation to see firsthand the conditions and the planning process in operation. He proved a useful ally in deciphering the rules and regulations related to the HUD 701 planning assistance grant and directed us through the maze of requirements for a subsequently funded Community Development Block Grant.

Results and Evaluation

The results of the planning program may be somewhat arbitrarily categorized as cultural, social, and material changes. By cultural change,

I mean change at the cognitive or ideational level that is generally distributed throughout the community. Social change refers to rear-rangements or modifications in the patterns of interaction between people. Material changes affect the physical characteristics of the community.

The most fundamental change was in the pattern and process of decision-making. This involved both cultural and social aspects and produced, in the end, material changes in the physical characteristics of the community.

The foremost cultural change was the development from a no-plan orientation to an attitude that a more desirable future could be planned and that the Kaibab Paiute people were not powerless to effect beneficial social and material changes in their community. The volume of ideas about undesirable and desirable attributes of life on the reservation increased and took form as *Punim Nuwu Kaivaneh:* The Kaibab Paiute Community Plan—1980. This document outlined precedent, present, and desired community conditions. It targeted, ranked, and scheduled developmental objectives in the areas of water resources, land use, shelter, public facilities, and health care.

A social transformation took place as well. First, the process of decision-making became more egalitarian and was thereby more har-monious with the indigenous pattern. Second, there were significant changes in power relations within the community and between the tribal and federal governments.

Prior to the program most decisions were made by elected tribal officials and appointed program managers. One family cluster was clearly more involved than the others in these positions of responsibility. The planning system allowed a more consensual approach in accord with traditional Paiute patterns of cooperative action. During the first year of the program sixty-six different adult members and an uncounted number of children took part in forty-nine meetings or special planning workshops. On the average, ten people participated in each event. As the year progressed the level of participation increased for the families previously left out. By the end of the year each of the five principal family clusters was sharing approximately equally in decision-making activities. As a result positions of responsibility were more widely shared as those families gained representation on the council and in paid positions in tribal programs.

The polarity of the federal-tribal power relationship was reversed. The Department of Housing and Urban Development listened to the tribe and followed community guidelines and priorities for developmental change. With the tribally generated comprehensive plan, other federal agencies were less inclined to impose their programs without considering tribally established goals.

Another important social change with economic implications took place in upgrading the tribal workforce. Before the planning program, maintenance of the physical facilities (roads, tribal housing, water works) was provided by unskilled dollar-an-hour workers. No program or organization was in charge of maintenance and operation of the community physical plant. Acting on the recommendation of the planning group, the tribal council passed a resolution creating the Department of Plant Management. As an arm of the tribe, this department was responsible for housing construction, road maintenance, water works renovation, and general management of all physical operations on the reservation. The wages of tribal maintenance and operations personnel were immediately raised to at least minimum wage levels.

The Department of Plant Management carried out many of the designated plans in physical community development. It engaged in several important enterprises, some profit making and others gratuitous. It contracted with the Forest Service to thin timber on the National Forest and on the side stockpiled about 100 cords of firewood for the community. It upgraded the water supply system from Moccasin Spring to the village at Kaibab, repaired the irrigation systems, and installed a pipeline and storage tank system that provided, for the first time, running water and fire protection to the village of Six Mile. It initiated a refuse collection program and operated the sanitary landfill. It remodeled a number of surplus tourist cabins obtained from Zion National Park and, by combining these small units, constructed five new houses that were rented to community members.

In 1984, I returned for a summer's fieldwork on the reservation. The purpose of this revisit was to observe and evaluate the consequences of the planning program initiated eight years earlier.

Between 1976 and 1984, the number of houses on the reservation increased from twenty-three to fifty-two units whereas the population increased only from 132 to 152 persons. Thus household density was reduced from 5.7 to 2.9 persons per household. The reduction in overcrowding is a significant benefit, and several new nuclear households were spawned from the extended family households in which they were imbedded. All housing units on the reservation, both old and new, are now well insulated, and most are supplied with woodstoves. As a result heating bills have been reduced from over $100 per month to less than $30.

Most of the new housing construction contracts were let to non-Indian contractors, and the local construction industry profited from the million-dollar housing expansion program. Some of the Indian men, having acquired skills while working in the Department of Plant Management, were employed by these outside contractors.

In 1984, the participation by community members in making decisions was greater than before the intervention but less intensive and less comprehensive than when it ended in 1978. At present, the tribe has a number of standing committees that have replaced the ad hoc planning group. These fixed membership committees now include a member of the Tribal Council who serves on the council as an advocate for the respective committee. This position has effectively closed the earlier gap between community and council.

But council meetings are still poorly attended, and to many members of the tribe's staff, the Federal Register is the gospel. Many of the decisions affecting the quality of life on the reservation are made through personal contacts between tribal administrators and federal program managers. Although this contact is important, it could reduce the attention to community interests.

The planning system was designed in accord with continuing patterns of Southern Paiute social organization. The planning system was intended to continue to operate as it had during the first year even in the absence of an anthropologist's continuing intervention. We did not intend to routinize the role of anthropological planning consultant to the point of creating a dependency relationship.

In broad perspective, some things worked and others did not. Citizen participation was dramatically enhanced as long as the anthropologist was directly involved. This correlation was not intended. Rather, we thought that we had discovered a principle of community decision-making that would function without continuing professional intervention. Could the role of the anthropologist be like that of a situational headman in that when he departed, the group of participants disbanded?

We had predicted that by involving the community in the planning process there would be a continuing exercise of grassroots power and that the many federal agencies would be pleased to follow the guidelines of the community. Instead federal presence on the reservation increased as did federal influence in setting the guidelines for development, defining the terms of employment, designing housing, and delineating roles for tribal employees.

New housing, for example, was not located in accord with community sentiments that called specifically for expansion of the existing villages. Rather, it followed plans that predated the inauguration of the new planning program. It was simply not feasible to stop programs already in the pipeline. Most of the new housing has been constructed at new subdivisions situated a mile or so apart, thus making the communication of information difficult in this face-to-face community with only a handful of telephones. Consequently, impromptu gatherings, long the norm, are less frequent, and people often are uninformed of community events. Visits between elders and extended family members require use of automobiles.

Life on the reservation is now more complex. In an earlier era a person possessed a home simply by occupying it. No longer can shelter be acquired merely by moving into a vacant house. Nowadays, however, the occupant must contend with the confounding intricacies of "negative rentals," "homeownership," "turnkey housing," "mutual help," and "sliding equity payments" to maintain a place to live. A complex tribal bureaucracy has emerged to manage housing. Did we discover the keys to the community and turn them over to more powerful agents of change whose policies and priorities are not attuned to small-scale American Indian communities?

More positively, the Kaibab Paiute Tribal Council is today more receptive to community ideas. It is much less reluctant to accept any or all federally sponsored programs without assessing their benefits and costs to the community. Nevertheless, a call continues for an independent perspective attentive to community culture.

Have the seeds of tribally guided developmental change been germinated? If so, they need to be nurtured by planners trained in the theories and methods of an anthropological praxis oriented toward tribally specific community development.

The Anthropological Difference

The problem of activating community participation in the reservation planning program was framed as one of cognitive and social organization. This perspective, though perhaps not unique to anthropologists, provides effective conceptual tools for the analysis of those behaviors needed for cooperation in the design of community plans and goals.

Planning is a cognitive process because it defines abstract goals and objectives. The Kaibab Paiute community came to see beyond its day-to-day life and to anticipate a more satisfactory future. Communal or cooperative planning is a social process because it involves the reorganization of interpersonal and intergroup alliances and directs their activities toward the identification and realization of community goals and objectives.

Some specific anthropological methods of generating data were deployed in this project. The first of these was to compile and analyze the existing ethnohistory and historic ethnographic sources. Before approaching the Kaibab Paiute community, my students and I engaged in library research on the Southern Paiutes. The students wrote a series of term papers on various topics including subsistence and trade, social and political organization, and religion and cosmology. The literature indicated that the Paiutes had been classic hunter-gatherers who exploited a wide range of ecological Life Zones. They had supplemented their local economy by trade with their neighbors, particularly the Hopi and Navajo. Their political organization had centered around a temporary or situational *niav* or leader whose authority was based on his or her expertise. We learned also that this adaptation had been seriously disrupted first in the eighteenth century by the Spanish slave trade and then in the nineteenth century by the expropriation of their water resources and land base by Mormon settlers.

The documentary record showed that although several attempts had been made recently to improve the quality of the Indians' lives through legislation, education, and religion, Paiute life continued to be distinctively different from that of the surrounding population. The Southern Paiute Indians still live within their aboriginal homelands, use their native language, and sustain a separate community life. In anthropological terms, they have a persistent culture.

On the reservation we used methods of ethnographic data collection and analysis. To discover politically relevant family relationships, we elicited kinship data. Family lines and clusters corresponded closely with alliances forming around personal issues. This configuration helped explain why some committees failed to function: Their membership consisted of people who had long been in competition. This aspect, I thought, was derived from an aboriginal pattern of familistic independence.

The methods of cognitive anthropology were used to discover categories of value relevant to the Kaibab Paiute people. Most categories of value relating to community change had been those of the sponsoring federal agencies and had little meaning to the Kaibab people. "Overcrowding," "substandard housing," "moderate income," and even "elderly" are simple examples. More abstract instances include "home-ownership" and "mortgage." Instead of these foreign concepts, Paiute concerns were for warm housing (*ka ni*) and clean water (*paa*).

The extent to which anthropology makes a discernible difference in the outcome in a program such as the Kaibab Project is perhaps not as readily apparent to an anthropologist as it would be to someone trained in another discipline such as economics, sociology, geography, or political science. These sister sciences do involve different fundamental assumptions from those of anthropology, and thus they have different approaches and different objectives.

Where an economist might focus on maximizing well-being through the control of material resources, the sociologist might seek organizational change. Where the geographer might focus on the relationship between the people and their land in order to secure better shelter and more effective agriculture, the political scientist might seek to amplify the voice of the people in decision-making. Although each of these methods is effective and their objectives potentially beneficial, they are specialized and focus on particularized results. In contrast, the anthropologist's approach is more generalized and the desired result is one that integrates material, social, and ideological well-being.

The anthropologist is guided by an assumption that those several elements are integrated into a mutually interdependent whole. This assumption of holism gives rise to the proposition that changes in one arena of community life will affect changes in the others. The integrating system is culture. In the context of community development, culture is the socially transmitted rule for decision-making, the guideline for behavior, and the conceptualization of the good life. The anthropologist working in a tribal community setting will therefore seek cultural rather than simply economic, social, or political change, although these latter should be corollary results.

I may conclude, then, that anthropology does not need to be relegated to providing the cultural context of development or the background exotica but can be the lead discipline that provides the general framework for other social scientists and their activities.

References

Gallaher, Art, Jr., and Frank A. Santopolo. 1967. Perspectives on Agent Roles. *Journal of Cooperative Extension* (winter):223–230.

Kimball, Solon T., and Marion Pearsall. 1954. *The Talledega Story: A Study in Community Process.* Montgomery: University of Alabama Press.

Turner, Allen C. 1985. Adaptive Continuity and Cultural Development among the Paiute Indians of the Grand Canyon's North Rim. *Tebiwa* 22:28–53.

———. 1985. The Kaibab Paiutes: An Ecological History. New Haven: Human Relations Area Files Press.

———. 1984. Research and Development Anthropology in the Kaibab Paiute Indian Community. In William Millsap, ed., *Applied Social Science for Environmental Planning*, Boulder, Colo.: Westview Press.

———. 1981. Housing, Water, and Health Care: The Anthropology of Planning in a Southern Paiute Community. Ph.D. dissertation, Department of Anthropology, University of Kentucky. Ann Arbor: University Microfilms.

———. 1980. *Punim Nuwu Kaivaneh:* The Kaibab Paiute Community Plan—1980. San Francisco: United States Department of Housing and Urban Development. Lexington: Applied Anthropology Archives, King Library, University of Kentucky.

————. 1979. The Kaibab Paiute Community Planning Process: A Descriptive Case Study. Phoenix: Inter-Tribal Council of Arizona.

————. 1979. The Kaibab Paiute Community Planning Handbook. San Francisco: United States Department of Housing and Urban Development. Lexington: Applied Anthropology Archives, King Library, University of Kentucky.

————. 1979. The Kaibab Paiute Tribal Specific Health Plan: A Health Ethnography. Phoenix: Indian Health Service. Lexington: Applied Anthropology Archives, King Library, University of Kentucky.

————. 1974. Southern Paiute Research and Development Program. Deans' Council, Southern Utah State College. Lexington: Applied Anthropology Archives, King Library, University of Kentucky.

————, and Richard A. Thompson. 1974. Proposed State College cooperation in the Kaibab Reservation Development Program. Manuscript submitted to Kaibab Paiute Tribal Council. Lexington: Applied Anthropology Archives, King Library, University of Kentucky.

10 / FJUA Relocation: Applying Clinical Anthropology in a Troubled Situation

Martin D. Topper

Problem and Client

Public Law 93-531 mandated that approximately 10,000 Navajos would have to relocate from 900,000 acres of reservation land in northeastern Arizona. The relocation was intended to provide a final and equitable solution to a 100-year-old land dispute between the Navajo and Hopi tribes over which tribe had the legal right to occupy lands ruled to be held jointly by both tribes. The Navajos occupied about 90 percent of this Federal Joint Use Area (FJUA), and in 1974 Congress decided that the lands should be split on a fifty-fifty basis, meaning that many Navajos would have to move.

As a federal mediator began the process of drawing a dividing line between the two tribes, an increasing number of potential relocatees were using Indian Health Service (IHS) facilities for the treatment of complaints stemming from the emotional stress of relocation. This observation raised questions about how these stresses were being manifested in physical and emotional illnesses. The IHS staff wondered what could be done to reduce the stress of relocation. To answer these questions, the Mental Health Branch of the Navajo Area Office of the Indian Health Service (NAIHS) hired an anthropologist. The anthropologist had three objectives. First, he was to gather data on problems experienced by relocatees and potential relocatees, including difficulties

This chapter represents solely the opinions of the author and does not represent the opinions of the federal government, the Indian Health Service, any tribal organization, or any other person.

with relocation housing, problems adjusting to off-reservation relocation homes, difficulties caused by mandatory livestock reduction in the FJUA, problems arising from a freeze on new construction in the FJUA, and stress resulting from the uncertainty generated by new regulations, continuing lawsuits between the two tribes, and modifications of the relocation law. Second, the anthropologist was to study the impacts of the requests by relocatees and potential relocatees on the operation of NAIHS mental health clinics. And, finally, the anthropologist was to provide consultation to NAIHS and other federal, state, and tribal agencies on reducing impacts of relocation to manageable proportions. The anthropologist's broad role required a variety of traditional and nontraditional skills.

Process and Players

Applied anthropology is not as much a field as a process. The process is usually composed of three stages during which the anthropologist, the work, and the situation all interact and evolve in a mutually beneficial direction. The stages—discovery/planning, intervention, and evaluation—do not always occur in perfect sequence. The work of each stage often requires that some work from one or more of the other stages be simultaneously undertaken. However, the work progresses more efficiently and effectively if the sequence is kept relatively intact.

Discovery/Planning Stage

The discovery/planning stage quickly showed that a great deal needed to be learned before any intervention would be possible. The complex issues surrounding the relocation were debated in both the courts and Congress, and they had been studied and discussed by lawyers for both tribes. Since the issues had been largely debated in legal terms, it was not surprising that the relocation law had been written by Congress mainly from the perspective of property rights. However, the human costs of relocating Navajos and the impacts of implementing a simultaneous program of livestock reduction were not well understood at the time that P.L. 93-531 was passed.

Therefore, the anthropologist's first step was to investigate the general situation and learn what was known about the health and human impacts of relocation. This information was then shared with other NAIHS staff so joint decisions about further research could be made. This initial information was gathered from a number of resources, some of which were traditionally used by anthropologists and others which were not. Although the anthropologist needed to develop an original data base on this subject, the necessary information probably could not be found in anthropological or other scientific journals because little documentation existed on the process of Indian relocation or its impacts on health and health care. Even the literature on recent relocations on other continents did not contain much information on health and health care impacts.

But if published literature was not very helpful, what would be? The first source for the original data base was local newspapers—a resource often ignored by anthropologists, who often feel that journalists are superficial or biased in their reporting. However, newspaper reports provide timely accounts whereas information in professional journals and books may be ten years old because of the lag between collection and publication. Anthropologists simply have to be careful to look for and discount the bias and superficiality that sometimes appears in these reports.

A second data source was interviews with workers from other government agencies including the Navajo and Hopi Indian Relocation Commission, the Bureau of Indian Affairs, the Navajo Tribal Land Dispute Commission, and several hospitals and clinics of the Indian Health Service. These employees were asked about relocation law and the regulations and procedures used to implement it and then about the impacts of relocation and the steps agencies were taking to alleviate them. The third data source was legal documents. All available court and legislative documents were assembled so that an objective evaluation could be made of the impacts of relocation and other attempts to solve the land dispute. The fourth data source involved studies commissioned by federal and tribal agencies to determine the impacts of livestock reduction and relocation. The final source of data was the statements of Navajos and Hopis involved in the dispute.

The discovery stage provided a rich fund of information for planning interventions. The results of data analysis indicated that relocated Navajos would probably experience significant psychological impacts. They also showed that despite the anxiety about relocation and the law suits brought by both tribes regarding relocation, many people were not well informed about what was happening. Because of these results, three specific interventions were suggested to Indian Health Service.

Intervention Stage

The first intervention—a monthly newsletter, the *JUA Report*—was aimed specifically at the lack of information concerning the relocation process. Developed by the anthropologist, the newsletter summarized information obtained through several sources: meetings with the lead agencies working with both tribes, official federal and tribal documents published during the month, and recent television and newspaper reports. Information was selected according to criteria. Most important, it had to conform to the journalist's criteria of "hard news": It had to be timely and important. News items were also selected if they were of interest to specific groups within the audience. For example, news items on the mental health of relocatees would be important to mental health workers but less interesting to other readers. Items of high interest to a minority of the readers were put on page two.

Besides the newsletter, the anthropologist held in-service training sessions for NAIHS staff and the staffs of other agencies to increase the flow of accurate information. These sessions provided summary statements of events in the FJUA, and staff members could ask questions and get immediate responses about such topics as health impacts, the location of the partition line, and recent court decisions.

In the second major intervention the anthropologist planned a research project to learn how the situation in the FJUA was impacting the NAIHS clinics. The project involved an in-house survey of the use of mental health staff to fill out questionnaires about their patients' problems. The study was designed to use available resources and did not call for long interview sheets or elaborate statistical analyses. Rather than acquiring a larger data base on the FJUA, the study simply investigated if relocatees were utilizing NAIHS Mental Health Branch services at rates higher than those for nonrelocatees or for Navajos in general. The data base provided a core of information on age, sex, occupation, community of residence, diagnosis, and summary of complaints that gave insights about who was using the NAIHS mental health services and why they were using them.

The third intervention provided ongoing consultation to non-NAIHS agencies. Informants in many non-NAIHS agencies were interested in the data from the clinic utilization survey and in anthropological consultations concerning decisions that they had to make within their own programs. They also consulted the anthropologist as a NAIHS staff member to help develop memoranda of agreement and other operating mechanisms by which they could regularize their working relationships with NAIHS on issues ranging from referral processes to the construction of sanitation facilities for relocatee housing. Although this intervention was not originally envisioned during the discovery phase, as the work progressed it gradually evolved as a very important part of the anthropologist's role.

Evaluation Stage

The survey yielded both expected and unexpected results. Although the anthropologist expected that relocatees were using mental health clinics at a higher rate, he did not anticipate the degree of emotional distress that they suffered. Also unexpected was the interest of lawyers, courts, and legislative bodies in the results of the research on clinic usage. Once the results were in, a fourth intervention evolved: that of anthropologist as neutral, expert witness.

Results and Evaluation

First Intervention

The best way to discuss results is to critically look at each intervention. The first intervention's goal was to increase the level of communication in the FJUA and disseminate accurate information. This intervention was highly successful because it provided an objective data source while developments in the FJUA were changing almost daily. It helped to substantially decrease the number of rumors and to provide a reliable source of information to which people could refer. It also caused the anthropologist to become a clinical resource. A number of patients and other individuals were referred to him for assistance in solving problems arising because of the land dispute. In addition, he became a networking resource for putting people with land dispute problems together with resources in both NAIHS and other agencies.

The first intervention lasted approximately three years. After a law to amend and clarify the Relocation Act was passed and the final federal partition line was drawn, the need for continuous updating decreased markedly. Therefore, the *JUA Report* was terminated, and in-service training sessions were held less frequently.

Second Intervention

The second intervention was also very successful. It produced data that conclusively indicated NAIHS Mental Health Branch clinics were being utilized by relocatees at a much higher rate than by nonrelocatees or by Navajos in general (Topper 1980:6). These data corroborated findings by Scudder et al. (1979). It also produced the first evidence that stress resulting from involuntary relocation is associated with the development of a specific type of mental illness. Potential relocatees from the FJUA developed depressive psychopathology at a rate up to 7.5 times that for nonrelocatees (Topper and Johnson 1979:6).

These results clearly showed that relocation had a mental health impact among potential relocatees from the FJUA. They also indicated that less acculturated individuals over forty were a high risk population for the development of mental depression.

Several approaches were taken by various organizations to determine what could be done for these individuals. Within NAIHS, efforts to increase services to the potential relocatees and to sensitize services to their needs occurred on both the areawide and the individual service unit level. Attempts at the latter level involved both sensitizing staff to the specific needs of relocatee patients and attempting to increase the size and degree of professional training of the staff.

Given the broad mandate of NAIHS and considerable limitations on program funding in fiscal years 1981–1983, a specialized NAIHS mental health program for the FJUA was not feasible. However, the Navajo tribe was developing a tribal system of behavioral health services and had expressed interest in providing direct mental health services to individuals who lived in the FJUA. In spring 1982 the Navajo tribe established its FJUA Mental Health Program, which employed three tribal social workers and three outreach aides. From the outset this program proved to be very valuable especially in early identification of health problems and early treatment of individuals. The anthropologist, who by this time had begun clinical services at the Winslow service unit in response to FJUA and other patient needs, consulted with the program's staff on difficult patient issues. As time went by, the anthropologist provided case review sessions for the tribal program, encouraged increasing involvement of the Winslow service unit mental health technician with it, and moved to establish a relationship between the tribal program and the Western Regional Program of the NAIHS Mental Health Branch. The response to the data uncovered in the second intervention can therefore be summarized as a joint NAIHS and Navajo tribal action to provide an increase in both the quality and the number of services to the high-risk population in the FJUA.

Third Intervention

The third intervention involved the anthropologist's consultations with other agencies. The anthropologist discovered that many agencies, such as the Tribal FJUA Mental Health Program and the Navajo Tribal Land Dispute Commission, had direct roles in promoting the physical and emotional health of the FJUA Navajos. The Navajo Tribal Land Dispute Commission, established by the Navajo tribe to act as its agent in all land disputes with the Hopi tribe, helped acquire resources for people displaced or otherwise affected by these disputes. This commission worked closely with the Navajo Area Office of the Bureau of Indian Affairs. Together these two agencies and NAIHS developed a $7.7 million proposal to provide services in the FJUA that would assist both tribes in overcoming the impacts of relocation, building freezes, and livestock reduction.

Other agencies that the anthropologist worked closely with included the Flagstaff Office of the Bureau of Indian Affairs (BIA), the Navajo-Hopi Relocation Commission, and Northern Arizona University (NAU). The Flagstaff office of the BIA was in charge of livestock reduction. When the staff needed ethnographic data to determine the number of sheep traditionally needed to support an individual Navajo household member at the subsistence level, it consulted the NAIHS anthropologist who used data from his dissertation and the existing literature to develop an estimate. The Navajo-Hopi Relocation Commission discussed various cultural issues in relocation with the anthropologist and asked him to help draw up a memorandum of agreement with NAIHS concerning medical examinations for Navajos applying for life estates under P.L. 96-305. It also discussed health issues related to relocation with him, and he drafted a plan for a multimillion dollar health center on new reservation lands acquired for Navajo relocatees under P.L. 96-305 by the Relocation Commission.

Finally, the anthropologist worked closely with other anthropologists, especially those at Northern Arizona University. NAU anthropologists, who had conducted studies of the impacts of livestock reduction and other subjects, worked together with the anthropologist to develop a mutually supportive and lengthy research collaboration. The anthropologist also worked with other anthropological and nonanthropological researchers in attempts to generate as many reliable data as possible about the impacts of the land dispute and the legal decisions and laws designed to produce a settlement between the two tribes.

Fourth Intervention

The fourth intervention was not planned during the discovery/planning stage. It arose from the needs of the Navajo tribe and its attorneys to use the research findings and clinical impressions of the anthropologist to seek relief for human suffering, which they felt was a direct result of the land dispute. This situation was sensitive for the anthropologist because NAIHS had a mission to provide care to all Indian beneficiaries and needed to remain impartial. Since the anthropologist was an employee of NAIHS, he shared the delicate position of his agency. On one hand, information gathered by the agency indicated that the dispute was having negative impacts on the mental health of some Navajos who were about to be relocated. On the other hand, the agency had to determine how to utilize and disseminate this information beneficially without becoming a major factor in the dispute itself.

The agency's solution was to make data available in an objective and impartial manner—in data summaries, research reports, and the *JUA*

Report. None of the information included confidential material. Because the research reports and the *JUA Report* were documents of a federal agency, they were all in the public domain and were available to any U.S. citizen under the Freedom of Information Act as nonclassified documents. The general public was made aware that these documents were available, and they were distributed to interested parties upon request.

A number of agencies expressed interest in the results of the research and in the *JUA Report*, including the Navajo tribe, various federal agencies, the White House, various federal courts, and the Senate Select Committee on Indian Affairs. Much of this interest was stimulated by lawyers who worked for the Navajo tribe; in many cases direct requests were made for an agency to enter a specific case or hearing on the side of the tribe. The information contained in the reports, after all, did support the case for developing means of reducing the impacts of relocation; however, how could the agency avoid the next step—arguing for a cessation of relocation and therefore generating emotional stress for the Hopi?

The solution to this dilemma was for the agency to act as a neutral witness to the extent possible. It presented the data and briefings with minimal interpretation. It required formal requests for hearings; for court hearings this meant that subpoenas were required; for U.S. Senate hearings a formal written invitation was required and testimony was submitted separately. In this way, data were released to those for whom it had direct relevance and interest and in a way in which it might be used in the decision-making process. However, it was not released in a manner that would violate the NAIHS trust relationship with any of its beneficiaries or the principles of Indian self-determination.

A number of lessons about the use of anthropological research in intergovernmental environments were learned during this work. First, such work is very complex. An anthropologist conducting such work within an agency must ask questions in which the agency is interested. These questions invariably deal with areas of policy, and agency policies frequently concern complex issues that have very unclear boundaries. Therefore, the anthropologist finds it is very difficult to define the work narrowly and conduct the project from an academic perspective, which calls for clearly defined hypotheses proposed after an exhaustive literature search. Instead, he or she must learn what questions can be asked and what questions are worth asking. In this approach the anthropologist must remember that doing nothing is a perfectly acceptable plan if the discovery process indicates that intervention will probably not produce beneficial changes in policy, procedures, or services. For this reason a careful, three-stage approach employing the processes of discovery/ planning, intervention, and evaluation was employed.

However, once it is determined that anthropological intervention can produce an improvement, the second lesson becomes apparent. Actions in the intervention stage are always actions of consequence. No matter how small the impact, interventions aimed at helping a human service agency more completely understand and develop ways of coping with the problems of the people it serves necessarily affect people's lives. And some individuals will perceive a positive impact and others a negative one.

This brings up the third lesson—that of balancing the client's and the general population's interests. Many people will attempt to use the study's results for their own benefit; they may even attempt to recast the interventions into instruments of action for purposes not always anticipated in the discovery/planning stage. However, when the anthropologist sees that additional interventions must be developed, he or she must formulate them in a manner that protects the client's interests while not obstructing processes that might ultimately have beneficial effects. The anthropologist should realize at the outset that he or she will not have the same control over the data that an anthropologist working in a university might. Therefore, issues such as confidentiality, protection of subjects, and dissemination of data assume an even greater than normal importance due to the synergism of imperfect control and unavoidable consequence.

The fourth and final lesson of this project is the limitations of its impact. Neither the anthropologist nor the client agency will be able to effect all the changes necessary to remedy all the problems inherent in a situation. The anthropologist and the client agency can deal directly with only such problems as increasing the flow of accurate information (as with the *JUA Report*). Other problems will require the assistance of other agencies, as in the joint NAIHS and Navajo tribal efforts to provide patient care to FJUA residents suffering from emotional problems. Still other problems like the legal difficulties of relocatees must be left to other parties.

As a group these four lessons indicate that clinical anthropological intervention on the agency level is often unlike anthropological research at the university level. The problems are more complex and less well defined, they often must be studied and resolved within strict time limits, and they often have unanticipated consequences that must be dealt with to prevent deterioration in the client's situation. This level of responsibility is not often encountered in more academic settings.

The Anthropological Difference

Anthropology played a very important role in this project. In fact, the work could not have been carried out without many kinds of anthropological involvement. During the discovery/planning stage anthropological data were vital. The work of Wood and Vanette (1979a) was very important in developing a demographic and economic understanding of the Navajos of the FJUA. The research of Scudder et al. (1979) concerning the expected impacts of relocation was also important in helping establish the overall framework for this project. Personal conversations with both Scudder and Colson concerning their research on compulsory relocation were also important. Finally, the understanding that the anthropologist acquired from over three years of fieldwork among the Navajos provided insights for hypotheses about impacts and offered a framework by which resulting data could be interpreted.

Anthropological perspectives were central in planning work with other government agencies. To study how the various agencies involved with the relocatees were organized and how they were or were not functioning, the anthropologist utilized the perspective of social anthropology. He then identified key positions and individuals within the organizations and worked with them to define and solve problems in their interrelations with each other and with the relocatees. This approach promoted the rapid development of a positive relationship between anthropologist, client, and agency.

Anthropological perspectives were central to all the interventions but were perhaps most critical in the second. Obviously the anthropological perspective was important in designing, administering, and analyzing the results of the patient questionnaire. However, the role of anthropology in delivering direct services to patients is not as apparent. Many of the most severely depressed patients were traditional Navajo women over the age of forty whose lifestyles were being severely altered because of livestock reduction and relocation. The anthropologist's experience of living with elderly Navajos in a traditional Navajo sheep camp provided him with an in-depth understanding of the magnitude of the changes in their lives and the emotional dislocation that these changes could produce. Such knowledge helped the clinic staff develop an empathic response to the problems of these patients and plan clinical treatments that met their specific needs.

Finally, the first intervention utilized a form of applied anthropology not commonly thought of in work among American Indians. The procedures employed in producing the *JUA Report* and in working with correspondents from such organizations as the *New York Times*, *Time Magazine*, and local media were developed according to the principles of media anthropology described by Eiselein and Topper (1976). This basic understanding of mediated communications was very helpful in organizing important information so that it could be conveyed in a clear and concise manner.

Because of its broad scope, the project might best be considered "action anthropology" as defined by Sol Tax (1975). As such, it demonstrates the usefulness of employing anthropology broadly to generate and communicate information and thereby stimulate action. Anthropology used in this way helped the project achieve its goals of helping provide better services to a group of people under severe stress.

References

Eiselein, E. B., and M. D. Topper. 1976. *Media Anthropology,* a special edition of *Human Organization,* June.

Scudder, T., D. Aberle, D. Begishe, E. Colson, C. Etsitty, J. Joe, M.E.D. Scudder, B.B.G. Tippeconnie, R. Walters, and J. Williamson. 1979. *Expected Impacts of Compulsory Relocation on Navajos With Special Emphasis on Relocation from the Former Joint Use Area Required by P.L. 93-531.* Binghamton, N.Y.: Institute for Development Anthropology, Inc.

Tax, S. 1975. "The Bow and the How: Reflections on Hunters, Villagers, and Anthropologists." In *Action Anthropology,* a special issue of *Current Anthropology* 16, no. 4, December 1975.

Topper, M. D. 1980. "Effects of P.L. 93-531 on Navajo Area Mental Health Patients from the Former Navajo-Hopi Joint Use Area: Final Report." Ms., Indian Health Service, Window Rock, Arizona.

Topper, M. D., and L. Johnson. 1979. "Effects of Forced Relocation on Navajo Mental Health Patients from the Former Navajo-Hopi Joint Use Area." Ms. Indian Health Service, Window Rock, Arizona (also published in the *White Cloud Journal* 1980).

Wood, J., and W. Vanette. 1979a. *A Socio-Cultural Assessment of the Livestock Reduction Program In the Navajo-Hopi Joint Use Area.* Flagstaff, Arizona: Flagstaff Office of the Bureau of Indian Affairs.

————. 1979b. "A Preliminary Assessment of the Significance of Navajo Sacred Places in the Big Mountain Area." Ms. Navajo and Hopi Indian Relocation Commission, Flagstaff, Arizona.

11 / A Case of Lead Poisoning from Folk Remedies in Mexican American Communities

Robert T. Trotter II

Problem and Client

Three sources of lead poisoning most commonly affect children in the United States: eating lead-based paint chips, living and playing near a smelter where even the dust has a high lead content, and eating off pottery with an improperly treated lead glaze. This chapter describes the discovery of a fourth source of lead poisoning, one resulting from folk medicine practices in Mexican American communities.

In summer 1981, a team of emergency room health professionals in Los Angeles discovered an unusual case of lead poisoning. They treated a child with classic symptoms of heavy metal poisoning. When they pumped the child's stomach, they found a bright orange powder. Laboratory analysis of the powder determined that it was lead tetroxide (PbO_4) with an elemental lead content of more than 90 percent. After being strenuously questioned, the child's mother admitted giving the child a powdered remedy called *azarcon.* She also said that the powder was used to treat a folk illness called *empacho,* which translates roughly as a combination of indigestion and constipation. Empacho is believed by people who treat it to be caused by a bolus of food sticking to the intestinal wall. Unfortunately, this case was not handled in a culturally sensitive way, and the child was not brought back for follow-up. However, a general public health alert was sent out (see MMWR 1981, 1982; Trotter et al. 1984).

As a result of the public health alert, a second case of lead poisoning from azarcon was discovered in Greeley, Colorado, by a nurse from the Sunrise Health Clinic who was culturally sensitive to the parents' claim that the child was not eating paint (the most commonly suspected cause). Having read about the azarcon case in Los Angeles, the nurse asked the mother if she was treating the child for empacho, and, when she answered yes, asked if the mother was using azarcon as a remedy. Analysis of the powder that the mother was keeping with the family's medicines confirmed that it was lead tetroxide.

Until this time, the use of lead as a home remedy had been assumed to occur only in isolated cases, and no anthropological input had been sought. However, additional questioning by the Los Angeles County Health Department and by individuals at the Sunrise Community Health Center turned up apparent widespread knowledge of azarcon in both Mexican American communities. The U.S. Public Health Service decided at this point that an anthropologist's study of this potential problem would be useful.

About six months after the azarcon problem was discovered, I was called by a friend who worked in the Region VI office for the Public Health Service (PHS) in Dallas. He asked me if I had ever heard of a remedy called azarcon while I was doing my research on Mexican American folk medicine. I had not. He then told me about the cases found in Los Angeles and Greeley and asked me to look for azarcon in south Texas.

I searched all the herb shops in four towns, including the one in the market in Reynosa, Mexico, and talked with *curanderos* (folk healers) living on the U.S.-Mexican border. I did not find azarcon nor did I find anyone who knew what it was. I reported this fact to my friend, and we both were relieved that the problem seemed to be confined to the western United States. Not long after I received a packet of information from the Los Angeles County Health Department, which had conducted a small survey on azarcon. Among other findings they had discovered some alternate names for the preparation. I went back to the herb shops to look for azarcon under its alternate names because the common names of remedies often change drastically from region to region.

The most important alternate name turned out to be *greta*. When I asked for greta in Texas I was sold a heavy yellow powder that, when analyzed, was found to be lead oxide (PbO) with an elemental lead content of approximately 90 percent. The shop owners told me that greta was used to treat empacho. So we now had confirmation that two related lead-based remedies were being used to treat empacho in Mexican American communities. In fact, a wholesale distributor in Texas, which was also selling over 200 other remedies to retail outlets, was supplying greta to more than 120 herb shops (*yerberias*). This finding drastically shaped both the scope and the content of the health education project that we started soon after this discovery. Because of the geographical scope of the problem and the multiple compounds involved, in the end six interacting clients utilized applied anthropology services to deal with the threat of greta and azarcon.

My first client was the Region VI Office of PHS. As previously described, it sponsored my initial narrowly focused ethnographic study to find azarcon—before our knowledge of greta. The second client group that requested my help was the task force formed to create and implement a health education project directed at eliminating the use of azarcon in Mexican American communities in Colorado and California. The project was sponsored through a federally funded migrant and community health center, the Sunrise Health Center, but was funded by the foundation of a private corporation. Our objective was to develop culturally sensitive health awareness materials that would reduce the risk of people using azarcon without attacking or denigrating the folk medical system. We knew that attacks on folk beliefs would produce strong resistance to the whole campaign and make people ignore our message. I was asked to participate because of my research on Mexican American folk medicine, in the hopes that my ethnographic data could be used to help design a health awareness campaign that would encourage a switch to non-poisonous remedies.

The technique behind this approach has been successfully used by all major advertising agencies for decades: It is relatively easy to get people to switch from one product to another when both products perform the same function. It is difficult or impossible to get people to stop using a product for which there is a felt need, regardless of the known potential for harm for that product, unless one provides an acceptable alternative. Thus, it is easy to get a smoker to switch from Camel filters to Winstons but very hard to get that person to stop smoking altogether. So we decided that we would attempt to give people the alternative of switching from greta or azarcon to another remedy for empacho, such as *te de manzanilla* (chamomile), known to be harmless, rather than trying to get people to stop treating empacho altogether.

The discovery of greta use in Texas and Mexico produced a third client. The Food and Drug Administration (FDA) decided it needed basic ethnographic information on the use of greta. It wanted to know who used greta, what it was used for, how it was used, and where it could be purchased. Lead oxide is most commonly used as an industrial compound (as an adherent in marine paints) and as a color component in the paint used to make the "no passing" stripes on U.S. highways. It has never been considered either a food additive or a potential drug. Therefore, the FDA needed verifiable data that the compound was being used as a "drug." The FDA asked me to conduct a short, thorough ethnography in the herb shops where I had found the greta. This study included collecting samples and interviewing the owners (and a number of clients who wandered in to buy other remedies) about the ways that greta was used, what it was used to treat, how it was prepared, and the size of dose given for children and adults. These data allowed the FDA to determine that greta was a food additive and enabled it to exercise its authority to issue a Class I recall to ban the sale of these lead compounds as remedies. The information I gathered was important because herbal remedies do not normally fall under the jurisdiction of the FDA,[1] except in terms of the cleanliness requirements surrounding their packaging.

The discovery of greta in Texas caused the regional office of Health and Human Services (HHS) to request my assistance in creating and executing a survey along the U.S./Mexican border to discover how much knowledge people had about greta and azarcon and how many people used them. HHS felt that the use might be much more extensive than was suggested by the relatively small number of poisonings discovered in clinics. The survey indicated that as many as 10 percent of the Mexican American households along the border had at one time used greta or azarcon. The survey also turned up several other potentially toxic compounds that included mercury and laundry bluing (Trotter 1985).

The fifth group to request data was the Hidalgo County Health Care Corporation, a local migrant clinic. It asked for a survey to determine the level of greta and azarcon use in the local population compared with their clinic population. The HHS regional survey had only sampled clinic populations. The Hidalgo County research project involved simultaneously sampling at the clinics and in the communities from which the clinic population is derived. Over a two-week period, a stratified random sample of informants at the clinic sites were given a questionnaire designed for the HHS regional survey. At the same time, a random stratified block cluster sample of households in the catchment communities were administered the same questionnaire. The results indicated that no significant difference existed between the two populations in terms of their knowledge about and use of greta and azarcon. The data showed trends that suggested that the clinic populations were more likely to treat folk illnesses than was the population at large.

My final client was the Migrant Health Service, a division of the PHS. The Migrant Health Service requested consultation on the necessity of a lead initiative for the entire United States, based on the results of the ethnographic and survey research conducted for other groups involved in the overall project. In the end, it was decided that a nationwide lead initiative was not necessary. Instead, the areas of high greta and azarcon use were targeted for a special initiative and received special notification of the problem.

Process and Players

The wide geographical distribution of greta and azarcon use, their employment as traditional remedies, and their inclusion in the treatment of a folk illness made this problem ideal for intervention by an anthropologist. Among other qualities, we tend to have a high ambiguity quotient: We tolerate poorly defined research objectives and virtually boundary-free problems that must be analyzed and solved simultaneously. The fact that the project rapidly developed a multiple-client base also made it very suitable for applied anthropology rather than for another social science. Anthropologists are often called upon to serve diverse, even conflicting, roles as culturebrokers. Multiple clients are no different from multiple community interest groups. Serving as a go-between in one setting develops the skills for doing so in any other setting.

From this perspective, my participation was requested by various clients because medical anthropologists have become known for being comfortable and competent in dealing with the types of issues presented by the greta and azarcon problem (problems that do not fit existing, well-defined categories or public health procedures). I did not become involved through a disguised or accidental process; my expertise was specifically sought because of the clients' recognition that they wanted a particular set of skills. This was particularly clear for the group creating the health education program. It deliberately sought an anthropologist with current knowledge about the Mexican American folk medical system. I was chosen because several people in the group had either read articles I had written or had heard me speak publicly about folk medicine. Likewise the migrant health program of PHS wanted someone with the same knowledge base, and I had previously worked with several of the individuals there.

My role evolved into a combination of researcher, consultant, communication bridge, and developer of program elements. My goal was to help create a culturally sensitive and effective method for reducing the use of these two folk remedies without interfering with the overall use of folk medicine. Another of my critical roles was that of information broker between the various client groups, some of which had not previously been in communication. Some of these groups had severe organizational barriers to communication with one another. One such barrier was simply organizational distance; the Washington-based migrant health officials only dealt with the local programs within certain contexts, such as regional and national meetings, or when a problem occurred in the operation of a clinic. I provided a good temporary (higher intensity) communication bridge to facilitate the exchange of information for this project. In the same way, the PHS and FDA had little need for contact, except for the temporary mutual need to solve different aspects of the greta/azarcon problem. But each of these groups found it useful to have the information available to, or available from, the others.

My final role was that of a scholar to publish the results of the study. The group developing the health education project wanted my findings published in order to disseminate the information about greta and azarcon as widely as possible. PHS wanted my results because it was finding it more and more difficult to put money into projects on the sole basis of an emotional appeal. The federal government (and increasing numbers of state and local governments) are reluctant to recognize "problems" that are not sufficiently documented and shown to be "real." One of the favored forms of documentation is publication in scientific journals. So following the normal process of publishing the results of an investigation allows an agency or organization to demonstrate a need for a specific program. The agency can support a request for a short-term (emergency) effort or can request a future increase in funds (or at least the maintenance of their prior funding levels). Scholarly documentation of problems and program effectiveness is particularly useful for programs that receive federal funds on an annual basis. When the preliminary results of my ethnographic research were published in *Medical Anthropology Quarterly* (Trotter et al. 1984), the officials in the migrant health program felt they could reasonably justify the expenditure of funds to deal with the part of the greta and azarcon problem that affected their clinics.

Publication can provide other long-term benefits. Naming members of the nonscholar staff as co-authors of publications not only gives them appropriate recognition for their contributions but also can increase the opportunities for future funding. Sharing a publication and its visibility tends to be excellent public relations. Clients can use the prestige of being an author in the development of their own careers. This tends to improve the chances of the anthropologist securing additional consultant work from that source. It produces a basic win/win situation.

Results and Evaluation

Because this project involved several clients, it also had multiple results and multiple levels of outcomes. The Sunrise Clinic health education project resulted in considerable media exposure on the existence and dangers of greta and azarcon. This exposure included radio public service announcements broadcast on Spanish radio stations, a special television program aired in Los Angeles county, and an information packet sent to migrant clinics. These informational campaigns contained the suggestion that people switch to other remedies because greta and azarcon were hazardous.

The other major accomplishment of the Sunrise project was the production and distribution of a poster designed by Mexican American commercial design students at Pan American University. The students were provided an in-depth briefing on the problem and our investigation; then were turned loose to create a culturally appropriate poster. A small cash prize was given to the student with the best design. Twenty posters were completed and turned over to a group of Mexican American clients and staff at the clinic to judge for most effective design. The final poster, which combines elements in two of the submissions, uses the culturally emotive symbol of La Meurte (a skeleton) to warn of the dangers of the use of greta and azarcon. The dominant impact of the poster is visual/emotional—to trigger the client into asking the clinic staff about greta and azarcon. The group felt that too many words would dilute the impact of the poster, so we did not attempt to incorporate the theme of product switch into the design. Posters with this design have been placed in over 5,000 clinics and other public access sites in each state with a concentration of Mexican Americans.[2]

The success of the overall campaign is demonstrated by the fact that some two years after the project was completed, interest had died down, and both greta and azarcon were hard to find in the United States. Another measure of the campaign's lasting success is illustrated by the doctor in El Paso who treated a child with classic lead poisoning symptoms. Not only did he recognize the probable cause of the symptoms (lead poisoning has such common symptoms that it is rarely suspected), he immediately asked the mother if the child was being treated with greta or azarcon. It turned out to be greta, and the child was immediately treated, with no serious long-term problems. The doctor was very happy that he had caught a problem that others might have missed, and we were pleased to discover that the project had at least a qualitative measure of success. Based on anecdotal information, the project appears to have had an important effect on public knowledge about these remedies and has reduced their use by some degree. However, no scientific effort was made to determine exactly how much change has occurred. Even with the increased information, these compounds will continue to be used regardless of the effectiveness of the campaign. Knowledge does not always drive behavior, as is evident in all the results of nonsmoking campaigns.

The work completed for the FDA was successful within the parameters set by the client. The data were sufficient to allow the agency to determine that the consumption of greta and azarcon fell within their jurisdiction, and it was able to successfully conduct a recall. Additionally, the data and the agency's recognition of its validity allow it to deal with future incidences of the sale of these two compounds as home remedies. This is a positive benefit because reuse of the compound is virtually assured by the fact that Mexico is the primary source of folk knowledge about the use of greta and azarcon and the source of the compounds themselves. Unfortunately, the public health sector in Mexico has not been able to devote many resources to this particular problem.

My work for the regional office of HHS resulted in data that allowed policy to be set and lead screening procedures to be amended at both national and regional levels to deal with this new source of lead poisoning. The basic policies dictated the creation of the new lead protocols. The agency pinpointed potential areas of high usage of the compounds and recommended cost-effective lead screening programs to be undertaken at selected sites. The screening is accomplished by drawing small samples of blood and testing it chemically for the effects or presence of lead. Because of the survey and accompanying ethnographic data the lead screening protocols for migrant and public health services were modified to include ethnomedical sources of poisoning, such as greta and azarcon. Clinics were alerted to this source, and a growing number of cases have subsequently been discovered that would have otherwise been overlooked.

The data provided to HHS also permitted cost avoidances. Just after the discovery of greta and azarcon there was a rush to do something, which included a preliminary decision to buy some very expensive equipment for a large number of clinics. However, the data allowed a more cost effective decision to be made: to only do lead screening in those areas where there was a demonstrated risk. This approach avoided the purchase of equipment that would have been misused or not used at all because no funds were available to train clinic staffs to use these complex instruments after they were purchased.

The survey of greta and azarcon use (Trotter 1985) turned out to be an excellent educational and informational device. It was conducted at thirty migrant and public health clinics in Texas, New Mexico, and Arizona. As a result of the open-ended ethnographic structuring of the survey instrument, several other potentially toxic compounds, with regional but not universal usage, were also discovered. This finding alerted the local clinics both to the current use of home treatments of illnesses in their area and to some of the specific health education needs of their clients. In my opinion, the education benefits of conducting this type of survey have an untapped potential as an educational device for health care service providers.

To disperse the data as widely and rapidly as possible, four different articles on greta and azarcon were submitted to a variety of journals. Each article was targeted for a particular audience. The most important audiences were thought to be health professionals, medical anthropologists, public health personnel, and an international pharmacological audience. Each audience needed to know about the data and had an opportunity to help solve the problem of lead poisoning caused by folk remedies. However, this process of multiple submissions conflicts directly with the practice of avoiding prior publication.

The Hidalgo County Health Care Corporation was provided with reports showing that greta and azarcon use was comparable between their clinic and catchment populations. These data were also passed along to the regional and national offices of PHS. In this case the client used the data to create priorities for the next funding cycle. Each funding request requires goals and priorities, and better funding opportunities exist if the clinic demonstrates changing as well as expanding needs and services, especially in the area of patient education. The data allowed it to successfully compete for funding for its patient education goals by demonstrating a need for further health education on home remedies.

Perhaps the most important overall result of this project was the increased awareness of the utility of anthropology in solving culturally related health care problems in at least one segment of the medical care delivery system. For many years anthropologists have been saying that knowledge of folk medicine was important to the delivery of health care. But the only examples of how such knowledge was useful were couched in terms of "better rapport" with patients, "potentially reducing recidivism," or were tied to the "interface between culture and psychological processes." Patient rapport is an abominably low priority for practicing physicians and for most health clinics that are experiencing a patient overload. Likewise the cultural/psychological aspect has low prestige and is of interest to a small group of practitioners but not to the larger group dealing with physical medicine.

Now anthropologists are becoming visible to the greater part of medicine. Our discovery of the use of greta and azarcon and the subsequent discoveries that similar remedies are causing lead poisoning in Hmong, Saudi Arabian, and Chinese communities have finally demonstrated a clear link between anthropological research and the dominant biophysical side of modern medicine. Anthropological knowledge, research methods, and theoretical orientations are finally being used to solve epidemiological problems overlooked by the established disciplines. For some of our potential clients, this approach, for the first time, makes anthropology a potentially valuable source for consultation and for funding.

A project is only half successful, regardless of its results, if it does not produce additional opportunities for anthropologists to practice anthropology. These serendipitous results can be as simple as further work for the same client or as important as the development of new theories for the discipline. Yet rarely are these spin-offs mentioned or considered an important aspect of anthropological praxis. Even when a project has clear closure (rare for many of the types of applied problems tackled by anthropologists), the process of solving the problem should set up personal and professional relationships that carry beyond that temporary closure. Regardless of the products they produce, successful applied scientists are process oriented; they are constantly moving from one point on a continuum to the next.

The additional opportunities created by the greta and azarcon problem may have more long-lasting effects on the cross-cultural delivery of health care in the United States than the original projects had. The first spin-off was an invitation to participate in a program review for the Migrant Health Services division of PHS in Washington, D.C. The program review brought together a group of experts from around the United States to review, revise, and set new policies for the delivery of health care services in all migrant health clinics in the United States. The policies that were adopted are strongly cross cultural. They include the development of a Public Health Service Corps provider orientation package that specifically addresses cultural sensitivity, basic anthropological concepts of culture, and awareness of the qualitative aspects of migrant lifestyles, health beliefs, and medical needs. I am in the process of developing this package. Other policies and goals include statements on program coordination, continuity of care, information needs (e.g., research), and services. All have been shaped by the participation of anthropologists in the policy-making body.

Additionally, Indiana Health Centers, Inc., a private, nonprofit corporation that runs the migrant health clinics in Indiana, asked me to spend a week as a consultant for its program. The primary purpose of the consultation was to conduct public and clinic seminars on ethnomedicine and its importance to the delivery of health care to Mexican Americans. A latent purpose was to legitimize the use of culturally appropriate health services and to integrate them into the scientific medical system. One indication that the process worked is the clinic's decision to incorporate four of the most common Mexican American folk illnesses into their diagnostic system, which includes a computer coding and retrieval system. At the end of the year, the clinics will use these to set goals, determine funding and educational needs, and determine policy for the program, along with all other diagnostic data derived from their computer system.

I was also invited by the Pennsylvania Department of Education, Migrant Education Division, to participate in its Project HAPPIER (Health Awareness Patterns Preventing Illness and Encouraging Responsibility). Project HAPPIER, which has a national scope, is funded through discretionary (143c) funds from the Office of the Secretary of Education. The objective of the project was to provide a major health resource guide and the data necessary to target health education in migrant clinics and for migrant educators, nationwide. My initial role was to conduct an analysis of national migrant health education needs, including an eight-state survey of migrant health beliefs and health education needs, as seen from the perspective of the migrants themselves. Although the survey provided excellent information, several important cultural groups were not well represented. Therefore, the following year I helped conduct a separate needs assessment in Puerto Rico to gather data on one of the underrepresented groups. The goals of the surveys were to improve our knowledge about migrant health status in all three migrant streams and to provide information that would allow the states and Puerto Rico to offer migrant children sufficient health education to improve the health status of the current and the next migrant generation. The preliminary results of the study indicate that migrants both want and need health education. This finding points up the possibility of exploring a number of areas for research and program development (spin-offs from spin-offs).

Other opportunities that resulted from the original project included the more traditional requests for speaking engagements, lectures, and so on. These occasions afforded visibility that created new project opportunities and acted as a source of income. In most academic settings these activities also count toward merit and promotion points.

Although it is very important to direct one's best effort toward each project, I feel that the best applied anthropologists also follow what I call the "basic fission theory of anthropological praxis." Each project undertaken by an applied anthropologist should produce at least four others (up to the capacity, skill, and time commitment available to the individual anthropologist). One indicator of success in anthropological praxis is a continued demand for the services offered; it is easiest to generate this demand by current success. An anthropologist should look for spin-offs during a project, not just after it is completed.

The Anthropological Difference

I believe that the anthropological difference I added to the greta/azarcon project comes from the training that all anthropologists receive. It includes our strong focus on culture combined with our willingness to innovate, to look for explanations in areas that have been neglected by other investigators. The difference is not so much a part of anthropological theory and methods as it is a part of the personal orientation many of us have and that we try to pass along to others. For example, the health officials who originally investigated the case of lead poisoning in Greeley assumed that the little girl could only have contracted lead poisoning in the same way all other children get lead poisoning—from the environment.[3] In her case, the only accessible source of lead was a fence some 200 yards from her house. Although her parents insisted that she never played near that fence, they were ignored until the child had gone through chelation therapy and, in a follow-up screening, was determined to have re-elevated blood lead levels without access to the fence. Then the publicity on the California case caused a culturally sensitive worker (who had been exposed to transcultural nursing concepts) to ask about azarcon, and the case was solved.

Another anthropological contribution to this project was in the design and administration of the research requested by the clients. The methodological contributions an anthropologist can make to a project may be as important or even more important to the client than his or her contributions of theory. It is relatively easy to find someone who has a theoretical explanation for known behavior; it is also easy to find someone who can administer surveys. It is much harder to find someone who can combine ethnographic data collection and theory grounded in real behavior with survey methodology that can determine the scope of a behavior. These projects demanded both types of expertise. I had to discover both the basic patterns of and reasons for the continued use of home remedies in an urban-industrial society and a cultural context within which the educational and intervention process could take place. At the same time, I had the vitally important task of discovering how widespread the use of these remedies had become and if other hazardous remedies were being used to treat the same folk illness. A combination of ethnography and survey accomplished these goals.

The final area of anthropological contribution was in the design of the educational material and the programmatic responses to the problem of greta and azarcon. The major contribution there was to ensure that the materials used or developed were culturally appropriate rather than trying to force inappropriate change on people who would resent it, making the effort useless in the long run.

In some ways this cluster of projects indicates a potential new era for anthropology in health-related fields. In these instances the services of an anthropologist were deliberately sought because of the clients' sophisticated knowledge of the type of services they needed and the exact type of expertise they wanted. They needed descriptive ethnographic data to determine a method in which to produce a product switch from one remedy to other, nontoxic ones. In addition they needed a survey built on a solid ethnographic base that did not presume a closed field of knowledge about the subject. More and more of today's anthropologists are equally comfortable with quantitative and qualitative methods of data collection. This combination of research methods is actually stronger than either pure ethnography or pure statistical analysis, but it requires a much more methodologically sophisticated researcher. In some ways, the flexibility of approach—an eclectic orientation to methodology and analysis—has always marked the anthropological difference and may herald a subtle but real advantage not only for anthropological praxis but also for the future employment of anthropologists in many industries. If, as many claim, we are now in an information-driven age, anthropologists should have an advantage in the information service market, given the importance or centrality of communications research and information handling in the history of anthropology.

Notes

1. Most of the people buying and selling greta and azarcon believe they are herbal compounds, probably because the overwhelming majority of Mexican American home remedies are botanicals.

2. Other Hispanic groups were not targeted for this campaign. A broad search among anthropologists working with other Hispanic populations in the United States indicated that the two compounds were not present in their ethnomedical pharmacopoeias.

3. Two traditional sources of lead poisoning are the consumption of lead paint chips, primarily by children living in dilapidated urban areas, and occupational exposure to high concentrations of lead by workers and children of workers in high lead use industries, such as battery manufacturing. The third source is environmental pollution. The most common victims of this type of poisoning are children whose normal hand-to-mouth activities give them an overdose of lead from playing on soil with a high lead content (such as that near heavily traveled roads or industries such as smelters that have high lead emission levels). Epidemiological investigations are conducted when a child or adult is detected as having high blood lead levels. These investigations invariably concentrate on discovering which of these sources caused the problem.

References

Ackerman et al. 1982. Lead poisoning from Lead Tetroxide Used as a Folk Remedy—Colorado. *MMWR* (Center for Disease Control, Morbidity and Mortality Weekly Report) 30(52):647–648.

Trotter, Robert T., II. 1985. Greta and Azarcon: A Survey of Episodic Lead Poisoning from a Folk Remedy. *Human Organization* 44(1):64–72.

Trotter, Robert T., II, Alan Ackerman, Dorothy Rodman, Abel Martinez, and Frank Sorvillo. 1984. Azarcon and Greta: Ethnomedical Solution to an Epidemiological Mystery. *Medical Anthropology Quarterly* 14(3):3,18.

Vashistha, et al. 1981. Use of Lead Tetroxide as a Folk Remedy for Gastrointestinal Illness. *MMWR* 30(43):546–547.

12 / Intercultural Mediation at Truk International Airport

Patricia L. Parker and Thomas F. King

Problem and Client

The government of the Trust Territory of the Pacific Islands planned to expand its airport in Truk, an island group in the central Caroline Islands. The people of the two villages targeted for construction objected: The project would destroy traditional fishing areas and important cultural landmarks and take land and food resources for which the villagers felt they would not be properly compensated. As a result, the government faced increasing civil disobedience and threats of litigation by the villagers. As anthropologists on the scene of the dispute, we became mediators between the parties in the standoff.

Since the end of World War II, the United States has administered most of the islands of Micronesia as the Trust Territory of the Pacific Islands (TTPI), under a trusteeship agreement with the United Nations. The trusteeship is scheduled to end soon, and for several years the United States has been installing roads, airports, and other capital improvements to provide a basis for economic development when the islands become self-governing. One of the new governments emerging from the TTPI is the Federated States of Micronesia; one of its states is Truk; the capital island of Truk State is Moen, and two of Moen's villages are Iras and Mechchitiw. In 1978 Truk International Airport was a coral runway within Iras village, barely long enough to handle the Boeing 727 airliners that landed there twice a day. The TTPI proposed to extend and improve the airport through construction contracts administered by the U.S. Navy.

The airport was originally built as a bomber-fighter airstrip by the Japanese in 1941; in building it, they displaced the Iras villagers from their shoreline homes and pulled down the adjacent slopes of Mt.

Tonaachaw to provide construction fill. In 1948 the people of Iras returned, but the U.S. and TTPI governments retained and rehabilitated the badly bombed runway, leaving the villagers to reestablish themselves on the quarried mountain slopes and in the filled-in taro swamps around the foot of the mountain.

The U.S. government reached a settlement with the people of Iras in 1956 by which they paid something less than $300 per acre for the right to "indefinite use" of the land under the airport. Few of the villagers understood the settlement, and those who thought they did, understood that they were to be paid annual rent. They soon found out that they were wrong, and they were bitter. There was little they could do, however, except shake their fists and shout "get off my land" to passing planes, until the early 1970s when lawyers from the newly formed Micronesian Legal Services Corporation took up their cause. The villagers filed suit against the TTPI in 1973, and after considerable maneuvering the case was referred to an impartial commission, which found against the government. The government promised to pay for proper leases but began dickering about the price. Each side brought in appraisers, whose methods of assigning values varied widely. By the end of the 1970s, the villagers still had neither their land nor their money. The generation that had seen the village razed by the Japanese was growing old in disappointment; their children were growing up in bitterness.

In 1978, the government unveiled its plans to expand the airport. By this time the plans had been developed in considerable detail; engineering drawings were prepared; and the Navy was ready to award a contract. The environmental impact statement on the project had been completed virtually without consultation with the villagers, and it was vague on a number of key points. Thousands of tons of coral fill were needed, for example, and would have to be dredged from the reef, but the location and boundaries of the dredge area were not identified. Noise impacts were discussed only very generally; a monitoring program was supposed to keep noise, dust, and other impacts under control, but its nature had not been established. Although strenuous objections had been raised to the environmental impact statement (EIS) by the villagers' lawyers, it had been accepted by the Federal Aviation Administration in 1976, and by 1978 the Navy was ready to proceed. The Navy's detailed plans, revealed to the villagers for the first time in a public hearing held by the U.S. Army Corps of Engineers, exposed a number of major problems for the villagers.

1. The entire reef flat in front of Mechchitiw village, just east of Iras, was to be dredged for fill. Trukese fish on the reef flat, especially around *púnúpún* (rock mounds constructed by women as artificial habitats). The

airport planners assumed that the villagers no longer fished on the reef flat, but no one had bothered to study the matter. In fact, the villagers continued to use the reef flat extensively, and as they pointed out, they obviously could no longer do so once it was dredged 40 feet deep.

2. The airport would be fenced for safety reasons; the fence would keep people from the rocks west of the runway, along the shore, where many went to relieve themselves. In a village without a sewer, concentrated in a filled-in but poorly drained taro swamp, this was the closest thing to a sanitary waste disposal system. The government proposed to do nothing about the problem, arguing that since such pollution of the lagoon was illegal, it would be inappropriate to address it.

3. The villagers would no longer be able to beach their boats along the shoreline west of the runway; they would have to walk a mile or so to the next available moorage.

4. The questions of land ownership and compensation were still not settled, and the airport would take still more land because it would require expansion of a nearby quarry. No provision had been made for acquiring the land or compensating the landowners, other than an assumption by the airport planners that the Truk State government would handle the matter.

5. The construction would destroy several landmarks important in the cultural history of the villagers and Trukese generally; notably, warning lights would be required on the peak of Mt. Tonaachaw, where the culture heros Sowukachaw and Sowuwóóniiras had had their meeting houses. Considerable magical power is ascribed to the peak of Tonaachaw and to various rocks and other sites on the mountain slopes and the reef; the airport had been designed without consideration for these locations.

6. The project would generate noise and dust during construction, and airport expansion would enable more and larger planes to land there, increasing the disturbance to the villagers. Camillo Noket, the young and sophisticated chief of Iras village, cited studies indicating a high incidence of psychological distress among people living near airports and asserted that a similar situation already prevailed in Iras. The airport planners countered that air operations around the new airport would be quieter than those on the old runway and that construction impacts would be carefully monitored; however, they were not specific about how these plans would be carried out.

Shortly after the public hearing, Chief Camillo led the people of his village to the airport in a mass demonstration of protest and threatened to block air operations indefinitely. Micronesian Legal Services Corporation prepared to seek an injunction to bar construction. The government could no longer ignore the problem.

Process and Players

We became involved in the project in a roundabout way. Late in 1977, Parker took up residence in Iras to conduct ethnographic research for her PhD dissertation, which concerns Trukese land law (Parker 1985). By the time of the public hearing in early 1978, she had become conversant in the Trukese language and had been adopted into a family and clan. King, Parker's husband, had been loaned to the TTPI by the U.S. Department of the Interior as a consultant in archeology and historic preservation, to help organize a historic and cultural preservation program and an archeological survey throughout Micronesia. Because of the historical significance of Mt. Tonaachaw and the archeological remains of Iras village that lay beneath the existing runway, the government was required by Section 106 of the U.S. National Historic Preservation Act to consider the effects of the project and consult about them with the U.S. Advisory Council on Historic Preservation. King was responsible for organizing this consultation.

King recognized, thanks to Parker's acquaintance with the villagers, that the sociocultural problems with the airport went beyond its impacts on historic places and archeological sites. King made an effort to bring these issues to light and seek their resolution through the Section 106 consultation process (see King 1981). At first, the government's response was relatively hostile, culminating in an effort to dismiss King and expel both authors from the islands. This effort, which met substantial objections from both the Department of the Interior and key Micronesian politicians, began to attract media attention on Guam. Meanwhile the problems presented to the project by the villagers showed no signs of going away, and in an abrupt turnabout the TTPI not only reinstated King to his position but charged the Historic Preservation Office with the responsibility of mediating between the government and the villages with respect to all airport impacts. Parker had no official role in the mediation process from the government's point of view, but it was tacitly recognized that she was the primary translator of the villagers' concerns into the government's language.

We have never inquired into the reconsideration of policy that must have been behind the government's change of heart. In the interests of working together, we all pretended that the unpleasantness surrounding the attempted ouster had never occurred; all concerned were treading on unfamiliar ground. Our charge was a broad one—to mediate the differences—and no one was specific about how to carry out this mission.

Clearly, the first step was to get the villagers to present their concerns in a way that the government could easily understand. Their deeply felt, but not very systematically expressed, outrage over what they believed the project would do to them had to be developed into a bill of particulars that could serve as a basis for negotiation. The government knew what it wanted: the airport. For an amicable solution to the conflict, the villagers' objections had to be broken down into a list of wants that could perhaps be met. To avoid charges by the government that the villagers were adding to their list of grievances as the negotiations proceeded, the list had to be as comprehensive as possible at the outset.

Developing the initial bill of particulars required a series of meetings in each village. Each had a different way of reaching consensus. In Iras the village council of senior men drafted a list of grievances under Chief Camillo's direction, and meetings of the whole village were held to discuss and refine them. Parker attended many of these meetings, sometimes with King, and provided him with outlines of the concerns as they developed. In other cases Parker was courteously excluded and then asked to transmit the results to King at the TTPI headquarters on Saipan. In Mechchitiw, a formal meeting of the entire village, with both of us in attendance, initiated the consultation process; later a working group of senior men under the leadership of Chief Chitaro William met with us regularly over coffee in a village store to focus the issues and negotiate.

On Saipan, King now enjoyed the full support of Trust Territory High Commissioner Adrian Winkel and Deputy High Commissioner Juan Sablan; as a result, the otherwise recalcitrant officials in charge of public works, transportation, and other programs with vested interests in airport construction were grudgingly cooperative. As the villagers' concerns were clarified, they were taken up by King with the responsible officials in a series of meetings. Parker, based on her daily interaction with the people of the villages, made sure that King understood their needs with precision. King, understanding the workings of the government and accepted (marginally) as an insider, tried to cast these concerns in terms the government could understand and to negotiate about them on behalf of the villagers. As government proposals to satisfy the villagers' needs were developed, King could usually judge which would be acceptable to the people; conversely, as the villagers began to develop proposed solutions, we could usually advise them about what would be acceptable to the government. Although many proposals and counterproposals flowed back and forth between Truk and Saipan, and King shuttled back and forth every few weeks, our understanding of the constraints and interests perceived by both sides of the controversy made it possible to handle most of the consultation informally and avoid the development of nonnegotiable demands manifestly unacceptable to either side.

In the end, the issues of concern to the villagers were handled as follows.

1. The dredge area on the Mechchitiw reef flat was redesigned to minimize the productive reef destroyed and to provide continued access for the villagers to the reef edge. This change cost the government several hundred thousand dollars because the Navy had already let the construction contract based on the original dredge configuration. The village was also given assistance in the construction of a seawall to halt shoreline erosion, which the villagers feared would increase as a result of the dredging.

2. Compensation was provided for the púnúpún that would be destroyed in both villages, at a rate of $90 per púnúpún. First, an accurate survey of púnúpún was made jointly by the Truk State government and the villages, each watching the other to guard against cheating. Next, a price had to be established by negotiation, with the government starting from a low point set in a several-year-old court case and the villagers starting from a high point based on estimates of fish yield per púnúpún and the cost of fish in the local market. The final figure was $40 per púnúpún higher than the government's starting point and $60 lower than the villagers'. Finally, the method of distribution had to be decided; consistent with our recommendation, the money was provided as a lump sum to each village, whose leaders were responsible for distribution to individual púnúpún owners, using their own systems of decision-making.

3. To compensate for food lost from the reefs, each village received a block grant of between $100,000 and $150,000 from the government after each chartered an agricultural and fishing cooperative with government advice and developed a proposal for capitalization. The grants were used to construct cooperative stores, to purchase tools, seeds, and other commodities, and, in the case of Iras, to construct a fishing boat and train its crew.

4. Construction priorities in the Truk State capital improvement program were shifted, and approval was obtained from the U.S. Environmental Protection Agency, to provide Iras with a modern sewer system at an early date. The village leaders, in turn, guaranteed that easements would be provided for the system across all private lands in the village. Until the sewer is complete, it was quietly and tacitly agreed that gates would be left open in the airport fence.

5. The government agreed to construct an anchorage and mooring area for the village's boats within one of the dredge areas that will be conveniently located for most villagers.

6. Although the overall question of compensation for land had to be left to continuing arbitration and action by the U.S. Congress on appropriations for Micronesia as a whole, an arbitration panel was established to rule on land claims arising from the construction itself.

7. After consultation with the Federal Aviation Administration confirmed that warning lights were not needed for airport safety, those on the summit of Mt. Tonaachaw were deleted from the project plans, thus avoiding the most objectionable impact on a place of cultural importance. We consulted with the villagers, especially local authorities on traditional history, to identify other landmarks; these included rocks on the reef associated with sailing directions, the arrival of culture heros, and metaphors equating the physical landscape and seascape with the traditional organization of Trukese society. The locations of such features were fed to the project planners so that they could be avoided in dredging and construction. An archeological salvage project was also conducted by the villagers under our supervision. This project studied the remains of prehistoric and early historic settlements within and around the impact areas of the airport and other planned improvements and relocated all human burials discovered during construction to safe new graves established by the kinspeople of the dead (see Parker and King 1981; King and Parker 1984).

8. Equipment was rerouted and measures were taken to minimize noise and dust impacts. Continuing consultation between the villagers and the Navy officers in charge of the project was arranged to address any noise and dust problems arising during the project.

Results and Evaluation

The success of the mediation effort can be evaluated from at least three points of view: those of the government, the villagers, and the anthropologists. From the government's viewpoint, the effort was successful: The enlarged, improved airport is now constructed and operating without litigation or project delay. However, many if not most government officials feel that too much money was spent to achieve a solution, that the villagers took the government for a ride, and that it was wrong to pay so much attention to the villagers' concerns. Some, although unsympathetic to the villagers, acknowledge that litigation over the project could have been more costly than the mediated solution and, as a result, see the exercise as a necessary evil.

The villagers were pleased with most of the results of mediation, though many still deeply resent the presence of the airport, the taking of land and reef, and the continuing lack of due compensation. As time goes by, their perceptions will probably be significantly colored by the success or failure of the agricultural and fishing cooperatives that were the most tangible results of the project. If the cooperatives succeed, the villagers probably will feel that they were winners; if they fail, the villagers may feel that they lost and their resentment will increase.

From our viewpoint, the effort was successful given the context in which it occurred. The costs of the government probably were greater than necessary, largely because the government ignored the problem until very late in project planning. Had the needs of the villagers for access to the reef been considered early, for example, the dredge area could have been designed with these in mind at the outset, and redesign costs would not have been incurred. Similarly, there might have been more cost effective solutions to the problem of compensation for lost food resources, but none could be found and implemented in the time available before construction made the existing resources unavailable. We are not optimistic about the economic future of the cooperatives, even though the Iras Producers' and Consumers' Cooperative cleared $34,000 during its first year. The economy of Micronesia and the economic and energy infrastructure of Truk are so fragile that one cannot comfortably place faith in any business enterprise there. Still, the cooperatives were the best available solution at the time, and thus far, they seem to be working.

A satisfying feature of the solutions, from our point of view, lies in certain things not done. Most important, cash payments to individuals were not made, except in the case of púnúpún compensation, and even in this instance, the payments were made not by the government but by the village leaders, according to their own systems. Cash payments to individuals have been made repeatedly in Micronesia by the U.S. government in connection with war claims and other compensation requirements. The results are generally destructive and counterproductive, breaking down traditional economic authority systems and creating "boom and bust" cycles and dependence on government largesse. At Truk Airport, payments were made instead to the villages as corporate entities, based on definite plans for investing the money in facilities and actions with the potential for long-term public benefit.

This approach is not exactly congruent with traditional Trukese practice because the "village" has a rather tenuous reality as a traditional organizational entity in Truk; local matrilineal clan segments are the major corporate decision-making entities. Because these segments are so small, however, separate negotiations with each would not have been logistically feasible and would have undercut the authority of the village chief and council, which are generally recognized as responsible for regulating affairs within the village and resolving disputes among resident clan segments. In all probability, the mediation process increased the stature and authority of the chiefs and their immediate advisers, at least to the extent that the villagers view the results of the process as successful. In turn local power may shift from the clan segments toward the chief and his advisers, with a variety of positive and negative ramifications, but at least with the positive effect of placing the villagers in a better position for future negotiations with the state and national governments.

It should be noted, in evaluating the success of the effort, that not all problems were resolved to everyone's satisfaction. Once construction was under way, the people of Mechchitiw became deeply upset by the noise of dredging and by the dangers posed by a high-pressure dredge pipe running just offshore. Efforts to work out a solution to this problem with the U.S. Navy and the construction contractor met with no success. Similarly in Iras, noise and dust impacts were much greater than anticipated and led to several near-violent confrontations between villagers and contractors. The construction contractor had little or no sensitivity to the concerns of the villagers and knew almost nothing about the consultation that had preceded construction; the naval officers responsible for contract administration were not much better. Construction by no means proceeded smoothly and the villagers were not happy with it, but dialogue was maintained between the villagers and the Navy, efforts were made to accommodate the villagers' concerns and to resolve day-to-day problems as they arose, and the project was completed without real violence or delay.

In summary, from our standpoint the effort was a success because the fundamental goals of both parties to the dispute were met in a manner that did minimal damage to the people of the villages and that involved minimal cost to the government.

The Anthropological Difference

We were able to operate effectively as mediators of the Truk Airport dispute largely because of the general anthropological principles and ethics we have absorbed as practitioners and because of the specific characteristics of Parker's dissertation research project in Iras. Parker had been trained as a cultural anthropologist with specialities in anthropology and law, ethnohistory, and the Pacific, and her study concerned the transformation of Trukese land law as a result of contact with Japanese and U.S. legal systems. She had become familiar with the dilemmas posed for newly independent nations by the need to design legal systems that preserve aspects of traditional law while carrying the legal freight generated by years of colonial rule and modern demands. She had absorbed the theoretical and methodological approaches that had come to the fore in anthropology in the mid-1970s that stressed the need to study substantive and procedural law at all levels within the social context (see Gluckman 1973; Holleman 1973).

Parker had focused her study on the legal domain of land because land is the most critical, culturally important of Truk's resources, and an exploratory visit to Micronesia had indicated that such a study would be welcomed by those responsible for developing and using the new legal systems of Truk and the Federated States. An underlying assumption of her research was that traditional Trukese methods of decision-making about land use differed from the traditional approaches of Euroamerican society that have led to the use of courts, land commissions, and in the case of Truk Airport, government planners, regulatory agencies, and public hearings. A further fundamental assumption was that the traditional Trukese methods were derived from, integrated with, and functionally important to the total fabric of Trukese society, that they therefore demanded respect, and that attention to them was basic to the satisfactory resolution of any conflict.

Parker chose Iras as her primary research site precisely because so much of its land had been taken by the Japanese and Americans for airport and other purposes. Although she was unaware of plans to enlarge the airport at the time her research began, she knew that the lands under the runway and the reef had originally been privately owned. From the available literature on Trukese land transactions, she expected that any effort by the government to take, use, buy, rent, or lease land would be fraught with difficulty. She had also learned from the literature and from her dissertation adviser, Ward Goodenough, about the hierarchical organization of Trukese lineages and the social significance of knowledge about land and history, which severely inhibits most Trukese from discussing such matters in any but general terms. These inhibitions, together with the suspicions generated by years of colonial rule and what the Trukese view as improper expropriations of land by outside administrative authorities, make it virtually impossible for a public hearing, consultation with elected government representatives, or short-term planning studies to generate accurate portrayals of public opinion about proposed land use actions.

King brought a different but compatible anthropological background to the controversy. Although his primary specialized training was in archeology, he had long before become involved in the U.S. historic preservation movement and had become familiar with the preservation and environmental laws and regulations that pertain to projects like the airport expansion effort. As a preservationist he had worked in negotiation situations with a wide range of agencies and interest groups. Most important, several years before he had become involved in the efforts of the Agua Caliente Band of Cahuilla Indians in California to block construction of a dam across a canyon of pivotal importance in their cultural traditions and subsequently with the Dry Creek Band of Pomo Indians in an effort to stop construction of Warm Springs Dam, which would flood both archeological sites and plant-gathering places vital to the Pomo's basketmaking and medicinal traditions. The Cahuilla were successful, the Pomo only partially so—causing the Corps of Engineers to relocate plant communities needed for their activities that would be flooded.[1] But the experience helped King translate traditional cultural concerns into terms understandable by U.S. planners, regulatory agencies, and courts of law.

Thus Parker arrived on the scene of the controversy prepared to observe and analyze the activities of the villagers, the chiefs, their lawyers, government officials, and anyone else involved in any land-related conflicts, armed with a substantial understanding both of Trukese society and of the kinds of problems that such conflicts present to their participants as recorded by anthropologists cross-culturally. King came with a much less detailed package of background knowledge and experience but with a general sensitivity to the kinds of issues involved and a practical understanding of how to deal with them in the context of U.S. law and planning practice. Our collective bundle of knowledge and experience was crucial to our work as mediators.

By contrast, planning for the Truk Airport project before 1978 was undertaken by U.S. engineers, planners, and environmental specialists in the context of American values and assumptions, with only the most marginal consideration for the possibility that Trukese approaches to such a project might be different. The U.S. group consulted only with government officials, who even if Trukese had been trained by Americans and had only American (and sometimes Japanese) models of planning and project design. The resulting set of planning and environmental documents failed even to reveal the potential for serious conflict and certainly did nothing to provide a basis for resolution. Although attorneys from the Micronesian Legal Services Corporation made a real effort to alert the airport planners to the potential for difficulty (MacMeekin 1973), their ideas seem to have been dismissed because as attorneys representing the villagers they were assumed to be trying to cut a better financial deal for their clients in the eventual land settlement.

Our approach recognized from the start that the concerns of a Trukese villager are likely to differ from, but be as legitimate as, those of a local government official, an airport planner, or an airline company. We further recognized that the concerns of the villagers would not necessarily work their way to the surface through local government processes in the way American models of local decision-making would lead planners to expect. Accordingly, we treated the villagers' concerns as legitimate and encouraged them to use their traditional decision-making processes—not those established by the government—to organize and refine their views and to evaluate those of the government. As a participant observer in the villages functioning as a member of Iras society but maintaining sufficient objectivity to describe and analyze what was going on, Parker was able to make the villagers' interests, needs, and values understandable to King, who played a somewhat equivalent participant observer role within the government. Parker's ability to function as a member of Iras village, combined with King's ability to be perceived as part of the government, provided a channel of communication for the identification and resolution of issues that would not otherwise have been available.

As it turned out, the mediation effort became an integrated part of both Parker's and King's research, and vice versa. The trust that the villagers developed for Parker because of her mediation efforts and their perception of King as a person with some power to advance their interests, together with the villagers' need to objectify their cultural concerns in a way understandable to the government, allowed Parker to gather data on land histories and genealogical relationships that were crucial both to her overall research and to her understanding, from the villagers' point of view, of the issues involved in the airport controversy. The same data served to structure the archeological salvage project that King directed, with traditional land plots serving as sampling units, recollections of village residents guiding the location of excavations, and the villagers both individually and corporately participating in the design and execution of the work. The archeological studies, conversely, stimulated the transmission of more historical information to Parker and tended to underscore the legitimacy of the villagers' claims about the cultural importance of the land under the airport. They also provided a context for the whole anthropological involvement in the project that was understandable to American planners and project managers, which would not have existed otherwise. The existence of U.S. historic preservation laws, which generated a legal requirement to be concerned with historic properties and archeological salvage, was a tangible reality in the eyes of the government and provided an initial rationale for King's involvement in the project. As the project progressed, the need to plan and then conduct the salvage research helped justify a continued anthropological presence in the villages. The opportunity to package archeological, ethnographic, and mediation activities in a mutually beneficial way came to us at Truk International Airport more or less by accident, but we suspect that such packages could be purposefully constructed in many project planning situations.

Interest in mediation and the ability to mediate among disparate interests are not unique to anthropology. In fact, our work has at least as much kinship with the emerging fields of social resource management (see Kent et al. 1979) and environmental dispute resolution (see Susskind and Weinstein 1981) as with the mainstream practice of applied anthropology. Although research interests and methods were important to our mediation efforts, we did not use our research skills for the sorts of description and evaluation central to much contemporary applied anthropology. The explicit intellectual roots of our work in anthropology lie in the interventionist strategies of the 1950s, which as van Willigen has recently noted, have had "remarkably little effect on the field" (van Willigen 1982:17). Our role was an active one, approximating one model of the mediator function identified by Susskind and Weinstein; according to this model:

> mediators should play an active role in identifying the parties to a dispute, arranging for their meetings and helping to sort (and even evaluate) the validity of technical information regarding the issues at stake. This undoubtedly makes the job of the mediator in environmental disputes much more complex than the job of the mediator in more typical collective bargaining situations. (Susskind and Weinstein 1981:348)

In a cross-cultural situation, in which many issues are cast in different terms and given different values by the participants because of the different cultural lenses through which they view them, an active mediator is necessary. It is difficult to imagine such a mediator being effective without the sensitivity and communications skills that anthropological training and experience impart. Ultimately, the success of any group of mediators "will depend on their ability to maintain a bond of trust with the participants" (Susskind and Weinstein 1981:349). Developing and maintaining such trust in a cross-cultural situation are skills that any ethnographer must develop, and they uniquely equip anthropologists for the mediator role.

Notes

1. See Chapter 16 of this book for a detailed description of the Pomo project from the perspective of the Corps of Engineers.

References

Gluckman, M. 1973. Limitations of the Case-Study Method in the Study of Tribal Law. *Law and Society Review* 7(4):611–642.

Holleman, J. F. 1973. Trouble-Cases and Trouble-less Cases in the Study of Customary Law and Legal Reform. *Law and Society Review* 7(4):585–610.

Kent, James A., et al. 1979. Social Resource Management Guidelines: a Ten-Step Process for a Social Impact Assessment. Report to the USDA Forest Service, Surface Environment and Mining Program, Billings, Montana. Denver: Foundation for Urban and Neighborhood Development.

King, Thomas F. 1981. Historical Preservation and Sociocultural Impacts: a Developing Relationship. *Practicing Anthropology* 3(4):6–8.

King, T. F., and P. L. Parker. 1984. PISEKEN NOOMW NOON TONAACHAW: Archeology in the Tonaachaw Historic District, Moen, Truk. Southern Illinois University, Carbondale, and Micronesian Archeologicial Survey, Saipan, Report no. 18.

MacMeekin, S., and D. MacMeekin. 1973. The people of Iras. Comment on draft environmental impact statement (EIS) on expansion of Truk International Airport. Appended to final EIS; prepared by Micronesian Legal Services Corp. in consultation with the people of Iras. Honolulu: Federal Aviation Administration.

Parker, Patricia L. 1985. PhD dissertation in progress, Department of Anthropology, University of Pennsylvania, Philadelphia.

Parker, P. L., and T. F. King. 1981. Recent and Current Archaeological Research on Moen Island, Truk. *Asian Perspectives* (Honolulu) 24(1):11–26.

Susskind, Lawrence, and Alan Weinstein. 1981. Towards a Theory of Environmental Dispute Resolution. *Boston College Environmental Affairs Law Review* 9(2):311–357.

van Willigen, John. 1982. The Great Transformation? Applied Training and Disciplinary Change. *Practicing Anthropology* 4(3/4):16–17.

13 / Promoting Socioculturally Feasible Housing and Community Upgrading Programs in Botswana

John P. Mason

Problem and Client

Urban growth in Botswana in the mid to late 1970s was proceeding at a very high, 12 percent, rate. To respond to this situation, the government of Botswana had invited the U.S. foreign assistance arm, the Agency for International Development (AID), to help. AID in turn asked my then-employer, the Cooperative Housing Foundation (CHF), to provide technical assistance in arriving at a solution to the rapid urban growth problem. (CHF is a not-for-profit technical assistance organization headquartered in Washington, D.C.) The result of this collaborative effort was the development and successful completion of an innovative, self-help urban shelter and community upgrading program. This program not only accommodated the housing demand of a growing population of squatters who were illegally occupying land in shanty structures they built on the fringes of Botswana's towns. It also met that demand in such a way that the houses and public facilities and services developed under the program were adapted to the socioeconomic and cultural conditions of low-income Botswana families.

Because of the success of the effort, the clients—the Botswana Ministry of Local Government and Lands (MLGL) and AID—asked my organization to document this shelter and upgrading program. The purpose of such a document was both promotional and educational: It informed other developing country planning officials, as well as donor agencies, of the technical, social, and administrative processes developed for reaching low-income populations in the delivery of economically feasible and socioculturally acceptable housing and community improvement programs.

174

I was designated by my organization to prepare the educational and promotional document requested by the clients. Before describing that document, its preparation, and the work and information on which it is based, I will first depict my long-term association with Botswana during the development of the country's shelter program. In that way, the reader will be apprised of the degree of knowledge, kinds of intercultural relationships, and modes of working necessary to carrying out what might appear a simple task—researching and writing a descriptive account of a self-help shelter and urban improvement program. I will also allude to some of my subsequent work in Botswana to illustrate the dynamics of international development consulting.

Process and Players

The program and resultant projects in self-help, low-income shelter and urban upgrading began in Botswana in the mid to late 1970s. They were a product of agreements among the government of Botswana, AID, and my employer, CHF. The Botswana government began the process of developing the program by requesting assistance from AID in stemming the rural-to-urban flow of migration. AID, through its regional housing office in Nairobi, Kenya, helped arrange a loan to the government for low-income housing. A loan, rather than an outright grant, was believed appropriate, given Botswana's reasonably good economic profile. That loan, made through a U.S. commercial bank and repayable at market rates over a thirty-year period, was directed at cost-recoverable projects. This meant that the low-income families building or improving their houses were expected to repay the loans, including interest for borrowing, so as to recover all the costs of the loan.

In addition to guaranteeing the commercial loan (in case of default), AID provided technical assistance funds in the form of a grant. These funds were used to employ a U.S. organization to help the implementing agency—the Ministry of Local Government and Lands (MLGL)—to improve its capacity to carry out the program in the future. An agreement was drawn up between MLGL, AID, and CHF for my organization to provide long-term resident advisers specialized in community-based, self-help, low-income housing in a developing country context. It included provision for a series of short-term advisers, such as myself, and also for legal, cost-accounting, architectural, community development, and audio-visual specialists to supplement the skills of the resident adviser.

The technical assistance funds provided for training of Batswana assigned to the project in three areas: (1) technical housing assistance, including design and planning, construction supervision, and self-help building techniques; (2) finance management methods, such as procurement, accounting, office procedures, and warehouse operations; and (3) community organization approaches, including interviewing, case work, group dynamics, and community sensitizing.

In 1977, in an ambience of trust and a willingness to learn from one another, the Batswana invited my employer, in concert with the AID housing guaranty loan, to assist them in establishing an innovative program that would demonstrate that low-income housing (costing about $700 per unit) was within the reach of most of Botswana's low-income families. Furthermore, the program would demonstrate that the preferences of a family and its ability and willingness to pay for shelter and services, as well as the adaptability of its sociocultural traditions, are not only useful but critical to successful planning and implementation.

My role consisted of assisting the Batswana staff of the MLGL housing division in the capital city of Gaborone and in the local housing agencies to design, conduct, and analyze sociocultural research. The purpose of that research was to ensure that the preferences of low-income families and measures of their willingness and ability to pay for new shelter and upgraded services were reflected in the physical design and implementation of the housing and community upgrading program.

That activity consisted of designing a strategy for observing and questioning families residing in low-income housing communities in Botswana's four principal towns. I developed a questionnaire with the helpful advice of Batswana housing staff, and it was translated into the national language, Setswana, and pretested in several neighborhoods. In addition, I helped train enumerators to administer the questionnaire. The questionnaire itself was designed to collect information about residents' willingness and ability to pay for certain house designs, plot sizes, water and sanitation, street construction, and street lighting.

This first effort might be called "quick and dirty" social marketing research, given the time limit of one month. It included not only the tasks of developing the questionnaire, pretesting it, and training enumerators; it also involved the following steps: fixing the sample; supervising eight to ten enumerators in interviewing over 200 respondents in about fifteen neighborhoods in four distant towns; rapidly analyzing the data and writing a report (Mason 1979) with detailed recommendations for use by architect/planners, engineers, and administrators for design and planning purposes. I also had to present the findings to a large meeting of Batswana and expatriate housing and town planning officials. (I have since learned to examine contract terms more carefully so that the time and work pressures are not so extreme.)

Subsequent to the social marketing research, I was invited by the ministry, MLGL, to head a team to carry out a socioeconomic feasibility and planning study (Mason 1981b). That study was directed toward developing a major village as a regional center that would attract rural migrants who would otherwise end up in Botswana's urban centers. Such a regional center was expected to relieve the growing pressures of rural-to-urban migration on those urban centers while stimulating rural development in the region.

The key ingredient of this part of the village planning study was the development of a survey instrument that could serve as a model for future major village socioeconomic feasibility studies. Basically, my role was to work with Batswana in the Applied Research Unit of MLGL to draft a questionnaire, fix the sample frame of 600 compounds based on an outdated, poorly resolved aerial photo, train seven interviewers, and supervise the six-week-long collection of data in the village of Mahalapye. The questionnaire sought specific information about villagers' attitudes toward change; the degree to which they were willing and able to participate in planned change of their village, from both social and economic perspectives; the kinds of physical design changes in the village plan that villagers preferred or would accept, including alterations in such conditions as their residential plot size and shape; and the role village political and business leaders would potentially play in shaping and administering the village development plan.

To collect the necessary information, we had to observe and ask questions about existing patterns of residence, compound use patterns, house types, and the division of labor on the plot for the 600 selected compounds. For individuals numbering perhaps four to five times the number of compounds, we asked questions about their jobs, earnings, expenditures, and consumption. Going beyond the perimeter of the compound, we talked to informants about their preferences for public service utilities and facilities, including residents' ability to participate in paying for such features as water and sanitation lines, roads, lighting, schools, clinics, and community centers.

A potential, downstream result of a more planned village community was the presumed desire by industry, manufacturing, and service employees to locate their economic activities in Mahalapye. This process would in turn draw off rural-to-urban migrants who presently moved into the major urban centers. Furthermore, the planning of this village with its townlike population of 25,000 would presumably contribute to the integration of Mahalapye into the national economy of Botswana.

Of special interest to me as an anthropologist was the contextualization of the village, the region, and the entire nation in a tribal-based setting (in which control of people, land, and cattle were functions of the tribe). For planning purposes, the implications of the tribe and its several divisions were important for several reasons. First, the tribe served as the basis for the spatial distribution of the village's inhabitants, namely in the form of ten clan quarters. Second, it provided the basis for the promotional campaign that announced and explained the survey, specifically through the tribal councils representing the subdivisions. And, third, the tribal subgroupings constituted the channel through which the survey findings were presented and discussed with the villagers. From the outset I regarded the tribal structure as critical for the research and was certain that structure would be highly influential in shaping the spatial distribution of public resources under any proposed plan. For these reasons, I obtained permission to broaden my original work contract by adding open-ended interviews with tribal section leaders, as well as with village business leaders and district political heads.

Yet another phase of my work in Botswana as an employee of CHF was to advise a Canadian International Development Agency (CIDA) planning team. Its work, which was a continuation of the social survey in Mahalapye, consisted of detailing selected topics highlighted in the earlier study. The Canadian study followed on the original research three years later—a testimony to the often slow pace of foreign assistance. My task with the CIDA team was to review their sociological survey work and to ensure that sociospatial considerations were reflected in the eventual plan for Mahalapye. For the latter purpose, I recommended that physical modeling experiments be carried out with residents so that they could see, touch, discuss, and select preferred models for plot boundaries, plot size, plot shape, access to the plot, residential plan, road system, and utilities and services.

The technique I recommended of using modeling as a mode of participation in human settlements research and planning in Mahalapye (Mason 1985) proved highly effective. Employing traditional tribal groupings for the purpose of testing physical planning and design issues also worked well. The choice of modeling itself as an approach to participatory planning was based on its practical utility in eliciting information, as well as on its sociocultural appropriateness to Botswana. Four models, illustrating physical planning factors, were designed using past and present settlement patterns as well as formal and informal discussions with the villagers. Advantages and disadvantages of each model were elicited in ward council meetings. Clearcut preferences emerged from the experiment concerning the physical factors listed earlier. Residents' preparation of the self-directed models provided corroboration of both the earlier research and the prepared models experiment. It also evoked a highly participatory mode of bottom-up planning. Although the planning research described here has not yet had a direct impact on the policy and planning process in Mahalapye—because insufficient time has elapsed since it was carried out—evidence indicates that local, regional, and national officials view it favorably.

Generally speaking, the officials of AID, MLGL, and Mahalapye, as well as village residents, have expressed a favorable reaction to my work as an anthropologist in the consulting roles depicted here. Although anthropology was rarely stated explicitly as the discipline employed in carrying out those roles, it was certainly recognized as an integral part of my knowledge and experience. The practical implications of the work, of course, were what was important.

Results and Evaluation

The request for an educational/promotional description of the self-help shelter and urban upgrading program was made jointly by the Botswana government (namely MLGL) and the AID Office of Housing and Urban Development. MLGL and AID officials wanted a document that would describe in "readable" fashion the technical, financial, and sociocultural features of the program so as to demonstrate that program's success, to suggest how it could serve as a model for sister developing countries experiencing similar conditions, and to depict the operations of major components of the program.

That program, it is recalled, was directed at low-income Batswana who had migrated to urban centers and who threatened to become permanent slum dwellers or squatters; its vehicle was a repayable loan to assist self-help construction of basic housing and public services and facilities; a major facet was the mobilization of families and communities to participate in building their own houses, using a loan equivalent to about US$700 to a family for purchase of building materials, at 9 percent interest for fifteen years (this is adequate for a two-room, 18-meters-square house and a pit latrine). Also, part of the program was the administration of public services and facilities through a pay-as-you-go monthly service fee of about US$5 for water from standpipes (one per twenty families), a toilet foundation for a pit latrine, refuse collection, road maintenance, street lights (where available), and the operational cost of the local housing agency. Finally, an integral feature included technical assistance to the local housing agency to help it design and implement a socioeconomically and technically feasible approach to working with low-income residents in providing them the wherewithal to improve their access to better housing and services.

The requested document was important in circulating the "news" of the success of the self-help program in delivering most of these features. Some of the important achievements of that program were

1. Eliminating the problem of squatter communities in the capital city of Gaborone through the allocation of several thousand self-help plots.

2. Recovering most of its initial costs based on monthly payments by families of their building material loans and service fees, making it a truly "developmental" program in terms of being self-supportive.
3. Eliciting residents' active participation through a community development subprogram in the self-help home construction activity.
4. Convincing skeptical politicians of the effectiveness of a strategy of low-income and minimal (but acceptable) physical planning and design standards for houses and services.

These were the kinds of development successes that the MLGL and AID wished to publicize and disseminate widely to housing and urban development officials in developing countries, as well as to donor and foreign assistance agencies.

As coordinator, author, and producer of the requested document, *Mansion in the Sky,* I was given considerable rein in defining the approach to the study, the methods used in obtaining information, and the way in which the story would be told. The only specified condition was that the document had to credit AID for its funding of the program and the cost of preparation and publication of the story itself. Unmentioned was the question of how to present some of the political sensitivities encountered in interviews and observations while researching the story. These sensitivities (described later) concerned certain politicians' perceptions of the program and their varying support for low-income, self-help solutions to the squatter problem.

In the description, I depicted those facets of Botswana[1] society that differentiated its human settlements pattern from those found elsewhere. For example, the role of multiresidence solutions for a Motswana family clearly influenced the process of developing a government-related shelter program. Many Batswana possess a village house, a cattle post, and an urban home, all used to "hedge their bets" in adapting to an economy based on, respectively, agriculture, cattle raising, and an urban cash income.

Another significant factor in the sociocultural description of the program was the depiction of the part played by women in the construction of the house. The Batswana women produced one type of thatched roofing for village houses and applied the exterior finish to the houses. These contributions are traditionally very important functions in giving the shelter its enduring quality and aesthetic character. Thus it was important for the self-help program to include the Botswana women's contribution to building a new house—thereby maintaining that traditional role.

Yet another feature characterized in the document was the community organization activity that was important for the success of the self-help program. It enabled housing officials in other developing countries to compare notes with the Botswana situation in order to assess the potential for a community development effort in their own settings. Although a major motive in the community development effort was to elicit participation of the squatters in improving their shelters and services, another motive was keeping plotholders in the mood to pay their building materials loans and monthly service fees. If these were paid, the program would have a much better chance of sustaining itself in the absence of external funding and technical assistance.

Problems besides those of good debt management had to be dealt with. What I have termed the "shock absorptive capacity" of the city in dealing with migrant villagers had to be supplemented. The community development staff helped greatly to offset some of the shock felt by villagers moving to the city. Working with the families in the self-help program on their specific needs greatly aided the rural-to-urban transition.

The section of the document that considered community development and its appropriate mode of organization is one of the richest parts of both the program and the document itself. Information in that section of the booklet was communicated in sufficient descriptive detail to evoke in readers similarities, as well as potential differences, in their own culture or societies that would have a bearing on the appropriate organization of a related program.

The publication stresses that among all the self-help purposes of the program, the educational one is perhaps the most important for the community development effort. The community development process works both ways: Residents must know what is expected of them before they can participate meaningfully in a self-help program; equally important is the community developers' need to know what residents expect of them in order to do their job effectively. In this context of mutual need and respect, community meetings were held with town councillors and residents to discuss needs, preferences, and other issues. Successful use was also made of such "show and tell" projects as a comic book format that describes in Setswana (the national language) the process of obtaining a plot and a building material loan, as well as advice on construction. Another comic book tells the builder how to construct a type B toilet. Tape-recorded instructions to plotholders explained how to use the self-help housing office, and popular theater in skit and play form underscored the overall benefit of the program to residents.

In describing the community development context, the document dealt frankly with the role of local and national politics in influencing the program. I felt that a sense of the political context would be useful to housing managers and urban planners and implementers in other developing countries as well as to bilateral and multilateral donors and lenders. The major rationale for including substantial material on this topic was to help such planners and donors become cognizant of how political influence might be wielded in a self-help program such as Botswana's and the necessity of investing significant project funding toward dealing with that influence.

In depicting the political forces on the program, the booklet looked specifically at those examples of influence that had to be recognized and dealt with in implementing the program. Such an example included the pressures brought to bear on the housing agency by both public and private interest groups for the scarce resources, namely, land (for plots), money (for materials loans), and personnel (agency staff). One particular political issue that had broad consequences for implementing the program concerned balancing the opposing forces of dependency and self-help. People perhaps naturally become dependent on government if it is "giving away" resources and creating dependence among its citizens; on the other hand, when a program is distinctly based on the principle of self-help (as this one is), such a principle would fly in the face of the notion of government as provider. That characterization is even more complex for Botswana because of its democratic process by which everyone from town councillor to national parliamentarian is voted into office through popular elections.

The booklet showed that politics was involved in the establishment and collection of service fees. Any fee, especially the $8 per month for all services, was anathema to the town council. Distraught by rising service fees, the councillors pleaded to the housing agency, "Do anything else but do not ask us to go to our constituents and ask for even $5.00!" No fewer than twenty meetings—many of them stormy—at various levels of government were held over this thorny issue. The issue, by the way, was mediated in such a way that the national policy of not subsidizing urban growth was basically kept intact, while the fee was raised to a level that did not lose the politicians' support, thereby allowing them to save face with their voters.

A specific goal of the booklet was to be instructive for those working to house the "poor majority" of the developing world. This goal was achieved by describing the successful Botswana program in terms of its (1) socioeconomic and political aspects, (2) formal, technical, and management organizational design, and (3) place in the context of general Third World development conditions. A second goal was to promote the kind of program depicted in the booklet from the perspective of the AID Office of Housing and my technical service organization. Third, the document aimed at characterizing the program as a human interest story for an audience dedicated to international development.

The purpose of the publication, then, was educational and promotional—to advocate a specific mode of project implementation that underscored the people-to-people side of foreign and technical assistance. On another level, its purpose was evaluative and educational—reaching a wide audience interested in broad issues of development, including the human dimensions.

The impact of an educational/promotional booklet such as *Mansion in the Sky* seems always difficult to determine with precision. Nevertheless, certain useful measures can be provided. For one, the client that financially supported the publication—the AID Office of Housing—distributed it widely as part of its promotion of the housing guarantee loan program. Another measure is that "Mansion" received widespread coverage in international development publications, including AID and World Bank house organs. In such coverage, the Botswana program was recommended as a model for low-income, self-help shelter and upgrading programs. And, as other indicators, letters commending *Mansion* were received from such leaders in development as former World Bank president Robert McNamara, former AID administrator Douglas Bennett, and several ministers of housing and other officials from developing countries. Requests for the booklet exceeded 4,000, requiring one reprinting and perhaps a second.

The Anthropological Difference

Before attempting to make sense of the anthropological difference in shaping the educational/promotional document described here, I wish to review the parts I played in carrying out my anthropological role. I also want to underscore the point that my role in the Botswana shelter program was much broader than what the term "anthropologist" might normally convey. I also served as a policy and program analyst, examining such issues as the costs of physical planning and design standards and the relationship of such costs to residents' ability to pay for them. In my task of recommending the adoption of what I considered the most "reasonable" standards for land use practices, shelter design, and public facilities and services planning—based on the socioeconomic studies I had worked on—I was in effect serving as a social planner. Of course, to some extent these functions of policy analyst and social planner probably come with the territory of the applied anthropologist.

From the more strictly anthropological perspective, I played several distinct roles, using the methods and techniques which in combination make our approach unique. First, I acted as ethnographic researcher, talking with, listening to, and observing Batswana living day to day in their houses and inside and outside their compounds. In that capacity, I tried to see how their values, preferences, and practices could best (including most economically) be reflected in the physical design and composition of the low-income housing program. My second role was survey researcher, carrying out sample surveys using questionnaires to determine such factors as house design preferences and acceptable trade-offs in the area of physical planning standards. For example, survey questions offered clear-cut alternatives such as "What would you prefer: a large plot with a pit latrine or a small plot with water borne sanitation?" My third role was trainer/teacher, in which I disseminated information and knowledge, as seen in the instruction I gave to numerous survey interviewers and in the production of *Mansion in the Sky*. My writing and production of this document were attributable mostly to my pre-viously described roles. I have no doubt that the "thick description" and sociocultural contextualization of the story told in *Mansion in the Sky* would have been impossible without the earlier sociocultural research.

Essentially, three broad types of anthropological knowledge and skills were used in the work that eventually led to the production of the booklet: (1) observational fieldwork, (2) sociocultural analysis, and (3) application of both the observations and analyses to the low-income, self-help urban and rural shelter and community upgrading programs in which I participated. For the first, I gathered ethnographic data over several consultancies as part of an examination of the shelter needs, market, preferences, and problems of low-income Batswana. In looking into these factors I framed questions concerning the social process such as, "Under what socioeconomic, political, and ecological conditions and as an expression of what cultural values is housing evolved or developed in different parts of Botswana?" To answer these questions, the traditional uses of a house were described, landholding patterns delineated, the role of rural-to-urban migration defined, and the place of farming, cattle, and mine work in South Africa explained. Also, the woman's role in traditional shelter activities was depicted, including her part in planning, constructing, and utilizing the house.

For the second type of anthropological knowledge and skills—socio-cultural analysis—I went to some length to demonstrate to the Motswana client (the low-income resident, local housing official, and ministry official) my knowledge and (at least partial) understanding of his or her society and culture. I always approached my analyses with modesty because I was not an expert in Setswana culture in the sense of having done previous long-term anthropological research in Botswana. Never-theless, my interpretations were received with sufficient confidence for me to be invited back to the country several times.

I must add that although a considerable degree of anthropological theory went into my analyses, most of it was frankly implicit. For example, theory on residence and kinship structure, ecological relationships, and the role of community were always a subconscious part of my tool kit. Given the work I was doing and my client, however, there was neither the request nor need to explicitly state the theories used. For ethnographic knowledge of the culture area and its role in giving context to the people and culture in which I was working, on the other hand, I always specified the applicable references.

On the level of application of anthropological knowledge to specific aspects of Botswana's low-income housing program, three major points of impact emerge. First, the collaborative research that I carried out with Batswana participation and the subsequent analyses influenced both national- and local-level government policy in fixing "appropriate" physical planning standards in its shelter program. Second, the work I did with the Batswana in surveying primary village socioeconomic and sociospatial patterns had a significant impact as a model for future village research and planning, as well as for the design and planning features of such villages. Third is the educational/promotional role I played as an anthropologist, also in collaboration with Batswana social resources personnel, in demonstrating the effectiveness of the Botswana low-income, self-help housing model for use in other developing country contexts.

In conclusion, it seems appropriate for me to highlight both the interdisciplinary and collaborative nature of the anthropological endeavor. On one hand, my reliance on architects, engineers, business managers, and community developers for their know-how was highly critical in both contextualizing specific socioeconomic, political, and spatial parameters of the shelter and upgrading program and in developing a consensus among such professionals as to appropriate solutions to the complex mix of social and technical problems. On the other hand, a collaborative relationship with low-income Batswana—the object of the entire endeavor—and Botswana government officials and politicians was of paramount importance to the sustainability of the program. Not to be omitted was the assistance of U.S. government officials who supported the effort financially, technically, and morally.

That my role as an anthropologist was so interdependent with all different kinds of people and professions is a reality that should be driven home. The anthropologist can not, need not, probably should not, stand alone in the type of work I was doing, for by its very definition of wholeness (wholism), anthropology thrives on the process of exchange. Nevertheless, as an anthropologist working in Botswana,

I believe that I have made a modest contribution in supporting the Batswana in their country's development.

Notes

1. The following terms are used throughout this chapter: Botswana (the country/nation); Batswana (the people living within the country/nation); Motswana (a person living in the country/nation); and Setswana (the national language).

References

Mason, John P. 1979. Social Research of Resident Preference, Need, and the Ability to Pay: Towards a Framework of Physical Planning Standards in Botswana's Sites and Services Areas. Washington, D.C.: Cooperative Housing Foundation.

————. 1981a. Mansion in the Sky: A Lesson in Self Help Housing from Gaborone, Botswana. Washington, D.C.: Cooperative Housing Foundation.

————, and Jesse Jones, Jr. 1981b. Priorities of Paced Growth in Mahalapye, Botswana: A Survey of Residents' Perceptions of Change and Its Affordability. Washington, D.C.: Cooperative Housing Foundation.

————. 1984. Report on Sociologist's Consultancy to the Mahalapye Village Upgrading Project. Washington, D.C.: Cooperative Housing Foundation.

14 / Designing Apache Homes with Apaches

George S. Esber, Jr.

Problem and Client

A man's home is his castle—or so the saying goes. That has not been the case, however, for Native Americans who, since the time of contact, have listened to unsolicited opinions about their homes and been subject to Anglo attempts to change their living conditions. Repeatedly, Indian houses have been referred to as "hovels," and as "unsanitary or substandard shacks." Colonists often felt that the promise of new, Anglo-styled homes could be used to entice tribal leaders to sign treaties that would cede land to the settlers (Washburn 1973:2310, 2333, 2507). Later, during the assimilationist era that began with Ulysses S. Grant's peace policy of 1867, more systematic attempts were made to pressure Indian peoples to restructure their lives by modifying their homes.

Surprisingly little has changed in the last 120 years. The U.S. government has continued to judge Native American homes unilaterally as inadequate and/or substandard and to pursue policies to rehouse Native Americans in Anglo-style housing. This approach has been followed without regard for Native American needs as dictated by cultural traditions or the architectural designs necessary to accommodate them. Rarely have Native Americans even been queried about their preferences for house types (Wulff 1973).

The goal of the Payson Project was to correct this problem by honoring Indian self-determination with respect to the home and community

---

The author wishes to acknowledge support for research on the Payson Project from the Comins Fund, the Doris Duke American Indian Oral History Project, the America the Beautiful Foundation, the Save the Children Federation, Mrs. Nan Pyle, and the Graduate Research Office and the Office of the Dean of Arts and Sciences, both of Miami University.

design for a new Tonto Apache camp. The setting for the project is the mountainous region of central Arizona where the *dilje* or true ones (renamed the Tonto Apache by the Spaniards) lived prior to contact with Europeans. Situated seventy-five miles north of Phoenix, Payson has a climate moderated by the mile-high elevation that makes its summers pleasant in contrast to the oppressive heat of Phoenix and the other valley cities to the south. On the north side of Payson is the Mogollon Rim, a spectacular ledge that begins the platform of the northern part of the state and through which cuts the Grand Canyon. Mesquite and oak trees grow on the south side of town, and Ponderosas are found to the north. The natural beauty of the country is special to the Tonto Apaches who know it as their homeland.

In a way, the Payson Project aimed at restoring a sense of self and home to the dilje, who came to be the clients in the project although they were not at first identified as such. In fact, when I first became aware of the design project, I was a graduate student at the University of Arizona, and one of my professors asked me to meet with some people in architecture about their working with a Native American group. In reluctantly agreeing to do so, I found myself working with clients who were architects working on a project having to do with Indians.

My anthropological training quickly alerted me to the missing native point of view. I knew that to be effective as an applied anthropologist, I would have to realign my position in relation to the architects and the Apache community and to establish the Indian community as the client. The designs would have to meet the Apaches' needs as understood from the Apache point of view; at the same time, the design decisions had to respect their right of self-determination. The realignment was not readily accomplished; it emerged as events unfolded.

Process and Players

The Payson Project was a piece of a larger, long-term community development effort whose goal was to improve the overall life conditions of one particular Apache group. Change began in the mid-1960s when a missionary organized the community as a religious and political unit. Later in the decade, a plan of action was outlined in conjunction with the people by which they would realize changes in their lives and their community.

When the project was begun, the people were living as squatters in the Tonto National Forest. Before settling there, their camp had been situated on highly desirable land in Payson, Arizona, that had been purchased by an Apache and former scout who was a member of the community. That land eventually fell onto the delinquent tax rolls and after ten years was purchased by a developer for the past due amount of $3.42 (Houser 1972:70). Subsequently, the people were literally bulldozed from their homes to make way for some of the more prestigious dwellings in Payson. The program that followed was, in part, an effort to correct this injustice.

The primary objectives of the community development project were to organize the community in a way that would enable the tribal leadership to articulate with Anglo society, to function as a political unity, to lobby for legislation to secure reservation land with full tribal recognition, and ultimately to develop the land and build a new settlement that would offer the comforts of modern living while still supporting the persisting Apache culture. The people agreed to the idea of securing specialists from outside the community whenever needed skills were unavailable from within the group (Keneally n.d.).

In this spirit, an architect and four architecture students were asked to begin planning community settlement. I was invited to join them as an anthropologist in an advisory capacity. This group formed the planning team whose mission was clear: to help plan and design a totally new reservation that would include both residential and community facilities, to satisfy as completely as possible the cultural needs of the Apache people, and to respect their right of Indian self-determination.

Problems became apparent very early. The architects began the planning process by following some of the same assumptions about needs that were considered in designing middle-class American homes. The variations that they anticipated were of the same order as those qualities that identify each real estate listing as unique—the number of bedrooms, the size of each room, the number of bathrooms and closets. Their only cross-cultural investigation of the Apache's needs was directed at learning what different activities the people engaged in and what arrangements were necessary to perform those functions. Interestingly, the Apache people did not have any better conception of what should constitute a home appropriate for their needs than did the architects. One woman suggested that we distribute a variety of house and home magazines that showed architectural photographs that could give people design ideas. Although this approach would have presented some at- tractive and eye-catching suggestions to the Apache, it would not touch on the real problems of identifying needs. The housing needs not being addressed were based on unconscious patterns of behavior and the demands that these practices would make on housing designs.

Communicating this anthropological thinking to both the architects and the Apache people became one of my first goals as a member of the design team. The Apache community readily heard and understood my concern for the design of a community to serve its needs. However, the suggestion that certain patterns of behavior were acted out unconsciously seemed an alien idea. On the other hand, I had no difficulty in gaining the Apache's recognition and acknowledgment of these patterns as they were pointed out in the course of my anthropological research. Whenever relevant behaviors were observed, identified, and described to Apache informants, they were always acknowledged by an enlivened, "Oh yeah, that's the way we do" (Esber 1977).

The architects, on the other hand, understood the anthropological concerns, and, having read Edward T. Hall's *The Hidden Dimension* (1966), they were aware of cross-cultural differences in the use of personal space. Consequently, the problem lay not with their ability to recognize the reality of such differences or to acknowledge their importance for design but rather with their not knowing how to elicit the appropriate cultural information from the Apache. Although the architects were trained to investigate the programmatic needs for particular activities, such as sewing and beading, they were not prepared to uncover the cultural requirements for personal space and social interaction or to translate such requirements into actual design elements.

I had to constrain the architects from moving forward with insufficient ethnographic data. Their frustrations mounted. The architect and his students were waiting to begin; in fact, they initially expected to complete a community design by the end of a school term, and, given the schedule usually allowed for design projects, that projection was not unrealistic. Because of that time frame, they felt compelled to proceed with or without anthropological input. Only through my firm insistence on restraint did they agree to wait for research to be conducted and results to become available. The timing, of course, now would depend on the Apache's interest and willingness to have the research done.

The architects still wanted to proceed and at least design the kitchens using the argument, "There are only so many ways you can use a stove, a sink and a refrigerator." Yet the anthropological literature is filled with examples of how creative people may be when adapting elements from an alien culture to their own. Once again restraint was demanded and an agreement reached but only after I consented to spend the next summer in the community to research behaviors and needs that would affect home and community designs.

That decision marked a turning point in the project: The architect and I agreed to a new plan of action with which we could both feel comfortable. The Apache leadership readily accepted our idea with the knowledge that only through close and extended contact could any cooperative, workable arrangement become a reality.

As fieldwork began, the usual anxieties that accompany cross-cultural experiences became apparent. I was eager to begin collecting data but recognized the Apache need to move slowly and deliberately in forming the relationships essential for learning about matters as personal as people's daily lives. My anthropological training enabled me to recognize these anxieties and to adopt the Apache's timetable. On the other hand, the architecture student assigned to the summer research project became impatient and subsequently lost favor with the Apache people. My persistence and adjustment to a different conceptual time frame paid off, and later in the summer I was able to use intensive, structured data collection procedures in addition to my ongoing participant observation.

I mapped the entire settlement to show the location of all the structures, and I identified the occupants of each home. I also conducted interviews to learn the relationships among the people of different households, and I mapped the interior and outside surroundings of each household to identify how space was defined and used. Later, I gave each family a model kit that consisted of a board with wall segments of various sizes that could be pinned in place. I also gave them scale size furnishings similar to what they had or wanted to have. I designed this methodology to collect data on culturewide housing preferences and patterns as well as on individual statements of preference. I photographed and analyzed each model plan and shared this information with the architect. Finally, ethnographic and ethnohistorical materials were studied and compared with modern-day living to identify continuing practices as well as changing ones.

Results and Evaluation

My research uncovered many features of Apache cultural life that were important determinants of design. Mapping revealed that the matrilocal pattern described by Goodwin (1942) was still being practiced. Not surprisingly, there were some exceptions to that pattern, but they could be explained by variables such as economic factors and marital status. For example, a few unmarried men lived on the fringe of the settlement, which in itself was a statement about their social status. Unmarried women, on the other hand, remained at home with their mothers until they married, at which time they built their own house (or moved into an already standing one) next to their mothers'. The matrilocal pattern was retained as an Apache preference in the new community plan. In fact, when the time approached for the people to select their new homesites, the older women of the community were asked to choose first and their daughters picked second and, in many cases, selected locations next to their mothers'.

The mapping of homes showed many regularities in the allocation of space for the various activities performed by each family. Comparisons with traditional Apache wickiups revealed several persistent patterns. For example, the most important division of space in a wickiup separated the sleeping area from the remaining larger space used for all daytime activities. Although this pattern was reflected in varying degrees from house to house, a preference toward fewer partitions was expressed. One woman specifically said, "If I were going to get a new home, I would want one big room for storage and one big room to live in." Many of the models that people built reflected the desire for a sense of openness in the living area rather than for partitions separating cooking, dining, and living areas.

Participation-observation made possible certain discoveries about the Apache use of space. For example, the negatively perceived personality trait of shyness so frequently attributed to Apaches by Anglos was found to be a function of the Apaches' definition of appropriate social interaction. Apache rules for conduct dictate that a slow, step-by-step approach should be used to enter a social situation with delays at periodic stations along the way. This pattern enables people to carefully assess a situation, to note the behavior of those present, and to make decisions about whether they wish to interact further. Apaches prefer large rooms and open spaces so they can have a full view of the social setting but can maintain enough distance from others so that verbal interaction is not necessary (Esber 1972). From this vantage point, the behavior of others comes to be known, and further social intercourse may follow from the judgments made.

Food often serves as the catalyst for bringing people closer together. This ethnographic fact was significant for my design suggestion that the cooking area should not isolate people from one another as they moved through the interaction process. This is especially important for host/ guest relations in which several weeks or months may have elapsed since their last gathering. A host always offers food and a guest rarely declines. Very little catching up on the past is done until the guests have eaten. The initial, relatively silent reunion is part of the reacquaintance process that ensures each party that relationships are much the same since they last saw each other. Apache homes need a cooking area to be part of the open space that permits people to be in full view of one another and to assess each other's behaviors. This persisting cultural pattern carries over from life in wickiups as Goodwin (1942:544–546) described it.

Although part of my role was to ensure that the desired Apache lifestyle was taken into account, I also had to consider how changes might be integrated into Apache life. For example, indoor plumbing, running water, and electricity would be incorporated with existing Apache patterns. New appliances and a more permanent cooking arrangement would result from these innovations, and the traditional practice of moving outdoors during the summer months might be affected. Interviews were used to bring this fact to the attention of the Apaches and also to elicit feelings from them about the possible resulting changes. Out of these discussions came the reaffirmation of the need to retain wood stoves for cooking because of the greater flexibility and portability that they offered, although other cooking appliances might be used in conjunction with them.

In some ways traditional space patterns were to change to become more like middle American patterns. For example, an Anglo home defines a master bedroom separate from others, thus offering privacy to a husband and wife. Apache society scorns any public or outward displays of affection, and people preferred the idea of separate bedrooms for the greater modesty that the arrangement offers.

I brought to the people's attention many such anticipated changes. As I researched traditional Apachean patterns, much of my work was to make explicit the behaviors that were not consciously played out or whose implications for design were not readily seen. The same theme had to be played out with respect to my identification of changes that would result from the new, more permanent camp. For example, whenever a person died in a wickiup, that home was burned immediately after the funeral. The Payson community modified that practice when they moved into the national forest because open fires were a violation of Forest Service regulations. Instead, community members tore down the home of the deceased. I asked what might be done in the future because Housing and Urban Development would frown on such a practice. After some thought, one person suggested that perhaps the surviving family members could stay elsewhere with relatives for a couple of weeks while other members of the community redecorated the home to give it a new appearance.

Examples such as this one illustrate the utility of bringing to the people's attention certain facets of life in which cultural change will occur. The direction of the change will necessarily be an Apache decision, but without these issues being raised, information bearing upon design decisions will not be available.

My anthropological research and design recommendations contributed to a successful planning effort and ultimately to a successful finished product. The actual construction of twenty homes was completed early in 1981, and families moved into their new homes in March and April. When I returned that summer for a postoccupancy evaluation, I found people who were genuinely excited about their new community and their new homes. Nearly every family symbolized their pride by hanging their own handmade name plates in front of their homes.

The differences in satisfaction level between Apaches living in the Payson housing designed with anthropological input and new housing in other Apache communities designed without anthropological input are instructive. Apaches in other reservations were reluctant or unwilling to move into new homes built for them. Those who tried Anglo housing found it unsuitable and soon moved back to their old homes. Government officials were unable to understand why new homes were being scorned because they assumed that anyone would like a new home. However, the issue was not one of having new quarters but rather of experiencing the comfort of home in culturally appropriate housing.

In contrast, the new homes in Payson, with their modern technologies and conveniences, were readily adopted and integrated into the Apache lifestyle. One obvious advantage was the readily available water supply that obviated the need for hauling garbage cans filled with water from the local sawmill where the men worked. No one seemed to miss a cold night's walk to an outhouse. The fact that people had running water in their kitchens meant that they could wash pots and pans easily. Although that may at first seem trivial, without anthropological input, conventional kitchen sinks would have been installed. Because of my research on social organization and community social life, the need for handling large quantities of food in large pots and pans was taken into consideration in the kitchen design, and extra large sinks and cupboards were installed. In contrast, in government housing on other Apache reservations I watched women washing vessels outside with a garden hose and storing them on open counter space because their cupboards were too small.

Social interaction, too, was comfortably managed in the new homes. On one ordinary evening, I counted twenty-six people in one home. The concept of open space permitted comfortable accommodations for everyone. From observations of Apache life in other government housing, I found that people would rather sit in separate rooms than crowd together in a smaller space. In one instance, people communicated across a partition separating one room from another without being able to see the person speaking.

These are but a few of many examples where anthropological research made apparent cultural needs that were easily accommodated through architectural design. Without the information or attention to special needs in cross-cultural design problems, the Payson houses would not have been comfortable homes for Apache living. Instead, the major problem that the Apaches encountered after moving in was that their new homes were too warm and not drafty like their old homes. During that first winter they cracked windows open just to feel at home.

The Anthropological Difference

Anthropological input helped direct the architect's attention to the culture-specific needs of the Apache people. The anthropological contribution drew upon knowledge in the areas of social organization and the social use of space, or proxemics. The knowledge of the dynamics of a matrilineal and matrilocal society informed the planners about why people chose to live where they did and what this residence pattern meant for social interaction. These factors were not considered in planning typical government housing because kinship and social organization were not included in the determination of people's needs.

Equally important to the Payson Project was the work of E. T. Hall on the cross-cultural differences in the social use of space. Interestingly, the concept of space provided the communication link between anthropology and architecture. Space is the central concept for design in the same way that culture is for anthropology. The added hidden dimension that anthropology contributed drew upon the knowledge that people in different cultures use space differently in their social interactions and that these patterns of behavior are practiced unconsciously (Hall 1959, 1964). My findings about Apache space use patterns were collected and summarized in a form that could be used to guide design decisions. Not only was that information useful to the architects, but it made the Apache people aware of their unconscious behaviors so that they could participate more fully in design decisions.

Perhaps more significant than the knowledge and data drawn from anthropology was my own active involvement as an applied anthropologist who could employ the methods for obtaining the information. The cross-cultural nature of the design project placed different demands on the architect, and though aware of these, he lacked the necessary knowledge for data collection. The field methods of anthropology coupled with this awareness made possible an exploration of Apache cognitions and behaviors with respect to their patterns of space use. Moreover, the fieldwork tradition of anthropology requires that rapport be adequate to allow the discovery of "the native point of view." The architect himself had very friendly relations with the Apaches, but the nature of the relationship was not such that ethnographic data were being revealed to him or that he was pursuing that data. He lacked training in anthropological field methods.

Finally, through anthropology I had the benefit of the tradition of a working relationship between members of my discipline and Native

American groups. The history of Anglo-Indian relations gave me the knowledge of current policy guidelines for fostering Indian self-determination. That translated into a real difference between the architects' readiness to design *for* while I was determined to have them design *with* the Apache people. Here, the anthropological difference was most clear. Other government housing was done for Indians without the involvement of Indian people. I adhered to the principle that the Apache people should be involved in making design decisions, and they were. Moreover, the self-knowledge that the Apache people gained about their unconscious patterns of behavior enabled them to know better their own needs. With that awareness, the people were truly in a position to make decisions about what they wanted and to use for their own purposes the knowledge that anthropology was able to offer.

References

Esber, George S., Jr. 1972. Indian Housing for Indians. *The Kiva* 37(3):141–147.
——— . 1977. *The Study of Space in Advocacy Planning with the Tonto Apaches of Payson, Arizona.* Ph.D. dissertation, University of Michigan Microfilms, Ann Arbor.
Goodwin, Grenville. 1942. *The Social Organization of the Western Apache.* Chicago: University of Chicago Press.
Hall, Edward T. 1959. *The Silent Language.* Greenwich, Conn.: Fawcett Publications.
——— . 1966. *The Hidden Dimension.* Garden City, N.Y.: Doubleday.
Houser, Nicholas P. 1972. "The Camp"—An Apache Community of Payson, Arizona. *The Kiva,* 37(2):65–73.
Keneally, Henry J., Jr. n.d. The Advocacy Team Concept: A New Look at Approaches to Problem Solving. Paper presented at the 99th Annual Forum and Exposition, National Conference on Social Welfare, Chicago.
Washburn, Wolcomb E. 1973. *The American Indian and The United States.* New York: Random House.
Wulff, Robert M. 1973. Housing the Papago: An Analytical Critique of a Housing Delivery System. International Housing Productivity Study, School of Architecture and Urban Planning, University of California, Los Angeles.

15 / Tribally Controlled Culture Change: The Northern Ute Language Renewal Project

William L. Leap

Anthropologists have long recognized the significance of language skills for all areas of the human experience. People talk, as anthropological linguist George L. Trager is fond of saying, and what they talk about is their culture. So anthropologists have not been surprised to find that speakers will view situations of imminent language death with great alarm. Loss of language skills is always associated with losses in other areas of social and cultural life, and replacements for such details, regardless of their emotional appeal, may not always restore continuity or stability within these cultural domains.

The case study at issue in this chapter offers an example of ways in which responses to losses in language and cultural tradition can be effectively implemented. At issue here are a series of efforts, some that are ongoing at this writing (November 1986) and others that have been replaced or phased out entirely. Input from a variety of sources has contributed to the success of these efforts. I was one of those sources, and this chapter describes the roles I played in this project and evaluates the outcomes of the project and my contributions to it from several points of view.

Problem and Client

The Northern Ute (officially designated the Uintah and Ouray Tribe of Ute Indians, Inc.) is a federally recognized Indian tribe, most of whose members live on or near the tribe's 971,000-acre reservation in northeast Utah. In terms of linguistic heritage, the Northern Ute language is said to be mutually intelligible with the Indian language spoken on Colorado's

Southern Ute and Ute Mountain reservations; even so, Ute speakers report that people from each tribe maintain distinct ways of structuring sentences, pronouncing words, and expressing their ideas. The Northern Ute language is closely related to those of the Chemehuevi and Southern Paiute, and then to the Shoshone, Comanche, and other languages within the Numic family. Ethnographers recognize this relationship when they include the Northern Ute people among the Indian tribes of the Great Basin. However, mountain and grassland ecologies as well as desert environments helped to shape traditional culture for this tribe, and they continue to influence Indian life on the reservation.

Traditionally, Ute social organization centered around a person's membership in one of fifteen bands, each with its own name, identity, territory, and characteristic way of speaking the Ute language. By 1890, ten of these bands had been settled on the Northern Ute reservation, and over time, because of intermarriage and other factors, the number of Northern Ute bands was reduced from ten to three. Even so, the principle of band membership remains a basic component of Northern Ute social life, and band-specific dialects of the Ute language continue to be maintained.

What has changed, particularly in recent years, is the number of speakers of these dialects. Even though contact with speakers of English began shortly after the creation of the reservation (1860), Ute continued to be the first language of most households, and the preferred means of public communication for most individuals until the mid twentieth century. Parents' interest in preparing their children for the rigors of an English-only school environment had much to do with this shift. More significant for the Northern Ute was the closing of the on-reservation boarding school in 1953. This move gave the county-operated public schools complete responsibility for the education of Ute young people. Attending public schools forced Ute students to function as members of a linguistic and cultural minority within an all-English-speaking, predominately non-Indian student population. Acquisition of a functional fluency in English was the only strategy for success that this institutional context allowed. Outside of the classroom, radio, motion pictures, and other popular media were making their impact on language skills development and use options. Likewise family decisions to move to Salt Lake City or other urban areas and then to return to the reservation when prospects for employment did not materialize were also important, as were the growth of the non-Indian communities in the area and the increasing significance of their role as commercial centers in the on-reservation economy.

By the end of the 1960s, even though the idea of Ute language fluency continued to be highly valued, the traditional relationship between being Ute and speaking Ute was no longer as widely evident on this reservation. Tribal members were aware of this change; yet their responses to it were not uniform. Some felt it best if the language disappeared because so many other facets of traditional culture had also passed away. Others agreed that a restoration of Ute fluency was needed, though they did not always agree about the way to obtain that goal. So for example, in 1971 a Ute woman and a non-Indian colleague began offering Ute-as-second-language classes as one of the electives at the local public high school. Tribal members applauded the program in concept, while objecting to its emphasis on written as well as spoken Ute language skills, to the presence of non-Indian students (and a non-Indian instructor) in the classroom, and to the fact that the program, being school-based, was operating independent of tribal control and tribal accountability. Despite the program's popularity among participating students, the instructors terminated it several semesters after it began. Such was the situation presented to me when I made my first trip to the Northern Ute reservation in 1978. By then, the language question had become a frequent topic for discussion throughout the Ute Division of Education (the component of tribal government that coordinates services in education on behalf of the tribal membership). The Johnson-O'Malley (JOM) committee (the group of Ute parents and educators that supervises federally funded tutorial services to Indian elementary and secondary school students) had decided that some action needed to be taken before knowledge of the language became lost entirely. So it proposed to hold a half-day discussion of options in language renewal. I was invited to participate in that discussion because of the success of my work in language education in other tribal contexts and the national credibility I had developed as an advocate for tribally controlled education programs. Other participants, in addition to members of the JOM committee, included the directors of the Ute Head Start project and other tribal education programs, the director of the Tribal Division of Education, parents from the on-reservation communities, and several tribal elders.

This meeting was, to the participants' knowledge, the first formal discussion of the Ute language problem ever held on this reservation; and it soon became clear that a one-afternoon meeting could not resolve the many policy questions surrounding the creation of a language renewal effort on any reservation. The discussion did, however, help participants identify some of the requirements for a successful language program whatever its design or orientation. According to that discussion, such a project would need to

- acknowledge the distinctiveness of the "band" dialects in all areas of instruction;
- respect oral traditions, and avoid emphasis on writing the language or on developing literary skills in it;
- maintain tribal control over the program at all costs and minimize the involvement of non-Indian institutions—particularly, the public school system;
- emphasize band, community, and family-level responsibilities and obligations in language and culture transmission.

The problem at issue in this project was twofold: Ute language loss and the need to counteract it. The intended beneficiaries were the members of the Northern Ute Tribe. My involvement in this project was not made official at this meeting; that I was to have a role in it was clear, however, because in good Ute fashion meeting participants told me that they could "use my help" with several of the meeting's follow-up tasks. Determining the client—who would take charge of the language renewal on this reservation (and, by extension, for whom I would be working)—was the first of those tasks to be addressed.

Process and Players

According to Ute tradition, decisions to take action on some problem can be made individually, provided the decision-maker is willing to assume responsibility for the outcomes of those actions. A more cautious, and ultimately more appropriate, alternative is to discuss intended actions with a large number of individuals and then pursue a plan of action that all parties are willing to endorse. The sensitive nature of the language renewal question (as seen, for example, in the earlier attempt to teach the language at the local high school) made it particularly appropriate to follow this second alternative in the earliest stages of planning. And so, rather than take responsibility for decision-making on their own, participants at the afternoon conference decided to sponsor a three-day, reservationwide language workshop during which all tribal members could explore and evaluate possible solutions for the tribe's language needs. Tribal educators and political and spiritual leaders were asked to attend this workshop and share their perspectives on the language issue with participants. Representatives of language renewal efforts underway on the Southern Ute and Ute Mountain reservations were invited to participate. And, as I suggested, because other tribes were also struggling with many of the same problems and questions, the representatives of other Indian language renewal projects were invited to describe the work being done by those projects and the ways their projects addressed questions of tribal control, community and family involvement, oral versus written instruction, and other issues.

The workshop was held in early March 1979. Workshop expenses were met in part through a grant from the Utah Endowment for the Humanities (the proposal for which I helped prepare) and through tribal funds. Members of more than 35 percent of the on-reservation households attended the three-day meeting. And, after listening to the discussion, participants agreed to support the Tribal Division of Education as it continued to explore the possibilities for language renewal on this reservation. The division now had a popular mandate to begin developing a plan of action.

Yet informed discussion of this issue could not continue until the extent of Indian language loss on the reservation had been assessed. Workshop participants knew that Ute language fluency was on the decline, but participants could not estimate the size or scope of the problem, nor could they agree on which factors had greatest influence over that decline.

I had developed an instrument for assessing language fluency patterns within on-reservation households while working with a Wisconsin Indian language census project in 1977–1978. The JOM committee, which continued to act as the focus for project decisionmaking within the Division of Education, reviewed the instrument and evaluated the clarity of the questions when translated into Ute. Then, after making minor adjustments in format, it sponsored a reservationwide language survey, the first ever attempted on this reservation. Members of the committee and other workshop participants served as enumerators; I provided them with orientation to the project and trained them in data-gathering skills, following the strategies I had developed during my work in Wisconsin. Fourteen percent of the households were randomly selected for survey purposes; enumerators contacted these households during April and May 1979. Students in the Department of Anthropology at the American University (Washington, D.C.) conducted a statistical analysis of the responses, and I supervised interpretation of those data and presented a summary of findings to the tribal membership during a second reservationwide language workshop in late June 1979.

Three of the points in my summary were particularly interesting to the workshop participants. First, the extent of Ute language loss versus language retention varies considerably among households, making residence-related patterns a highly significant descriptor when discussing distribution of Indian language fluency on this reservation. Age-level and generational position, found to be significant descriptors at other Indian sites, are much less closely tied to the distribution of language skills in this instance. Second, inability to speak the Ute language does not automatically imply absence of Ute language skill. Many members of the tribe were reportedly able to understand Ute when it is spoken to them, even though they could not respond to speakers in the same linguistic terms. Third, parents reported that children who speak Ute experience many fewer problems with English in the school classroom than do monolingual English-speaking students; cross-checks of drop-out rates, frequency of teacher-initiated parent conferences, and other measures confirmed the patterning of these reports.

The first two findings suggested that knowledge of the Ute language was not disappearing, even though the use of that language was certainly on the decline. Apparently, some tribal members, including young people who otherwise appeared to be English monolinguals, had already acquired a "passive fluency" in Ute language, which could be expanded into an "active fluency" if appropriate language-learning activities could be arranged. The third finding provided a compelling—and completely unexpected—reason for setting up access to such activities as soon as possible.

The discussion at this workshop developed into unanimous support for tribal government to create a Ute language renewal program within the tribal Division of Education. A second matching grant from the Utah Endowment for the Humanities provided funds to hire a project staff and to meet other start-up costs. The JOM committee selected a project director, a fluent Ute speaker in her mid-twenties. She began to assemble the information on the Ute language already in print, and, at my suggestion and with the endorsement of the newly constituted Ute Language Committee (composed of members of the JOM committee with particular interests in the language questions), she began tape-recording speech samples, personal narratives, recipes, and other Ute language materials from fluent speakers.

The director of the Education Division had already asked me to serve as consulting linguist for the language program, and, with the endorsement of the director and the language committee, he set aside a small portion of the program's operating budget to cover travel costs and other expenses, so I could commute from Washington, D.C., to the reservation at six-week intervals. Initially, my work centered around three tasks: staff training workshops in linguistic transcription and grammatical analysis; technical assistance in the design of a practical writing system for the language (even though the tribe was "officially" opposed to a written Ute language, project staff found it impractical to work with the language on an exclusively oral basis); and supervision of the data-gathering sessions with fluent speakers. I had chosen these tasks deliberately, and the project director and the language committee had agreed with my rationale: Work in these areas would increase technical understanding of a language whose structure and usage patterns had never been formally analyzed and amass data around which a Ute-as-second-language curriculum could be constructed.

Work within this second domain moved much more rapidly than I had originally expected. Although the director of the language program was interested in technical research, she was more interested in providing language development services, where needed, to tribal members. She was still intrigued by the fact that, according to the household language survey, students who spoke Ute have an easier time in school than do students monolingual in English. I suspected, based on my research at other sites, that part of the problem might lie in the monolingual students' "passive" knowledge of Ute grammar. The project director took that idea and developed it into a proposal for a bilingual education project to be based in the on-reservation public elementary school. The U.S. Office of Bilingual Education agreed to fund that proposal, and the county school authorities agreed to sponsor the grant. In fall 1980, the Wykoopah (two paths) language project began providing developmental Ute and English instruction to Ute Indian children (and to interested non-Indian classmates) at Todd Elementary School.

Wykoopah's parent advisory committee (PAC) asked the director of the tribe's language program to become Wykoopah director. She agreed. She then asked me to serve as Wykoopah's staff linguist and work with her in training the Wykoopah language teachers (all of whom were Ute, but none of whom held degrees in elementary education) in developing procedures for diagnosing and describing Ute student English language problems, and in designing an integrated Ute/English language arts curriculum. This resulted in a six-year research effort involving Wykoopah staff, elementary school teachers, and Ute and non-Indian students, many technical reports and in-service workshops, and several publications.   •

Meanwhile, the tribe's Ute language committee began interviewing candidates for a new director for the Education Division's language program. The woman the committee selected was familiar with the program and for some time had been concerned that parents and community members were not more involved in its activities. To address this problem, she proposed the preparation of a practical Ute language handbook—*Poopah Noochee ah Puhgkuhn* (The way the Ute speaks). This handbook, published in summer 1982, contained games, exercises, language drills, self-guided creative projects, and other activities that parents and grandparents could use to broaden the children's Ute language learning experiences within the home.

I had been interested in seeing such a "deliverable" prepared by the tribe's language program for some time and had written the proposal to the Utah Endowment for the Humanities that secured funds to support its publication. And, at the request of the program director, I supplied examples for several sections of the handbook from my research files, drafted the discussion that introduced the reader to basic grammatical rules, and helped the staff make spelling decisions and solve layout problems.

The program director realized that the publication of *Poopah Noochee ah Puhgkuhn* might appear to be in conflict with Wykoopah's work in oral language development. So, once the handbook was distributed across the reservation, the program director and her staff focused their work around other areas of Ute expressive culture. Project activities over the next several months included sponsorship of community-based workshops to train tribal members in beadwork, bustle-making, traditional design, and other creative themes; support, through small grants in aid, for the work of tribal artists and craftspersons (at one point, four Ute artists-in-residence were associated with the program); and preparation of a calendar illustrated with photographs and drawings that reflect various aspects of Ute traditional knowledge.

Creating this division of labor helped minimize (for a while, at least) friction that might have developed between these two language programs. However, by 1983–1984 other educational programs on the reservation had also become interested in Ute language instruction. Teachers in the tribe's Head Start program were regularly including Ute words and phrases in their preschool reading readiness activities, for example; and students in the tribe's vocational education program were requesting that Ute as well as English language skills be addressed in the basic education component of that program's curriculum. Unfortunately, no centralizing mechanism was used to coordinate the work of each of these projects, and when conflicts grew out of these differing approaches to language renewal—for example, disagreements over "proper spelling," which had already led Wykoopah, the Education Division's programs, and Head Start staff to develop individually distinctive writing systems for the Ute language—no procedures were in place to resolve them.

The solution to this problem came about as a result of another component of the tribe's language renewal effort. The 1979 language workshops had given the Education Division a mandate to work in these areas. The Tribal Business Committee, the official governing body of the Northern Ute tribe, had yet to take any official stand on the language question or on the importance of efforts to address it. So in

1982, it asked me to prepare what became the preliminary text for a tribal language policy that would, among its other points, affirm the value that Northern Ute people see in retention of Ute language fluency and describe the procedures that any party—tribal member, school official, church leader, or researcher—would need to follow before becoming an active participant in any language renewal-related activity. Wykoopah's Parents Advisory Committee reviewed the text, as did the advisory committee for the Education Division's language program. Both committees recommended additions and modifications in the text, to make certain that the cultural as well as linguistic dimensions of language renewal were addressed by the policy and to clarify the functions of the Ute Language and Culture Committee, the component of the Education Division which would be given responsibility for overseeing all language renewal efforts carried out on this reservation.

The Business Committee reviewed the policy in fall 1983 but declined to take any action on it. Among its concerns were the following: The policy identified Ute as the "official language" of the tribe; Business Committee members feared that all tribal business would have to be conducted, and reported out, in Ute—something they feared would offend tribal members who were not fluent speakers of that language. Second, the policy imposed certain requirements on (non-Indian) teachers of Ute students within the on-reservation public schools, something Business Committee members felt they lacked authority to impose or monitor. Finally, the policy represented a new direction for Ute tribal government, and some Business Committee members were not certain that tribal government should be venturing into language-related domains.

Clearly, members of the several language renewal projects felt otherwise. We caucused at some length throughout fall and winter 1983–1984, before coming up with responses to each of those concerns. Public review of the policy during a third reservationwide language workshop (November 1983) provided further perspective for our counterarguments: Describing Ute as the "official language" was a goal statement, not a reference to current condition; and by affirming this goal in the language policy, the Business Committee validated all the renewal efforts that had emerged on the reservation since 1978. Stating minimal requirements for teacher preparation on the reservation was a legitimate use of self-determination and sovereignty; if the tribe did not take the responsibility for setting minimum standards, what entity would? In fact, from the point of view of the actors in Ute language renewal, Business Committee endorsement of the proposed language policy was a highly appropriate move; by doing so, the Business Committee made it clear that language renewal was in the best interests of the tribe as a whole. Reconsideration of the policy in spring 1984 was swayed by these arguments; on April 10, 1984, the Northern Ute Tribe became the first Indian tribe in the United States officially to affirm the right of its members to regain and maintain fluency in the ancestral language and their right to use that language as a means of communication throughout their lives.

Results and Evaluation

The preceding section, which reviews Northern Ute efforts at Indian language renewal during the period 1978–1984, makes clear that, by the end of this period, the idea of language renewal had undergone a dramatic transformation on this reservation. Language development projects were in place within the on-reservation elementary schools, the tribe's Head Start program, and the tribal Division of Education. Federal as well as tribal revenues were supporting these projects, and persons with varying degrees of familiarity with the Ute language were participating in them. Several practical writing systems had now emerged, and project staff and other individuals were becoming literate in what was formerly an "unwritten" language. A tribally sanctioned language and culture committee now coordinated and monitored the work being done with language-related questions on this reservation. And underlying all these efforts was the Ute language policy, endorsing the tribe's work in this area and authorizing such work to continue. In other words, by 1984 language renewal had ceased being merely a topic for discussion and concern; now it was a rallying point for tribal activity, with a considerable amount of effort being directed toward this goal.

The significance of this shift in attitude can best be understood by focusing briefly on three of its major components: the emergence of a popular mandate for language renewal, the acceptance of Ute language instruction within the public schools, and the development of a written Ute language.

A Popular Mandate for Ute Language Renewal

In 1978, any discussion of language renewal needs on the Northern Ute reservation ultimately came back to a single theme: Home, family, and community contexts should serve as the focal point for Ute language learning, and any external involvement in that process constituted an unwarranted interference with the responsibilities properly assigned to those domains. Discussions during the Ute language workshops never contradicted that idea directly but did make clear that, before Ute language proficiency could begin to expand on this reservation, opportunities for language learning had to increase significantly. Even if language renewal efforts were confined to traditionally acceptable contexts, some entity on the reservation would have to take responsibility for increasing Ute language visibility within those domains. From the outset, the tribal Division of Education seemed the logical focus for this responsibility. Language services were not a part of the division's mandate, and the Business Committee had yet to include language renewal within the tribe's educational priorities. And even if that mandate were provided, mechanisms to deliver language services to the people, without running into conflict with more traditional language learning activities, had yet to be put into place.

Two reservationwide workshops, careful public scrutiny of data from the household language survey, and considerable public discussion (in Ute as well as English) were required before tribal members gave their support for a division-based renewal effort. By doing so, participants at these workshops took the first step in a lengthy process that would culminate, five years later, in the Business Committee's endorsement of the tribal language policy. During the interim (1978–1984) the people developed greater acceptance of a tribal role in language renewal, and the tribal government developed greater clarity regarding the contributions that it could make to this endeavor.

The emergence of the popular mandate for language renewal was the critical element in the success of the movement. This point is clearly illustrated by the tribal response to the Business Committee's 1983 proposal to balance its budget for the coming fiscal year by eliminating its support for "nonessential" tribal programs. The Education Division's Ute language program was one program targeted for elimination under this plan. Public opposition to the proposal was mobilized through discussions at a third reservationwide language workshop. That discussion led to a series of one-on-one contacts with Business Committee members (not all of whom, incidentally, were speakers of the Ute language) and ultimately a restoration of funding for that program and deeper budget cuts in other domains. The Business Committee made the decision to restore those funds, but the catalyst in the process was public opinion— specifically, the people's demand that language renewal not be excluded from the essential business of tribal government. Passage of the tribal language policy six months after this event can be seen as an additional response to public concern.

Ute Language Instruction Within the Public Schools

As previously described, Ute language instruction had been offered to high school students during the mid-1970s. Two instructors had taught this course under their own initiative, had allowed non-Indian students to participate in their classes, and had emphasized written as well as spoken Ute language skills in their curriculum. Tribal objections to the course focused on all three of these themes, and public pressure was the deciding factor in the termination of these classes after three semesters.

Tribal reaction to the Wykoopah project's work in Ute language development was considerably more supportive—even though, as before, there were non-Indian participants in the program and written language skills were emphasized. There was a critical difference, of course: Wykoopah grew out of a tribally sanctioned language initiative, its director was the original director of the Education Division's language program, and any number of provisions were now being made to keep tribal members informed about Wykoopah activities and to use tribal priorities as guides for project decision-making. Unlike the situation ten years earlier, the school-based Ute language project was no longer intruding into the private affairs of family and community; this time, the project's mandate, its director, and much of its plan for daily operations were grounded in the tribal domain. If anything, Wykoopah constituted an intrusion of the tribe and its educational priorities into the day-by-day concerns of the school system. And the tension that resulted from this intrusion was a factor leading Wykoopah staff to shift their base of operations back to the Education Division, once the funding for that project came to an end.

Development of a Written Ute Language

Among the constraints placed on the language renewal effort at Northern Ute was a prohibition against any form of written language instruction. Ute people were part of an oral language tradition, the argument ran, and that language tradition should be maintained in that format. Wykoopah was the first project to "violate" this constraint. And Wykoopah would have maintained an exclusively oral approach to language instruction if the participating students (Indian as well as non-Indian) had not asked for help in writing the language. The students had been trying to take notes during language classes, following their own sense for "proper" spelling. For them, formal literacy training served to stabilize something that they had begun under their own initiative.

Parental acceptance of a written Ute language grew out of a different set of arguments. English spelling had long been a school subject that plagued Ute students, and traditional classroom remedies for improving spelling skills were not leading to meaningful results in most cases. Ute language literacy, on the other hand, offered an appealing way of building Ute students' interest in the spelling process, in helping them make sound/letter associations, and in getting them to think about language in standardized as well as visible formats. Wykoopah staff became adept at introducing this argument in their parent training sessions. By doing so, staff were giving Ute parents a chance to build their familiarity with written Ute while they learned about the advantages of such knowledge for their children's education. Written Ute remained a nontraditional language skill, even within this context, but the non-traditional skills were now being directed to a nontraditional need—school success. Parental acceptance of this component of the Wykoopah project shows how effectively Wykoopah made its case on these grounds.

That the idea of a written Ute language is no longer an alien concept on this reservation is now clear. The Education Division's language project, initially sensitive to the tribal prohibition on written language materials, chose a written language format for the deliverable they prepared for reservationwide distribution in 1982. Project staff have largely avoided publication of Ute language materials since completion of the handbook. Other persons, however, have taken up the challenge: Now the tribe's newspaper includes Ute words and phrases in its editorials and guest columns each month, and word puzzles and other language related activities are often included in the reports from the several language projects. Posters advertising special events on the reservation, announcing plans for ceremonial activities, or urging tribal members to "get out the vote" do so in Ute as well as in English. Of course these developments cannot be taken out of context; tribal members were opposed to the use of written Ute in any form in 1978, and many have remained opposed to it since that time—making the growing interest in these elementary forms of Ute language literacy all the more intriguing.

The Anthropological Difference

The focal point for efforts toward language renewal on the Northern Ute reservation has been a theory of language acquisition that is heavily anthropological in orientation. This theory stresses the innate ability of human beings to acquire language skills, as well as the need for any language renewal project to organize its work in terms of this innate human potential. All members of the Northern Ute tribe, by this argument, are capable of being fully competent users of Ute (as well as of English), so if a tribal member's language skills are not meeting that expectation, the problem has as much to do with the influence of contextual factors on individual behavior as it does with that person's strengths and weaknesses. Thus the challenge facing Ute language renewal was twofold: first, to identify those factors impeding the acquisition of Ute language skills within the on-reservation speech community, and second, to develop necessary mechanisms to allow Ute language acquisition to occur in spite of those factors.

Ironically, most of the language renewal activities during the initial years of this effort were directed toward the second of these goals: The Education Division's community-centered programs, the school-based Wykoopah project, Head Start's language classes, and the other language development activities described in this chapter were designed to create opportunities for language learning where opportunities did not already exist. These projects were not expected to determine why they did not already exist, however; and even when they did come up with specific causes for Ute language loss, participants were quick to point out that they could not bring about the necessary changes in those conditions on their own.

From the beginning of this project, each discussion of Ute language needs ended with a plea for tribal-level leadership on this issue. As in other contexts, tribal leadership meant that the Ute people would make decisions at each stage of project activities. It also meant that Ute people would participate in these projects, not as individuals, but as members of family, kin, community, and band. This made validation of a proposed action as important to the planning as were the specifics of the activities being proposed, so no new renewal effort could be implemented without first weighing the consequences of the event for the actors and any others associated with its outcome. Thus consultation was a particularly appropriate decision-making strategy for the project, even if it meant that decisions themselves became buried beneath seemingly endless rounds of discussion, disagreement, and (at times) even personal confrontation.

Kin-and-community reference, validation, and consultation may not seem particularly efficient ways to manage a language renewal project, particularly when so many different agencies and individuals were involved in each facet of the effort. These are the management principles that the Ute people themselves built into this project. The preamble to the tribal language policy eloquently explains the significance of this position:

> The Ute language is a blessing given to our people by the Creator. It is spiritual and must be treated as such. It is a part of our land as well as a part of our people. There is no way that our language can be separated from our traditional beliefs and practices. Our language and our culture are one. Because we believe that education is the transmission of culture and that all our people must have genuine freedom of access to education we assert that all aspects of the educational process shall reflect the beauty of our Ute values and the appreciation of our environment. These language

policies shall manifest consideration of the whole person, taking into account the spiritual, mental, physical and cultural aspects of the person within the Ute family and Tribe. We, therefore, set forth the following policy statements to re-affirm our commitment to the promotion, preservation and enhancement of our language, culture, and traditions as a blessing for the future generations.

To work as a linguist at Northern Ute, I had to respect and agree to be guided by the political as well as emotional implications of this statement. Anthropology, given its orientation to the whole of the human experience and to the commitments people make to maintain that whole, was a particularly useful frame of reference for both of those ends.

16 / Preserving Plants for Pomos

Richard N. Lerner

Problem and Client

The 1969 National Environmental Policy Act (NEPA) requires both the government and the private sector to "preserve important historic, cultural and natural aspects of our national heritage, and maintain, wherever possible, an environment which supports diversity and variety of individual choice." To meet this requirement, the U.S. Army Corps of Engineers sponsored cultural investigations in association with the planning of a large dam and reservoir. The project, Warm Springs Dam–Lake Sonoma, is located on about 17,500 acres of land approximately ninety miles north of San Francisco.

Before they were forced out of the area by the mid-nineteenth century by Hispanic and then Euroamerican settlers, Southern Pomoan groups occupied the project's land. They were speakers of one of seven related languages, which early American scholars grouped as "Pomo." Archeologists and linguists believe they were descendants of "Hokan" speakers who moved into the region about 5,000 years ago.

Although not recognized by its initial studies, the Corps' later cultural surveys, which included ethnographic and ethnohistorical research, determined that Mihilakawna, Makahmo, and descendants of other Pomoan tribelets had continued to utilize the project area for collecting plants used for economic, ritual, and medicinal purposes. Of special importance was that Pomoan basketweavers still selectively harvested and made extensive use of rhizomes (reproductive roots) from a certain species of sedge (*Carex barbarae*) found within the project. Pomoan basketry constitutes a major cultural tradition and provides many Pomo with an important source of income; their craft is recognized worldwide for its skilled techniques and aesthetic artistry and is sought by museums and private collectors. Because virtually all existing sedge habitats in the project were to be destroyed by construction of the dam or by the reservoir's formation, the corps' San Francisco office agreed to undertake a program to mitigate the loss of these sites.

Overall, the Corps of Engineers is responsible for providing engineering services to the Army and other military and civil agencies of the United States and other countries. The San Francisco District of the corps is principally engaged in civil works projects related to the waterways and coast of northwestern California, including construction, operation, and regulatory projects and programs. Because many of the water projects with which the corps is involved, such as port development and flood control, have wide-ranging effects on land use, specialists from many academic disciplines are kept on staff and/or are hired under contract to participate in planning, review, and implementation.

I am a civil service employee of the corps' San Francisco District office. My role as district anthropologist is to advise about sociocultural factors associated with water resources programs and projects in northwestern California. These factors involve both social organization and values on behavioral science issues, as well as values associated with properties of historical or cultural significance.

In the case of Warm Springs Dam–Lake Sonoma, the corps' problem was to find alternative sources of the plant materials and/or to establish the plants in new locations. I was given the responsibility to develop and implement such a mitigation program. The issues that I needed to address included determining what and how many plants were being used and by whom; assessing cultural values and horticultural requirements associated with the plants; identifying alternative sources currently and potentially available; and analysing economic data concerning current benefits to users and potential cost for various mitigation alternatives.

Process and Players

The Corps

It was particularly timely that the corps hired me in early 1974. The environmental impact statement (EIS), which the Corps of Engineers had prepared in 1973 on the Warm Springs Dam–Lake Sonoma project, had just been challenged by archeologists and Native Americans as inadequately addressing cultural concerns. They joined with those who had other objections to the project and brought suit in federal district court within a few months after I was hired. Although the corps had one or two staff archeologists in the United States at that time, the closest was in Tulsa, Oklahoma, and I became the first social anthropologist hired by the corps.

The court found the EIS adequate in all areas except archeology and related cultural resources and directed the corps to undertake new, comprehensive studies at the project. Until then, the corps' San Francisco District had relied on a department of another federal agency, the National Park Service (NPS), to conduct and/or manage all its major cultural studies. The NPS office involved was then composed primarily, if not exclusively, of archeologists, and all their research concerned prehistoric archeology. Because living Native Americans were obviously concerned with the Warm Springs project, and the NPS indicated that it was not interested in managing nonarcheological research, I was given the responsibility of developing and managing ethnohistoric and ethnographic studies that would provide sufficient information to make the environmental impact statement adequate and would complete the planning phase of the project. The most important of these studies was reported in "An Ethnographic Survey of the Mahilkaune (Dry Creek) Pomo" (Theodoratus et al. 1975), which documented the collection of basketry and other plant materials in the project area. This report was described by the keeper of the National Register of Historic Places as "the first time a Federal agency has integrated ethnographic studies into its cultural resources program" (Murtagh 1975).

After the comprehensive archeological, ethnographic, and other studies were completed in 1976, I supervised and helped write a new National Register of Historic Places nomination form and included the basketry materials as an historic property. Mitigation for impacts on this historic property was therefore necessary, and I wrote a draft management plan for all the cultural resources at the project. After review by the California State Historic Preservation officer, the Advisory Council on Historic Preservation, and the U.S. Department of the Interior, as well as professional, Native American, and public review and a public hearing, the management plan was incorporated into a memorandum of agreement, which the corps signed in 1976. This document provided the basis for a supplement to the environmental impact statement, which the federal court then determined in 1977 to adequately address its concerns. The plan committed the corps to an ethnobotanical mitigation program.

The Pomo and the Plants

During the late 1970s, new, more detailed studies were sponsored to determine what biological and cultural factors were associated with management of ethnobotanically important plants and how new preserve areas might be established. Although some of the plants proved to be relatively common, Pomoan weavers selectively harvest and cultivate the same plants and areas for long periods of time, enhancing the quality and quantity of the plants and the ease of collection. Although at one time sedge beds, both cultivated and uncultivated, were common alongside streams and rivers throughout the region, agricultural clearing, gravel mining stream beds, and other degradation had made good accessible sites rare. The future reservoir zone included some of the best remaining beds, and weavers from three counties either came personally to dig roots or traded for or purchased coils of runners that other weavers had obtained in the project area.

Through the ethnological research, users of the plants were identified, and cultural factors associated with the plant material collection and utilization were described (Peri and Patterson 1979). In 1979, the sedge and willow that weavers were able to collect in the project area, which otherwise had no commercial value, were estimated to generate over $68,000 in income. These receipts, distributed among fifty-six weavers, were derived from the manufacture and sale of baskets, the sale of partially processed weaving materials, and teaching and demonstration fees. In addition to the weavers themselves, at least seventy-four of their dependents were principally or partially supported by the basketry income. Given the extensive labor required to produce a basket, no one was getting rich from this work. However, because of the scarcity of other sources of income and the psychosocial benefits of maintaining a highly skilled craft, the benefits derived from project area basketry materials were great.

Because the plants were never cultivated by anyone other than Pomoan specialists, no body of horticultural information appeared to be in existence. Biologists, native plant specialists, and landscape architects, as well as soils experts, were therefore consulted. Most of the research related to cultural factors was done under contract with Sonoma State University Academic Foundation, Inc.; horticultural aspects were studied and managed by a private environmental planning firm. A Native American professor of anthropology, David W. Peri of Sonoma State University, a specialist in ethnobotany, served as project director for the foundation, and many other Native Americans were employed or otherwise directly involved.

Even though detailed ethnographic and botanical studies were under way by outside experts, I undertook an extensive survey of stream banks owned by the federal government for the reservoir project, which would be either upstream of the reservoir or downstream of the dam. My survey work also involved contacting local and state agencies in the region to locate similar, publically owned habitat and personally surveying potential areas. In spring 1978 with a corps biologist, I also transplanted a small number of sedge plants downstream of the dam to see what the process might entail and how the plants would react to transplanting.

The 1978–1979 studies confirmed that all plants in question were essentially wild, that the only direct experience in their propagation was that of the Pomo, and that scientific experience with related species had limited value. Although no alternative sources for the four types of plants were found to exist either on or near project land, horticulturally compatible sites were located within the project area, and both the corps and the Native American Ethnobotanical Advisory Council agreed that relocation of the plants to these sites was desirable and had a high likelihood of success. The council was composed of representatives from the principal families of Mihilakawna and Makahmo Pomo and other traditional users of the project's ethnobotanical resources. Participants received small stipends for attending monthly meetings to provide advice for contractors and the corps about the implementation of the ethnobotanical program.

A variety of experimental transplanting techniques were developed and implemented in 1978–1980 (Peri et al. 1980). An elaborate testing procedure was developed to evaluate the suitability of lands downstream of the dam and to develop procedures for the establishment of new preserve areas. In spring 1979 over 1,000 plants were dug up and relocated. Work was done by corps staff, Native Americans, and specialists under contract. Many small plots were established, varying in factors such as soil composition, exposure to sun, and types of maintenance required.

After a year of studying the effectiveness of transplanting and maintenance variables, major transplanting was done in fall 1980 and 1981. As had been done in 1979, special ceremonies were conducted prior to participation by the weavers in the transplanting. One aspect of the ceremonies was to prepare special foods and hold a dinner as a means of sacrificial offering to the Spirit. All those participating in the transplanting, Indian and non-Indian alike, including all levels of corps personnel, participated in such dinners, which, it was believed, helped ensure the well-being of the plants and the people doing the transplanting. Attendees at one such dinner included the Corps of Engineers brigadier general in charge of the regional office as well as his wife and children. To further help consecrate the new sites before transplanting began, Pomo elders offered prayers in Southern Pomo and in English, and a lecture was given about proper rules of behavior.

Results and Evaluation

As a result of these efforts, over 48,000 sedge plants were relocated onto nearly three acres of project lands downstream of the dam. An irrigation system was installed and a gardener was hired by the corps to water and weed the plants for two years until they became established and could grow on their own. In addition to sedge, three other species of plants were studied, experimental plantings were conducted and were transplanted to new preserve locations: two herbs important for ritual and medicinal purposes, *Angelica tomentosa* (150 plants relocated) and *Lomatium californicum* (250 plants relocated); and a species of willow used as the foundation rods for almost all Pomo baskets. Some of the willow trees (*Salix hindsiana*) were already growing near the new sedge beds, and they were pruned back to encourage the type of growth needed for baskets and some of the prunings planted in additional areas (Peri et al. 1982). The riparian area in which the sedge and willow sites are located was dedicated as a preserve, and basketweavers were given special access to it.

Degree of survival of the plants has ranged widely. Although the survival of the lomatium was extremely high, by 1984 the plants had not as yet increased in numbers, making long-term harvests questionable. Although most of the angelica plants lived for a year or more, they appeared to be gradually dying and not reproducing. Further investigation of the causes of failure and possible additional mitigative actions are under consideration.

Transplanted willow trees also have not survived well; however, two sites on which they occur naturally were expanded, and with increased stream flows after the dam began operating in 1985, this species was expected to increase greatly on the banks both on and off corps land. Principally because of the need for this species by basketmakers, the corps selected it as the principal plant to be used to stabilize banks along fourteen river miles associated with the project downstream of the dam. As a result of this plan far more plants will potentially be available to weavers, who believe that they will be able to obtain sufficient access to the willow.

The sedge is growing vigorously and has reproduced heavily. Initial harvest by eight weavers took place in September 1983, and they reported that the material was of excellent quality. Groups of weavers have been returning each year since then. Because the sedge is the plant of principal concern to the greatest number of Native Americans of the region, it would appear that the ethnobotanical mitigation program was largely successful.

Evaluation of the ethnobotany program reveals benefits that extend far beyond the immediate plant and cultural needs of Native Americans. One of the principal purposes of the corps project is recreation, including swimming, boating, camping, and hiking. When the Lake Sonoma visitor center opened in 1980, an exhibit was installed describing and illustrating the transplanting program and Pomo basketry. The exhibit used materials that had been commissioned by the corps and purchased for the exhibit. It included varying styles of baskets and weaving techniques. Some partially processed plant material and partially made baskets were obtained, so that the steps of manufacturing could easily be seen. The exhibit has been a source of pride for visiting Pomo and of great interest to other visitors. During its first year, over a half-million people came to visit the project. The number had grown to near a million by the mid-1980s and was expected to pass 1.5 million after the reservoir is in full operation in the late 1980s. Hundreds of thousands of these people go through the visitor center each year.

Another recreation-related benefit has been the development of an ethnobotanical-riparian trail through part of the sedge and willow preserve area. Although most of the preserve has been reserved for native collectors, it was mutually agreed that the general public should have access to the rich vegetation and wildlife surrounding some of the relatively highly cultivated ethnobotanical beds. Future plans call for an elevated boardwalk, suitable for the handicapped, to be built a short distance from the visitor center, with trail guides and markers to interpret both the natural and cultural values of the area.

An even more far-reaching effect of the ethnobotanical program was its influence on land management of the 13,000 acres of corps land that will remain above the reservoir. In 1976 and 1977, while the early ethnobotanical studies were under way, California was subjected to two years of severe drought. This phenomenon led to a need to reevaluate the land restoration and management techniques developed and approved more than a decade earlier. A contract was issued to prepare a new vegetation management plan, with the contractor directed to consider using native plants and ethnobotanical needs. The plan did just that, recommending that native plants be used exclusively and identifying many particular species that would have high value to Native Americans. The use of controlled burning—a long-neglected means of keeping a balance of field and forest that had been commonly practiced by Native Americans of the region—was also recommended by the consultants and adopted by the Corps of Engineers.

A very different contribution of the mitigation program illustrates how anthropological practice can feed back knowledge into anthropological theory and advance the discipline. Anthropologists concerned with California have been provided a new perspective on horticultural practices of Indians of the North Coast Range. In general, Indians of this region have been described as exhibiting classic hunting and gathering means of subsistence, rather than as practicing agriculture. It became clear during the ethnobotanical research for this project that Pomo groups had developed long-term plant management techniques involving repeated, selective harvesting from the same plant beds and plants, accompanied by the removal of unwanted plants and rocks. Recognition of such practices has helped students of California's cultural history avoid oversimplified categorization of hunting-gathering versus agrarian and gain greater appreciation of the complexity of Pomoan and other Native American cultures. This new information and perspective have also contributed to similar reexaminations of various styles and phases of subsistence patterns that archeologists and ethnologists are making of cultures in many other parts of the world.

The Anthropological Difference

The ethnobotanical program provides a rich example of the application of anthropological knowledge. In particular, it highlights the value of the anthropologist being part of an agency's in-house, permanent staff. Principally because the staff lacked an anthropologist the corps was taken to court in 1974, prior to my being hired, and the corps' environmental impact statement was found to be inadequate in the area of cultural resources.

A cross-cultural perspective, with awareness of the internal social organization and values of both the highly organized Corps of Engineers and the highly segmented Native American people of the region, was essential to the effective development and implementation of this mitigation program. Because the program required cooperation of groups with a legacy of conflict—the U.S. Army and California Indians—traditional anthropological interactional field research techniques were vital not only for basic data collection but also to establish rapport and trust between the groups. Many cross-cultural stereotypes had to be overcome and innovations molded and presented in ways most acceptable to the frames of references of each principal group—the corps' being that of federal laws and regulations and the stated and unstated sociopolitical views and values of corps managers; those of the Native Americans being a mixture of traditional Pomoan values and technologies, as well as their more contemporary religious beliefs and socioeconomic requirements. Some techniques used to help this process included circulating the minutes of Native American Advisory Council meetings among corps staff and holding joint meetings periodically over a five-year period (1976–1980) to plan the mitigation program.

I served as an intermediary and facilitator: The perspectives of the Pomo had to be conveyed to the corps, and the regulations and operating procedures of the corps had to be conveyed to the Pomo. An outsider, no matter how enlightened and well intentioned, would find it almost impossible to get timely access to knowledge about impending actions in the midst of a large, complex construction project. In addition to just being part of the staff, I was conscious of the need to gain the trust of the project's construction personnel so they would see me as part of their team and not merely an agent for the Indians. At least in some measure, I believe I was successful, and this contact provided me greater access to information. As a trusted staff member, I was much more likely to become aware of proposed changes in project plans, construction schedules, and locations of work, and to provide rapid feedback about how these changes might affect existing or proposed ethnobotanical sites. I knew who to see and how to phrase suggestions for alternatives that would be less damaging to the plants and the interests of the Pomo.

Three specific examples can be given to illustrate this.

1. The dam was built of rolled (highly compacted) earth, and its construction required the excavation of soils from many of the sites where sedge, willow, angelica, and lomatium were growing. These sites were flagged and protected for as long as possible during the construction of the dam (1978–1982), allowing for maximum harvest by Native American users and retention of stock for transplanting to new sites.

2. The principal relocation area for sedge had been initially proposed as a place for stream access by the public for water recreation. Instead, in part because of its being needed for a transplant site, the area was dedicated in the reservoir's master plan as an ethnobotanical-riparian preserve and interpretation area.

3. In the case of land management, as information about Native American use of native plants became available, I was able to call it to the attention of biologists and managers in the corps and to help define the scope of new vegetation studies. The awareness generated by the ethnobotanical program thus led to the reevaluation of all land management at the project.

Because my job was to change the relationship between the corps and the Pomo from opponents in court to coplanners, it was important for me not only to participate in nearly endless meetings within the corps but also to learn about Pomoan traditional and contemporary culture and to become personally acquainted with and trusted by Pomoans. Some of the specific steps I took included

1. Participating with Pomoans intimately in the experimental transplanting program, showing care and concern as I handled the plants and as I physically helped elderly basketmakers (several were in their seventies and eighties) reach transplanting sites.

2. I arranged to have a Northern California Indian hired and work directly for me as a civil service employee at the project as the representative of the corps' Environmental Branch. Although not from the

immediate area, he was highly versed in the traditions of his own Indian culture and very respectful of the local Pomo. One of his jobs was to escort basketmakers through the construction zones to reach traditional collecting areas before they were destroyed and the mitigation program implemented.

Despite the great disappointment and even bitterness felt by Pomo about the coming loss of their traditional gathering sites, their participation in every step in the transplanting program was essential for it to be both botanically successful and of real use in the eyes of the weavers. In addition to secular aspects of their plant use, Pomo weavers perceive plant cultivation and weaving as spiritual activities, guided by supernatural beliefs and rules, violations of which lead to failure to find good roots and bring physical harm to the weavers. For example, beliefs of the weavers concerning menstruation and sexual activity and the timing of being in contact with sedge plants had to be identified and conveyed with sensitivity to corps personnel. The rituals shared by those participating in the transplanting were the culmination of several years of building mutually understanding and trust between the corps and the Indians.

It is hard to imagine ethnobotanical mitigation achieving such a fairly high measure of success, or even taking place at all, without the presence of an anthropologist throughout the process. Certainly the Corps of Engineers itself acknowledged the value of the program; both its regional and national offices made special awards to the corps' San Francisco District for the ethnobotanical program.

Although Native Americans had been forced out of the project area more than a century before the Corps of Engineers project began, and technically did not own the sedge and other vegetative materials so important to them, the facts gathered through anthropological study and presented to the responsible corps office convinced it that such significant cultural resources should be preserved. The ethnobotanical program incorporated highly technical ethnographic, historical, and botanical study with the knowledge, concerns, and participation of Native Americans themselves. It thus provides a model of applying anthropology to help a federal project meet both the letter and the spirit of the National Environmental Policy Act's historic, cultural, and natural environmental objectives, as well as those defined by the Historic Preservation Act of 1966, which declared that "the historical and cultural foundations of the Nation should be preserved as a living part of our community life and development in order to give a sense of orientation to the American people."

References

A 38-minute film entitled *The Environment and Engineers at Lake Sonoma,* which shows the plant preservation program being implemented, can be obtained by contacting Richard N. Lerner, U.S. Army Corps of Engineers, 211 Main Street, San Francisco, California 94105-1905.

Murtagh, William J. 1975. Letter of September 11 to Richard Lerner.

Peri, David W., and Scott M. Patterson. 1979. Ethnobotanical Resources of the Warm Springs Dam–Lake Sonoma Project Area, Sonoma County, California. San Francisco: U.S. Army Corps of Engineers. 152 pp.

Peri, David W., Scott M. Patterson, and Jennie L. Goodrich. 1980. History of the Transplanting of Sedge, Angelica and Lomatium, Warm Springs Dam– Lake Sonoma Project. San Francisco: U.S. Army Corps of Engineers. 105 pp.

———. 1982. Ethnobotanical Mitigation, Warm Springs Dam–Lake Sonoma, California. San Francisco: U.S. Army Corps of Engineers. 134 pp.

Theodoratus, Dorothea J. 1975. An Ethnographic Survey of the Mihilakawna (Dry Creek) Pomo. San Francisco: U.S. Army Corps of Engineers. 408 pp.

17 / The Domestication of Wood in Haiti: A Case Study in Applied Evolution

Gerald F. Murray

Problem and Client

Expatriate tree lovers, whether tourists or developmental planners, often leave Haiti with an upset stomach. Though during precolonial times the island Arawaks had reached a compromise with the forest, their market-oriented colonial successors saw trees as something to be removed. The Spaniards specialized in exporting wood from the eastern side of the island, whereas the French on the western third found it more profitable to clear the wood and produce sugar cane, coffee, and indigo for European markets. During the nineteenth century, long after Haiti had become an independent republic, foreign lumber companies cut and exported most of the nation's precious hardwoods, leaving little for today's peasants.

The geometric increase in population since colonial times—from an earlier population of fewer than half a million former slaves to a contemporary population of more than six million—and the resulting shrinkage of average family holding size have led to the evolution of a land use system devoid of systematic fallow periods. A vicious cycle has set in—one that seems to have targeted the tree for ultimate destruction. Not only has land pressure eliminated a regenerative fallow phase in the local agricultural cycle; in addition the catastrophic declines in per hectare food yields have forced peasants into alternative income-generating strategies. Increasing numbers crowd into the capital city, Port-au-Prince, creating a market for construction wood and charcoal. Poorer sectors of the peasantry in the rural areas respond to this market by racing each other with axes and machetes to cut down the few natural tree stands remaining in remoter regions of the republic. The proverbial snowball in Hades is at less risk than a tree in Haiti.

Unable to halt the flows either of wood into the cities or of soil into the oceans, international development organizations finance studies to measure the volume of these flows (50 million trees cut per year is one of the round figures being bandied about) and to predict when the last tree will be cut from Haiti. Reforestation projects have generally been entrusted by their well-meaning but shortsighted funders to Duvalier's Ministry of Agriculture, a kiss-of-death resource channeling strategy by which the Port-au-Prince jobs created frequently outnumber the seedlings produced. And even the few seedlings produced often died in the nurseries because peasants were understandably reluctant to cover their scarce holdings with state-owned trees. Project managers had been forced to resort to "food for work" strategies to move seedlings out of nurseries onto hillsides. And peasants have endeavored where possible to plant the trees on somebody else's hillsides and to enlist their livestock as allies in the subsequent removal of this potentially dangerous vegetation.

This generalized hostility to tree projects placed the U.S. Agency for International Development (AID)/Haiti mission in a bind. After several years of absence from Haiti in the wake of expulsion by Francois Duvalier, AID had reestablished its presence under the government of his son Jean Claude. But an ambitious Integrated Agricultural Development Project funded through the Ministry of Agriculture had already given clear signs of being a multimillion-dollar farce. And an influential congressman chairing the U.S. House Ways and Means Committee— and consequently exercising strong control over AID funds worldwide— had taken a passionate interest in Haiti. In his worldwide travels this individual had become adept at detecting and exposing developmental charades. And he had been blunt in communicating his conviction that much of what he had seen in AID/Haiti's program was precisely that. He had been touched by the plight of Haiti and communicated to the highest AID authorities his conviction about the salvific power of contraceptives and trees and his determination to have AID grace Haiti with an abundant flow of both. And he would personally visit Haiti (a convenient plane ride from Washington, D.C.) to inspect for himself, threatening a worldwide funding freeze if no results were forthcoming. A chain reaction of nervous "yes sirs" speedily worked its way down from AID headquarters in Washington to a beleaguered Port-au-Prince mission.

The pills and condoms were less of a problem. Even the most cantankerous congressman was unlikely to insist on observing them in use and would probably settle for household distribution figures. Not so with the trees. He could (and did) pooh-pooh nursery production figures and ask to be taken to see the new AID forests, a most embarrassing request in a country where peasants creatively converted daytime reforestation projects into nocturnal goat forage projects. AID's reaction was twofold—first, to commission an immediate study to explain to the congressman and others why peasants refused to plant trees (for this they called down an AID economist); and second, to devise some program strategy that would achieve the apparently unachievable: to instill in cash-needy, defiant peasant charcoalmakers a love, honor, and respect for newly planted trees. For this attitudinal transformation, a task usually entrusted to the local armed forces, AID/Haiti invited an anthropologist to propose an alternative approach.

Process and Players

During these dynamics, I completed a doctoral dissertation on the manner in which Haitian peasant land tenure had evolved in response to internal population growth. The AID economist referred to above exhaustively reviewed the available literature, also focusing on the issue of Haitian peasant land tenure, and produced for the mission a well-argued monograph (Zuvekas 1978) documenting a lower rate of landlessness in Haiti than in many other Latin American settings but documenting as well the informal, extralegal character of the relationship between many peasant families and their landholdings. This latter observation was interpreted by some in the mission to mean that the principal determinant of the failure of tree planting projects was the absence among peasants of legally secure deeds over their plots. Peasants could not be expected to invest money on land improvements when at mildest the benefits could accrue to another and at worst the very improvements themselves could lead to expropriation from their land. In short, no massive tree planting could be expected, according to this model, until a nationwide cadastral reform granted plot-by-plot deeds to peasant families.

This hypothesis was reputable but programmatically paralyzing because nobody dreamed that the Duvalier regime was about to undertake a major cadastral reform for the benefit of peasants. Several AID officers in Haiti had read my dissertation on land tenure (Murray 1977), and I received an invitation to advise the mission. Was Haitian peasant land tenure compatible with tree planting? Zuvekas' study had captured the internally complex nature of Haitian peasant land tenure. But the subsequent extrapolations as to paralyzing insecurity simply did not seem to fit with the ethnographic evidence. In two reports (Murray 1978a, 1978b) I indicated that peasants in general feel secure about their ownership rights over their land. Failure to secure plot-by-plot surveyed deeds is generally a cost-saving measure. Interclass evictions did occur, but they were statistically rare; instead most land disputes were intrafamilial. A series of extralegal tenure practices had evolved—preinheritance land grants to young adult dependents, informal inheritance subdivisions witnessed by community members, fictitious sales to favored children, complex community-internal sharecropping arrangements. And though these practices produced an internally heterogeneous system with its complexities, there was strong internal order. Any chaos and insecurity tended to be more in the mind of observers external to the system than in the behavior of the peasants themselves. There was a danger that the complexities of Haitian peasant land tenure would generate an unintended smokescreen obscuring the genuine causes of failure in tree planting projects.

What then were these genuine causes? The mission, intent on devising programming strategies in this domain, invited me to explore further, under a contract aimed at identifying the "determinants of success and failure" in reforestation and soil conservation projects. My major conclusion was that the preexisting land tenure, cropping, and livestock systems in peasant Haiti were perfectly adequate for the undertaking of significant tree planting activities. Most projects had failed not because of land tenure or attitudinal barriers among peasants but because of fatal flaws in one or more key project components. Though my contract called principally for analysis of previous or existing projects, I used the recommendation section of the report to speculate on how a Haiti-wise anthropologist would program and manage reforestation activities if he or she had the authority. In verbal debriefings I jokingly challenged certain young program officers in the mission to give me a jeep and carte blanche access to a $50,000 checking account, and I would prove my anthropological assertions about peasant economic behavior and produce more trees in the ground than their current multimillion-dollar Ministry of Agriculture charade. We had a good laugh and shook hands, and I departed confident that the report would be as dutifully perused and as honorably filed and forgotten as similar reports I had done elsewhere.

To my great disbelief, as I was correcting Anthro 101 exams some two years later, one of the program officers still in Haiti called to say that an Agroforestry Outreach Project (AOP) had been approved chapter and verse as I had recommended it; and that if I was interested in placing my life where my mouth had been and would leave the ivory tower to direct the project, my project bank account would have, not $50,000, but $4 million. After several weeks of hemming and hawing and vigorous negotiating for a leave from my department, I accepted the offer and entered a new (to me) role of project director in a strange upside-down world in which the project anthropologist was not a powerless cranky voice from the bleachers but the chief of party with substantial authority over general project policy and the allocation of project resources. My elation at commanding resources to implement anthropological ideas was dampened by the nervousness of knowing exactly who would be targeted for flak and ridicule if these ideas bombed out, as most tended to do in the Haiti of Duvalier.

The basic structural design of AOP followed a tripartite conceptual framework that I proposed for analyzing projects. Within this framework a project is composed of three essential systemic elements: a technical base, a benefit flow strategy, and an institutional delivery strategy. Planning had to focus equally on all three. I argued that defects in one would sabotage the entire project.

Technical Strategy

The basic technical strategy was to make available to peasants fast-growing wood trees (*Leucaena leucocephala, Cassia siamea, Azadirachta indica, Casuarina equisetifolia, Eucalyptus camaldulensis*) that were not only drought resistant but also rapid growing, producing possible four-year harvest rotations in humid lowland areas (and slower rotations and lower survival rates in arid areas) and that were good for charcoal and basic construction needs. Most of the species mentioned also restore nutrients to the soil, and some of them coppice from a carefully harvested stump, producing several rotations before the need for replanting.

Of equally critical technical importance was the use of a nursery system that produced light-weight microseedlings. A project pickup truck could transport over 15,000 of these microseedlings (as opposed to 250 traditional bag seedlings), and the average peasant could easily carry over 500 transportable seedlings at one time, planting them with a fraction of the ground preparation time and labor required for bulkier bagged seedlings. The anthropological implications of this nursery system were critical. It constituted a technical breakthrough that reduced to a fraction the fossil-fuel and human energy expenditure required to transport and plant trees.

But the technical component of the project incorporated yet another element: the physical juxtaposition of trees and crops. In traditional reforestation models, the trees are planted in large unbroken mono-cropped stands. Such forests or woodlots presuppose local land tenure and economic arrangements not found in Haiti. For the tree to make its way as a cultivate into the economy of Haitian peasants and most other tropical cultivators, reforestation models would have to be replaced by agroforestry models that entail spatial or temporal juxtaposition of crops and trees. Guided by prior ethnographic knowledge of Haitian cropping patterns, AOP worked out with peasants various border planting and intercropping strategies to make tree planting feasible even for small holding cultivators.

Benefit Flow Strategies

With respect to the second systemic component, the programming of benefit flows to participants, earlier projects had often committed the fatal flaw of defining project trees planted as *pyebwa leta* (the state's trees). Authoritarian assertions by project staff concerning sanctions for cutting newly planted trees created fears among peasants that even trees planted on their own land would be government property. And several peasants were frank in reporting fears that the trees might eventually be used as a pretext by the government or the "Company" (the most common local lexeme used to refer to projects) for eventually expropriating the land on which peasants had planted project trees.

Such ambiguities and fears surrounding benefit flows paralyze even the technically soundest project. A major anthropological feature of AOP was a radical frontal attack on the issue of property and usufruct rights over project trees. Whereas other projects had criticized tree cutting, AOP promulgated the heretical message that trees were meant to be cut, processed, and sold. The only problem with the present system, according to project messages, was that peasants were cutting nature's trees. But once a landowner "mete fos li deyo" (expends his resources) and plants and cares for his or her own wood trees on his or her own land, the landowner has the same right to harvest and sell wood as corn or beans.

I was inevitably impressed at the impact that this blunt message had when I delivered it to groups of prospective peasant tree planters. Haitian peasants are inveterate and aggressive cash-croppers; many of the crops and livestock that they produce are destined for immediate consignment to local markets. For the first time in their lives, they were hearing a concrete proposal to make the wood tree itself one more marketable crop in their inventory.

But the message would ring true only if three barriers were smashed.

1. The first concerned the feared delay in benefits. Most wood trees with which the peasants were familiar took an impractically long time to mature. There fortunately existed in Haiti four-year-old stands of leucaena, cassia, eucalyptus, and other project trees to which we could take peasant groups to demonstrate the growth speed of these trees.

2. But could they be planted on their scanty holdings without interfering with crops? Border and row planting techniques were demonstrated, as

well as intercropping. The average peasant holding was about a hectare and a half. If a cultivator planted a field in the usual crops and then planted 500 seedlings in the same field at 2 meters by 2 meters, the seedlings would occupy only a fifth of a hectare. And they would be far enough apart to permit continued cropping for two or three cycles before shade competition became too fierce. That is, trees would be planted on only a fraction of the peasant's holdings and planted in such a way that they would be compatible with continued food growing even on the plots where they stood. We would then calculate with peasants the potential income to be derived from these 500 trees through sale as charcoal, polewood, or boards. In a best-case scenario, the gross take from the charcoal of these trees (the least lucrative use of the wood) might equal the current annual income of an average rural family. The income potential of these wood trees clearly far offset any potential loss from decreased food production. Though it had taken AID two years to decide on the project, it took about twenty minutes with any group of skeptical but economically rational peasants to generate a list of enthusiastic potential tree planters.

3. But there was yet a third barrier. All this speculation about income generation presupposed that the peasants themselves, and not the government or the project, would be the sole owners of the trees and that the peasants would have unlimited rights to the harvest of the wood whenever they wished. To deal with this issue, I presented the matter as an agreement between the cultivator and the project: We would furnish free seedlings and technical assistance; the cultivators would agree to plant 500 of these seedlings on their own land and permit project personnel to carry out periodic survival counts. We would, of course, pay no wages or "Food for Work" for this planting. But we would guarantee to the planters complete and exclusive ownership of the trees. They did not need to ask for permission from the project to harvest the trees whenever their needs might dictate, nor would there by any penalties associated with early cutting or low survival. If peasants changed their minds, they could rip out their seedlings six months after planting. They would never get any more free seedlings from us, but they would not be subject to any penalties. There are preexisting local forestry laws, rarely enforced, concerning permissions and minor taxes for tree cutting. Peasants would have to deal with these as they had skillfully done in the past. But from our project's point of view, we relinquish all tree ownership rights to the peasants who accept and plant the trees on their property.

Cash-flow dialogues and ownership assurances such as these were a far cry from the finger-wagging ecological sermons to which many peasant groups had been subjected on the topic of trees. Our project technicians developed their own messages; but central to all was the principle of peasant ownership and usufruct of AOP trees. The goal was to capitalize on the preexisting fuel and lumber markets, to make the wood tree one more crop in the income-generating repertoire of the Haitian peasant.

Institutional Strategy

The major potential fly in the ointment was the third component, the institutional component. To whom would AID entrust its funds to carry out this project? My own research had indicated clearly that Haitian governmental involvement condemned a project to certain paralysis and possible death, and my report phrased that conclusion as diplomatically as possible. The diplomacy was required to head off possible rage, less from Haitian officials than from certain senior officers in the AID mission who were politically and philosophically wedded to an institution-building strategy. Having equated the term "institution" with "government bureaucracy," and having defined their own career success in terms, not of village-level resource flows, but of voluminous and timely bureaucracy-to-bureaucracy cash transfers, such officials were in effect marshaling U.S. resources into the service of extractive ministries with unparalleled track records of squandering and/or pilfering expatriate donor funds.

To the regime's paradoxical credit, however, the blatant openness and arrogance of Duvalierist predation had engendered an angry willingness in much of Haiti's development community to explore other resource flow channels. Though the nongovernmental character of the proposal provoked violent reaction, the reactionaries in the Haiti mission were overridden by their superiors in Washington, and a completely nongovernmental implementing mode was adopted for this project.

The system, based on private voluntary organizations (PVOs), worked as follows.

1. AID made a macrogrant to a Washington-based PVO (the Pan American Development Foundation, PADF) to run a tree-planting project based on the principles that had emerged in my research. At the Haiti mission's urging, PADF invited me to be chief of party for the project and located an experienced accountant in Haiti to be financial administrator. PADF in addition recruited three American agroforesters who, in addition to MA-level professional training, had several years of overseas village field experience under their belts. Early in the project they were supplemented by two other expatriates, a Belgian and a French Canadian. We opened a central office in Port-au-Prince and assigned a major region of Haiti to each of the agroforesters, who lived in their field regions.

2. These agroforesters were responsible for contacting the many village-based PVOs working in their regions to explain the project, to emphasize its microeconomic focus and its difference from traditional reforestation models, to discuss the conditions of entry therein, and to make technical suggestions as to the trees that would be appropriate for the region.

3. If the PVO was interested, we drafted an agreement in which our mutual contributions and spheres of responsibility were specified. The agreements were not drafted in French (Haiti's official language) but in Creole, the only language spoken by most peasants.

4. The local PVO selected *animateurs* (village organizers) who themselves were peasants who lived and worked in the village where trees would be planted. After receiving training from us, they contacted their neighbors and kin, generated lists of peasants interested in planting a specified number of trees, and informed us when the local rains began to fall. At the proper moment we packed the seedlings in boxes customized to the particular region and shipped them on our trucks to the farmers, who would be waiting at specified drop-off points at a specified time. The trees were to be planted within twenty-four hours of delivery.

5. The animateurs were provided with Creole language data forms by which to gather ecological, land use, and land tenure data on each plot where trees would be planted and certain bits of information on each peasant participant. These forms were used as well to follow up, at periodic intervals, the survival of the trees, the incidence of any problems (such as livestock depredation, burning, disease), and—above all—the manner in which the farmer integrated the trees into cropping and livestock patterns, to detect and head off any unintended substitution of food for wood.

Results and Evaluation

The project was funded for four years from October 1981 through November 1985. During the writing of the project paper we were asked by an AID economist to estimate how many trees would be planted. Not knowing if the peasants would in fact plant any trees, we nervously proposed to reach two thousand peasant families with a million trees as a project goal. Fiddling with his programmed calculator, the economist informed us that that output would produce a negative internal rate of return. We would need at least two million trees to make the project worth AID's institutional while. We shrugged and told him cavalierly to up the figure and to promise three million trees on the land of six thousand peasants. (At that time I thought someone else would be directing the project.)

Numbers of Trees and Beneficiaries

Though I doubted that we could reach this higher goal, the response of the Haitian peasants to this new approach to tree planting left everyone, including myself, open mouthed. Within the first year of the project, one million trees had been planted by some 2,500 peasant households all over Haiti. My fears of peasant indifference were now transformed into nervousness that we could not supply seedlings fast enough to meet the demand triggered by our wood-as-a-cash-crop strategy. Apologetic village animateurs informed us that some cultivators who had not signed up on the first lists were actually stealing newly planted seedlings from their neighbors' fields at night. They promised to catch the scoundrels. If they did, I told them, give the scoundrels a hug. Their pilfering was dramatic proof of the bull's-eye nature of the anthropological predictions that underlie the project.

By the end of the second year (when I left the project), we had reached the four-year goal of three million seedlings and the project had geared up and decentralized its nursery capacity to produce several million seedlings per season (each year having two planting seasons). Under the new director, a fellow anthropologist, the geometric increase continued. By the end of the fourth year, the project had planted, not its originally agreed-upon three million trees, but twenty million trees. Stated more accurately, some 75,000 Haitian peasants had enthusiastically planted trees on their own land. In terms of its quantitative outreach, AOP had more than quintupled its original goals.

Wood Harvesting and Wood Banking

By the end of its fourth year the project had already received an unusual amount of professional research attention by anthropologists, economists, and foresters. In addition to AID evaluations, six studies had been released on one or another aspect of the project (Ashley 1986; Balzano 1986; Buffum and King 1985; Conway 1986; Grosenick 1985; McGowan 1986). As predicted, many peasants were harvesting trees by the end of the fourth year. The most lucrative sale of the wood was as polewood in local markets, though much charcoal was also being made from project trees.

Interestingly, however, the harvesting was proceeding much more slowly than I had predicted. Peasants were "clinging" to their trees and not engaging in the clear cutting that I hoped would occur, as a prelude to the emergence of a rotational system in which peasants would alternate crops with tree cover that they themselves had planted. This technique would have been a revival, under a "domesticated" mode, of the ancient swidden sequence that had long since disappeared from Haiti. Though such a revival would have warmed anthropological hearts, the peasants had a different agenda. Though they had long ago removed nature's tree cover, they were extremely cautious about removing the tree cover that they had planted. Their economic logic was unassailable. Crop failure is so frequent throughout most of Haiti, and the market for wood and charcoal so secure, that peasants prefer to leave the tree as a "bank" against future emergencies. This arboreal bank makes particular sense in the context of the recent disappearance from Haiti of the peasant's traditional bank, the pig. A governmentally mandated (and U.S. financed) slaughter of all pigs because of fears of African swine fever created a peasant banking gap that AOP trees have now started to fill.

Strengthening Private Institutions

Before this project, PVOs had wanted to engage in tree planting, and some ineffective ecology-cum-conservation models had been futilely attempted. AOP has now involved large numbers of PVOs in economically dynamic tree planting activities. Though some of the PVOs, many operating with religious affiliation, were originally nervous about the nonaltruistic commercial thrust of the AOP message, the astounding response of their rural clientele has demolished their objections. In fact many have sought their own sources of funding to carry out this new style of tree planting, based on microseedlings made available in large numbers to peasants as one more marketable crop. Although these PVOs are no longer dependent on AOP, it is safe to say that they will never revert to their former way of promoting trees. AOP has effected positive and probably irreversible changes in the behavior of dozens of well-funded, dedicated local institutions. And by nudging these PVOs away from ethereal visions of the functions of trees, AOP has brought them into closer dynamic touch with, and made them more responsive to, the economic interests of their peasant clientele.

Modifying AID's Modus Operandi

AID has not only taken preliminary steps to extend AOP (some talk is heard of a ten-year extension!); it also has adapted and adopted the privatized AOP delivery model for several other important projects. The basic strategy is twofold: to work through private institutions but to do it in a way consistent with AID administrative realities. AID missions prefer to move large chunks of money with one administrative sweep. Missions are reluctant to enter into separate small contract or grant relationships with dozens of local institutions. The AOP model utilizes an "umbrella" PVO to receive and administer a conveniently large macrogrant. This PVO, not AID, then shoulders the burden of administering the minigrants given to local participating PVOs.

Though it would be premature to predict a spread effect from AOP to other AID missions in other countries, such a spread is not unlikely. What is clear, however, is that the modus operandi of the Haiti mission itself has been deeply changed. In the late 1970s we were fighting to give nongovernmental implementing goals a toehold in Haiti. In the mid-1980s, a recent mission director announced that nearly 60 percent of the mission's portfolio was now going out through nongovernmental channels.

The preceding paragraphs discuss positive results of AOP. There have also been problems and the need for midcourse corrections.

Measurement of Survival Rates

A data-gathering system was instituted by which we hoped to get 100 percent information on all trees planted. Each tree-promoting animateur was to fill out data forms on survival of trees on every single project plot. The information provided by village animateurs on survival was inconsistent and in many cases clearly inaccurate. Project staff members themselves had to undertake separate, carefully controlled measures, on a random sample basis, of tree survival and tree growth. Such precise measurement was undertaken in the final two years of the project.

Improvement of Technical Outreach

The original project hope had been for an overall survival rate of 50 percent. The rate appears lower than that. The principal cause of tree mortality has been postplanting drought. Also in the early years the project was catapulted by peasant demand into a feverish tree production and tree distribution mode that underemphasized the need for careful instruction to all participating peasants about how to plant and properly care for the trees planted. In recent years more attention has been given to the production of educational materials.

Reduction of Per Household Planting Requirements

In its earliest mode, the project required that peasants interested in participating agree to plant a minimum of 500 trees. Peasants not possessing the fifth of a hectare were permitted to enter into combinational arrangements that allowed several peasants to apply as a unit. This mechanism, however, was rarely invoked in practice, and in some regions of the country poorer peasants were reported to have been denied access to trees. In more cases, however, peasants simply gave away trees for which there was no room on their holding.

In view of the pressure that the 500-tree requirement was placing on some families and the unexpected demand that the project had triggered, the per family tree allotment was eventually lowered to 250. This reduced the number of trees available to each farmer but doubled the number of families reached.

Elimination of Incentives

I had from the outset a deep anthropological suspicion that Haitian peasants would respond enthusiastically to the theme of wood as a cash crop. But to hedge my bets I recommended that we build into the project an incentive system. Rather than linking recompense to the planting of trees, I recommended a strategy by which participating peasants would be paid a small cash recompense for each tree surviving after nine and eighteen months. Some members of the project team objected, saying that the tree itself would be sufficient recompense. I compromised by accepting an experimental arrangement: We used the incentive in some regions but made no mention of it in others.

After two seasons it became clear that the peasants in the nonincentive regions were as enthusiastic about signing up for trees as those in incentive regions and were as careful in protecting the trees. I was delighted to back down on this incentive issue: The income-generating tree itself, not an artificial incentive, was the prime engine of peasant enthusiasm. This was a spectacular and rewarding confirmation of the underlying anthropological hypothesis on which the entire project had been built.

The Anthropological Difference

Anthropological findings, methods, and theories clearly have heavily influenced this project at all stages. We are dealing, not with an ongoing project affected by anthropological input, but with a project whose very existence was rooted in anthropological research and whose very character was determined by ongoing anthropological direction and anthropologically informed managerial prodding.

My own involvement with the project spanned several phases and tasks:

1. Proposal of a theoretical and conceptual base of AOP, the concept of "wood as a cash crop."
2. Preliminary contacting of local PVOs to assess preproject interest.
3. Identification of specific program measures during project design.
4. Preparation of social soundness analysis for the AID project paper.

5. Participation as an outside expert at the meetings in AID Washington at which the fate of the project was decided.
6. Participation in the selection and in-country linguistic and cultural training of the agroforesters who worked for the project.
7. Direction and supervision of field operations.
8. Formative evaluation of preliminary results and the identification of needed midcourse corrections.
9. Generation of several hundred thousand dollars of supplemental funding from Canadian and Swiss sources and internationalization of the project team.
10. Preparation of publications about the project (Murray 1984, 1986)

In addition to my own participation in the AOP, four other anthropologists have been involved in long-term commitments to the project. Fred Conway did a preliminary study of firewood use in Haiti (Conway 1979). He subsequently served for two years as overall project coordinator within AID/Haiti. More recently he has carried out revealing case study research on the harvesting of project trees (Conway 1986). Glenn Smucker likewise did an early feasibility study in the northwest (Smucker 1981) and eventually joined the project as my successor in the directorship. Under his leadership many of the crucial midcourse corrections were introduced. Ira Lowenthal took over the AID coordination of the project at a critical transitional period and has been instrumental in forging plans for its institutional future. And Anthony Balzano has carried out several years of case study fieldwork on the possible impact of the tree-planting activities on the land tenure in participating villages. All these individuals have PhDs, or are PhD candidates, in anthropology. And another anthropologist in the Haiti mission, John Lewis, succeeded in adapting the privatized umbrella agency outreach model for use in a swine repopulation project. With the possible exception of Vicos, it would be hard to imagine a project that has been as heavily influenced by anthropologists.

But how specifically has anthropology influenced the content of the project? There are at least three major levels at which anthropology has impinged on the content of AOP.

1. *The Application of Substantive Findings.* The very choice of "wood as a marketable crop" as the fundamental theme of the project stemmed from ethnographic knowledge of the cash-oriented foundations of Haitian peasant horticulture and knowledge of current conditions in the internal marketing system. Because of ethnographic knowledge I was able to avoid succumbing to the common-sense inclination to emphasize fruit trees (whose perishability and tendency to glut markets make them commercially vulnerable) and to choose instead the fast-growing wood

tree. There is a feverishly escalating market for charcoal and construction wood that cannot be dampened even by the most successful project. And there are no spoilage problems with wood. The peasants can harvest it when they want. Furthermore, ethnographic knowledge of Haitian peasant land tenure—which is highly individualistic—guided me away from the community forest schemes that so many development philosophers seem to delight in but that are completely inappropriate to the social reality of Caribbean peasantries.

2. *Anthropological Methods.* The basic research that led up to the project employed participant observation along with intensive interviewing with small groups of informants to compare current cost/benefit ratios of traditional farming with projected cash yields from plots in which trees are intercropped with food on four-year rotation cycles. A critical part of the project design stage was to establish the likelihood of increased revenues from altered land use behaviors. During project design I also applied ethnographic techniques to the behavior of institutional personnel. The application of anthropological notetaking on 3-by-5 slips, not only with peasants but also with technicians, managers, and officials, exposed the institutional roots of earlier project failures and stimulated the proposal of alternative institutional routes. Furthermore ethnoscientific elicitation of folk taxonomies led to the realization that whereas fruit trees are classified as a crop by Haitian peasants, wood trees are not so classified. This discovery exposed the need for the creation of explicit messages saying that wood can be a crop, just as coffee, manioc, and corn can. Finally, prior experience in Creole-language instrument design and computer analysis permitted me to design a baseline data gathering system.

3. *Anthropological Theory.* My own thinking about tree planting was heavily guided by cultural-evolutionary insights into the origins of agriculture. The global tree problem is often erroneously conceptualized in a conservationist or ecological framework. Such a perspective is very short-sighted for anthropologists. We are aware of an ancient food crisis, when humans still hunted and gathered, that was solved, not by the adoption of conservationist practices, but rather by the shift into a domesticated mode of production. From hunting and gathering we turned to cropping and harvesting. I found the analogy with the present tree crisis conceptually overpowering. Trees will reemerge when and only when human beings start planting them aggressively as a harvestable crop, not when human consciousness is raised regarding their ecological importance. This anthropological insight (or bias), nourished by the aggressive creativity of the Haitian peasants among whom I had lived, swayed me toward the adoption of a dynamic "domestication" paradigm in proposing a solution to the tree problem in Haiti. This evolutionary

perspective also permitted me to see that the cash-cropping of wood was in reality a small evolutionary step, not a quantum leap. The Haitian peasants already cut and sell natural stands of wood. They already plant and sell traditional food crops. It is but a small evolutionary step to join these two unconnected streams of Haitian peasant behavior, and this linkage is the core purpose of the Agroforestry Outreach Project.

Broader anthropological theory also motivated and justified a nongovernmental implementing mode for AOP. Not only AID but also most international development agencies tend to operate on a service model of the state. This idealized model views the basic character of the state as that of a provider of services to its population. Adherence to this theoretically naive service model has led to the squandering of untold millions of dollars in the support of extractive public bureaucracies. This waste is justified under the rubric of institution building—assisting public entities to provide the services that they are supposed to be providing.

But my anthropological insights into the origins of the state as a mechanism of extraction and control led me to pose the somewhat heretical position that the predatory behavior of Duvalier's regime was in fact not misbehavior. Duvalier was merely doing openly and blatantly what other state leaders camouflage under rhetoric. AID's search of nongovernmental implementing channels for AOP, then, was not seen as a simple emergency measure to be employed under a misbehaving regime but rather as an avenue of activity that might be valid as an option under many or most regimes. There is little justification in either ethnology or anthropological theory for viewing the state as the proper recipient of developmental funds. This theoretical insight permitted us to argue for a radically nongovernmental mode of tree-planting support in AOP. In short, sensitivity to issues in anthropological theory played a profound role in the shaping of the project.

Would AOP have taken the form it did without these varied types of anthropological input? Almost certainly not. Had there been no anthropological input, a radically different scenario would almost certainly have unfolded with the following elements.

1. AID would probably have undertaken a reforestation project—congressional pressure alone would have ensured that. But the project would have been based, not on the theme of "wood as a peasant cash-crop," but on the more traditional approach to trees as a vehicle of soil conservation. Ponderous educational programs would have been launched to teach the peasants about the value of trees. Emphasis would have been placed on educating the ignorant and on trying to induce peasants to plant commercially marginal (and nutritionally tangential) fruit trees instead of cash-generating wood trees.

2. The project would have been managed by technicians. The emphasis would probably have been on carrying out lengthy technical research concerning optimal planting strategies and the combination of trees with optimally effective bench terraces and other soil conservation devices. The outreach problem would have been given second priority. Throughout Haiti hundreds of thousands of dollars have been spent on numerous demonstration projects to create terraced, forested hillsides, but only a handful of cooperative local peasants have been induced to undertake the same activities on their own land.

3. The project would almost certainly have been run through the Haitian government. When after several hundred thousand dollars of expenditures few trees were visible, frustrated young AID program officers would have gotten finger-wagging lectures about the sovereign right of local officials to use donor money as they see fit. And the few trees planted would have been defined as *pyebwa leta* (the government's trees), and peasants would have been sternly warned against ever cutting these trees, even the ones planted on their own land. And the peasants would soon turn the problem over to their most effective ally in such matters, the free-ranging omnivorous goat, who would soon remove this alien vegetation from the peasant's land.

Because of anthropology, the Agroforestry Outreach Project has unfolded to a different scenario. It was a moving experience for me to return to the village where I had done my original fieldwork (and which I of course tried to involve in the tree-planting activities) to find several houses built using the wood from leucaena trees planted during the project's earliest phases. Poles were beginning to be sold, although the prices had not yet stabilized for these still unknown wood types. Charcoal made from project trees was being sold in local markets. For the first time in the history of this village, people were "growing" part of their house structures and their cooking fuel. I felt as though I were observing (and had been a participant in) a replay of an ancient anthropological drama, the shift from an extractive to a domesticated mode of resource procurement. Though their sources of food energy had been domesticated millennia ago, my former village neighbors had now begun replicating this transition in the domain of wood and wood-based energy. I felt a satisfaction at having chosen a discipline that could give me the privilege of participating, even marginally, in this very ancient cultural-evolutionary transition.

References

Ashley, Marshall D. 1986. A Study of Traditional Agroforestry Systems in Haiti and Implications for the USAID/Haiti Agroforestry Outreach Project. Port-au-Prince: University of Maine Agroforestry Outreach Research Project.

Balzano, Anthony. 1986. Socioeconomic Aspects of Agroforestry in Rural Haiti. Port-au-Prince: University of Maine Agroforestry Outreach Research Project.

Buffum, William, and Wendy King. 1985. Small Farmer Decision Making and Tree Planting: Agroforestry Extension Recommendations. Port-au-Prince: Haiti Agroforestry Outreach Project.

Conway, Frederick. 1979. A Study of the Fuelwood Situation in Haiti. Port-au-Prince: USAID.

_____ . 1986. The Decision Making Framework for Tree Planting Within the Agroforestry Outreach Project. Port-au-Prince: University of Maine Agroforestry Outreach Research Project.

Grosenick, Gerald. 1985. Economic Evaluation of the Agroforestry Outreach Project. Port-au-Prince: University of Maine Agroforestry Outreach Research Project.

McGowan, Lisa A. 1986. Potential Marketability of Charcoal, Poles, and Planks Produced by Participants in the Agroforestry Outreach Project. Port-au-Prince: University of Maine Agroforestry Outreach Research Project.

Murray, Gerald F. 1977. The Evolution of Haitian Peasant Land Tenure: A Case Study in Agrarian Adaptation to Population Growth. Ph.D. dissertation, Columbia University, New York.

_____ . 1978a. Hillside Units, Wage Labor, and Haitian Peasant Land Tenure: A Strategy for the Organization of Erosion Control. Port-au-Prince: USAID.

_____ . 1978b. Informal Subdivisions and Land Insecurity: An Analysis of Haitian Peasant Land Tenure. Port-au-Prince: USAID.

_____ . 1979. Terraces, Trees, and the Haitian Peasant: An Assessment of 25 Years of Erosion Control in Rural Haiti. Port-au-Prince: USAID.

_____ . 1984. The Wood Tree as a Peasant Cash-Crop: An Anthropological Strategy for the Domestication of Energy. In A. Valdman and R. Foster, eds., *Haiti—Today and Tomorrow: An Interdisciplinary Study.* New York: University Press of America.

_____ . 1986. Seeing the Forest While Planting the Trees: An Anthropological Approach to Agroforestry in Rural Haiti. In D. W. Brinkerhoff and J. C. Garcia-Zamor, eds., *Politics, Projects, and Peasants: Institutional Development in Haiti.* New York: Praeger, pp. 193–226.

Smucker, Glenn R. 1981. Trees and Charcoal in Haitian Peasant Economy: A Feasibility Study. Port-au-Prince: USAID.

Zuvekas, Clarence. 1978. Agricultural Development in Haiti: An Assessment of Sector Problems Policies, and Prospects under Conditions of Severe Soil Erosion. Washington, D.C.: USAID.

PART 4
EVALUATION: ASSESSING
WHAT HAPPENED

18 / A National Ethnographic Evaluation of the Career Intern Program

David M. Fetterman

Problem and Client

The Career Intern Program (CIP), an alternative high school program for dropouts and potential dropouts, is designed to enable students to work at their own pace to earn a high school diploma. The program allows most students to complete their educational program in a shortened period—two years for many. The program serves the "whole person," addressing aspects of both the students' academic and personal lives, and provides almost as many counselors as teachers to help students cope with their problems. Because the program emphasizes career preparation, students are typically placed in jobs or admitted to colleges after completing the CIP.

The CIP represents one of the few exemplary educational programs for disenfranchised and economically disadvantaged minority youth. Moreover, it is an important social and educational experiment in the United States. Policymakers have been interested in the program as a viable response to serious labor market problems—high dropout rates and high youth unemployment. Social reformers, however, have viewed the program as a vehicle to redress historically based social inequities and promote upward social mobility for minority groups. Researchers have regarded this program and the evaluation as an opportunity to explore equal opportunity in the United States.

I am indebted to G. D. Spindler, J. L. Gibbs, G. K. Tallmadge, Lee J. Cronbach, and D. S. Waxman for their assistance in the preparation of this manuscript.

243

The evaluation problem was to determine if this program could be successfully replicated in four sites across the United States: Bushwick, New York; Poughkeepsie, New York; East Detroit, Michigan; and Seattle, Washington. The evaluation was divided into four major sections. The first part focused on the implementation of the program—evaluating how successfully each new site matched the original prototype from start-up to full-operational levels. The second part was concerned with statistical outcomes in mathematics, reading, and various attitudinal tests. Ideally, students would have higher test scores after taking a mathematics course in the program. The third part of the evaluation was the ethnographic component for which I was responsible. This portion of the evaluation was charged with identifying interrelationships between the descriptive implementation and the statistical measurement sections of the study. The fourth part of the evaluation compared this program with similar programs for dropouts.

Although the ethnographic portion of this study had multiple clients, the most important were the students. Programmatic feedback was designed to assist them in the program. Students provided the most significant insights into the structure and substance of the program: They told us when a teacher was not on their wavelength, if a counselor was exceptional, if they took the program seriously, and whether they had changed as a result of the program. In return I provided them with my assessments of their performance and the program's performance at their request. This form of reciprocity was usually accomplished in a verbal manner.

Teachers, counselors, and directors constituted the second programmatic level of clients. They shared their successes and failures with me throughout the evaluation. Similarly, I reported my interpretation of their progress and development in interim reports that analyzed and evaluated each major component of their program. The purpose of this early feedback was to inform them of problems and useful approaches so that the programs could be improved before the end of the evaluation. These findings and recommendations were generally well received because they were given in the spirit of constructive criticism and collaboration.

The local- and national-level managers of these programs—Opportunities Industrialization Centers (OIC) and Opportunities Industrialization Centers of America (OIC/A), respectively—represented another level of clients. They were responsible to the monitoring agency, the National Institute of Education (NIE), the funding agency, the Department of Labor (DOL), and the evaluators, RMC Research Corporation, for the success of this effort. They were being evaluated by NIE, DOL, and RMC in their capacity as disseminators of the program. They knew that if they could successfully monitor and manage the program at these four sites they would have the opportunity to disseminate it on a much wider basis across the United States.

The ethnographic portion of the evaluation also had NIE as a direct client and DOL as a secondary client. NIE selected RMC to evaluate the program; therefore NIE was technically and contractually the primary client. DOL periodically wanted information from RMC on the progress of a specific site and—given its funding role—merited RMC's attention.

Having this many masters created some conflicts. Our responsibility to inform NIE of the status of the program conflicted with our responsibilities to the disseminators and the local program people. A poor report about a site could close it down before the evaluation was complete. At the same time, NIE needed to know the status of the sites to make timely reports to Congress. Discretion and judgment were essential in reporting findings. Idiosyncratic or one-time experiences, such as a drunk teacher, were not reported. However, problems that became routine in certain programs—such as high teacher turnover and a poor record of job placement for students—were reported. These latter findings, although negative, were characteristic of certain programs and required attention for the program to survive and serve students.

Process and Players

As the individual in charge of the ethnographic portion of the evaluation, I was responsible for producing case studies of each of the four sites and analyzing all the players—the students, the teachers, the counselors, the directors, the disseminators, the monitors, the funders, and RMC itself—to identify the interrelationship between program components and student outcomes. The ethnographic portion of the evaluation relied on data collected from each section of the study, including the outcome or psychometric testing section of the evaluation. In practice, therefore, the ethnographic portion of the study overlapped with each section of the total evaluation.

This evaluation represents one of the earliest substantive attempts to apply ethnographic techniques and anthropological concepts to a large-scale project within the time frame of a more traditional educational evaluation. Ideally, much more time and additional ethnographers would have been available for a study of this type. Although there are many drawbacks to reducing time normally required to conduct extensive fieldwork, this evaluation suggests what can be done ethnographically within an extremely limited time.

Ethnographic data collection instruments, methods, and perspectives were employed. I used traditional techniques such as participant observation, nonparticipant observation, key informants, triangulation, and structured, semistructured, and informal interviews to elicit data from the emic or insider's perspective.

The most significant adaptation of ethnographic methods involved the schedule of the fieldwork. I made intensive two-week visits to each site every three months for three years, instead of staying at each site for three to six months or longer. This approach enabled me to contribute ethnographic insights to the project and not burden the project's budget through the tremendous number of billing hours that would have resulted from a traditional fieldwork schedule of three to six months. It also let me compare across sites and reflect on my observations from a distance after intensive involvement in the site.

The visits were unusually successful approaches to collecting abundant amounts of data for two reasons: I knew I did not have much time to spend with program participants and the participants knew I would be available only for a short time. The initial ice-breaking periods took as long as they do in regular ethnographic work: I talked with students in the cafeteria, played basketball with students and teachers, and visited students' and teachers' homes for dinner. However, after a rapport was developed, key informants brought me up to date on all the changes and gossip since the last visit. Students made sure that they let me know how they were doing in the program. Teachers and counselors would grab me in the hallways to talk with me privately about problems in the program or successful innovations.

In addition to this intermittent participant observation, I maintained regular contact with participants through telephone, correspondence, and special visits. The study attempted to be nonjudgmental, holistic, and contextual in perspective. A tape recorder and camera were invaluable in collecting and documenting the data. (See Fetterman 1980 for additional details about the methodology.)

The interim findings were reported at the end of each site visit in an exit conference. Formal interim findings were reported in detail in a written report. Drafts of the reports were reviewed by the program administrators and the disseminators. Similarly, final reports were reviewed by participants to ensure accuracy and to provide additional balance to our interpretations.

Results and Evaluation

Ethnographic evaluation views education as a process of cultural transmission that is concerned with how institutions socialize individuals (transmit the appropriate cultural knowledge) to enable them to function in their culture. Although cultural transmission is a life-long process, this evaluation focuses on those elements of cultural transmission found in formal schooling, specifically in this experimental school for dropouts and potential dropouts.

The evaluation documented the role of program ethos as a critical component of the program. Teachers maintained high expectations of their students; at the same time, teachers, counselors, and administrators created a supportive environment. The long list of program rules and regulations—ranging from "no hats or sneakers" in one program to "no unexcused absences" in another—provided students with guidance and a sense that someone cared about them.

The ethnographic evaluation also recognized the role of rituals in the program. Student council elections were one of the most common rites of solidarity that created a sense of group identity and loyalty to the program. Basketball games and bake sales also provided useful rites of solidarity. The single most identifiable communal rite of solidarity was the monthly CIP-is-Hip day, which involved recognition and appreciation of some achievement. Activities included the awarding of prizes for such achievements as best attendance, most talkative, best personality, teacher's pet, always on time, enthusiastic about CIP, likely to succeed, class participation, leadership ability, always late, sleeping in class. The names of winners were posted, stimulating much joking and arguing about the awards and general involvement in the excitement. The teachers and counselors often prepared a dinner for the students on these occasions. The ritual often required a reversal of roles as well: Students prepared a dinner for the teachers and counselors and bestowed special awards on them. This ritual helped to strengthen the group, bringing a sense a unity and purpose to the entire school.

Rites of passage were also identified. Moving from the new group status (in the program for a few months) to the old group status (in the program for several months) was an important rite of passage for students. They knew they could make it all the way through the program if they could cross this hurdle. A more significant rite of passage was the graduation ceremony itself. The students recognized the difference between passing an equivalency examination and getting a real diploma, in terms of both personal self-worth and employment, and they were in the program to earn the diploma. The graduation ceremony marks the transition from young adult to adult for many, from failure to success for others, and from dropout or potential dropout to high school graduate and either employee or college student.

Numerous program outcomes (or approximations of outcomes) were important measures of the program's success. The ethnographic evaluation outcomes included dramatic attitudinal transformation, increased attention span, acquisition of cognitive skills, enhanced communication skills, improved self-presentation skills, and ability to cope with authority. A number of formal and quantifiable measures of program success and stability were also documented in this evaluation, including attendance, staff turnover, graduation, and placement. Poor attendance was a criterion for referral to the CIP. Satisfactory to good attendance was in itself a measure of improvement. Actual dropouts represented a more extreme example of behavior change in the program: Some changed from nonattendance to 70 percent or 90 percent attendance rates. The investigation attempted to break down the quantitative-qualitative dichotomy by reporting both types of program outcomes.

Finally, the study provided programmatic and policy recommendations. Two of the most important personnel findings that we documented involved management and staff turnover. The high turnover rate of management was directly attributable to poor screening techniques. The staff turnover rate was often attributable to competing salaries and benefits of local public schools. Therefore, we recommended that program disseminators

1. Improve screening and selection procedures for management of programs by focusing on administrative experience and educational background (Fetterman 1981b:269).
2. Establish equitable salaries and yearly schedules comparable with the local educational agencies to prevent demoralization, burnout, and turnover (Fetterman 1981b:269).

The ethnographic evaluation also made a number of policy recommendations, ranging from the use of the experimental design to the use of the concept of replicating social programs. One of the most significant policy recommendations was to

abandon the use of randomized treatment-control designs to evaluate social programs, particularly when ethical standards have been violated. All available program positions should be filled; individuals should not be excluded from participation in a program for the sake of constructing a control group. (Fetterman 1981b:268)

This problem is discussed in greater depth later in this chapter. However, my primary concern was that dropouts and potential dropouts were being needlessly and wrongly turned away from the program to maintain an experimental design for the evaluation.

The Anthropological Difference

The first major contribution that anthropology made in this evaluation was conceptual. As an anthropologist I rejected the conception of four sites replicating a prototype. Although this is a useful concept in the biological sciences, it is less useful in the sociological and anthropological sciences. I focused the evaluation on adaptation instead of replication. The initial comparisons of the new sites with the prototype made the new sites look terrible. Even though some of the sites were thriving, the evaluation descriptions made them appear to be in trouble because they did not correspond with the prototype. The funding and monitoring agencies viewed these deviations from the model as failures and threatened to terminate the sites.

When I changed the focus of the evaluation from replication to adaptation, the site descriptions more accurately reflected the success that the program was achieving in school enrollment, school climate, community acceptance, and various other criteria. This change in focus helped provide a more accurate picture of the success of the sites as they adapted to new environments and helped the schools maintain their funding.

Ethnography's talent for detail helped explain puzzling psychometric or outcome findings. Although the students' math scores were improving steadily, during one testing period their scores were unexpectedly low. The psychometrician on the team asked me if I had any explanation for these test results. I reviewed my field notes for the period and found a simple and compelling explanation: The program had no math teacher during that period. Although the explanation was simple, it required detailed notes based on direct observation of the program. Without such information, the program failure would have gone unexplained or been misattributed. The ethnographic approach represents an improvement over correlational analysis of survey data or predetermined observational category systems. The ethnographic explanation provided program personnel and policymakers with levers of action to remedy the situation immediately.

The ethnographic portion of the evaluation also provided a description of the neighborhoods of the program to illuminate the program's physical context. A description of the inner city—where pimping, prostitution, murder, and theft are common occurrences—provides insight into the influences shaping many urban youths and challenging any educational program. This description and the slides that accompanied it had a powerful impact on policymakers, reminding them that the program does not function in a vacuum. Educational programs must contend with many compelling influences on students if they are to win against the powerbrokers of the streets in the competition for inner-city youth.

In addition, the ethnographic portion of the evaluation provided context for the conventional program attendance statistics. Some sites established an exceptional attendance record by almost any standard—90 percent. Other programs maintained an attendance record of 60 percent to 70 percent. The funding agency planned to terminate one of the programs with the worst attendance record. However, the ethnographic portion of the evaluation provided a crucial piece of information that made the statistics meaningful. In response to the funding agency's interpretation of the attendance statistics, I reported the figures with reference to a baseline. The baseline attendance figure for dropouts is zero. They simply did not attend. A 70 percent attendance figure gains significance for policy decisionmakers when compared with a zero attendance baseline figure. This contextual piece of data saved the program from extinction.

The ethnographic portion of the evaluation discovered a few external influences on program operation that would have otherwise gone unnoticed and damaged the credibility of the program. RMC's psychometric or outcome portion of the test required each program to wait until fifteen students were interested in their program before the firm would test them to determine their eligibility for the program (minimum scores in reading and mathematics). Unfortunately, students became disinterested and disillusioned waiting for the firm's "critical mass" of people to accumulate to make the testing economical. Consequently, the students drifted away. This pattern made it look like the programs had difficulty recruiting students or—worse—that students were not interested in the program. In fact, although they were interested in the program, they simply were not interested in the testing or in waiting around to find out if they were eligible. This information was fed back into the evaluation, and testing was conducted on an on-demand basis for each student expressing an interest in the program. Even though this process was much more expensive for RMC, there was no moral or academic alternative.

The ethnographic portion of the study also recorded the interagency rivalry between the funding agency and the monitoring agency. An argument between the two agencies resulted in inadequate funding for the sites. This situation left some of the sites unable to pay their teachers and buy paper for classroom work. A simplistic description of the classrooms would have made the programs look like educational chaos: Teachers were not showing up, students were hanging out in the hallways, and everyone appeared demoralized. An exploration into the context of this condition revealed the funding problem, which reached to the highest levels of the evaluation. Once this situation was reported, the funding problem was solved. In the meantime, the program descriptions were placed in context.

Finally, the ethnographic perspective examined the psychometric or outcome portion of the study itself. The outcome section of the study required students to undergo testing before they entered the program and then to be assigned to a treatment group (students who entered the program) or a control group (students who were told they would not be allowed to enter the program). Ideally, this test would demonstrate whether the students who received the treatment were more or less successful than students who were not allowed to enter the program (the control group). I pointed out that this design was methodologically unsound and ethically dangerous in the larger social context. First, the experiment was not a double-blind experiment. (In such experiments, no one is supposed to know who is receiving or not receiving the treatment—in this case, the educational program.) However, students admitted to the program knew they were receiving the treatment, and students turned away knew they were being systematically denied this educational opportunity. In addition to the academic problems with this social experiment, this type of testing procedure created obstacles for the program's recruitment effort. How many students who were not achieving in the school system would want to endure long hours of testing just to be told they had not made it? The test would be interpreted as another opportunity to fail.

Ethically, this test raised additional concerns. Most of these children were giving society another chance by approaching this experimental educational program. Could we afford the cost of turning away these students who viewed this opportunity as their last chance? On a more personal note, mothers of these children often characterized assignment to the control group as "a slap in the face." The problems with this evaluation approach for these students were discussed in detail in the report and various journals (see Fetterman 1981a, 1981b, and 1982). This finding resulted in more appropriate alternative research strategies.

This study also offered a rare opportunity to replicate anthropological research. The Career Intern Program was studied in its prototype form by one contract firm (Gibboney 1977) and at four replication-demonstration sites by RMC Research Corporation (Fetterman 1981b). The present study can thus be regarded as a partial replication of the ethnographic portion of the study of the prototype. As such, it is significant that the two investigations identified identical components as key to the program's success. This agreement demonstrates that issues of reliability can be successfully addressed in the field of anthropology.

In conclusion, this national ethnographic evaluation served multiple audiences and a variety of purposes. Most notably, it represented an important shift in emphasis from the urban educational anthropology research of the previous decade because it focused on school success for minority youth rather than school failure. In analyzing the way educational differences are related to social stratification, this evaluation challenged the traditional assumption of horizontal social mobility by demonstrating how an alternative school can socialize economically disadvantaged youth for vertical (upward) mobility. It differed from the traditional ethnography of schooling in incorporating findings from a multidisciplinary evaluation effort. The research concerned not a single school but an entire demonstration project in several cities. The analyses examined classrooms, program components, community environments, local and national affiliates, governmental agencies, and evaluators. The study differed also in its multidimensional emphasis, discussing federal involvement, evaluation design, and the role of reinforcing world views. It represented both an opportunity for and a test of ethnography in its emerging role in educational evaluation (see also Fetterman 1984; Fetterman and Pitman 1986; and Fetterman in press).

References

Fetterman, D. M. 1980. Ethnographic Techniques in Educational Evaluation: An Illustration. In Alanson A. Van Fleet, ed., *Anthropology of Education: Method and Applications.* Special Topic Edition of the *Journal of Thought* 15(3):31–48.

————. 1981a. Blaming the Victim: The Problem of Evaluation Design and Federal Involvement, and Reinforcing World Views in Education. *Human Organization* 40(1):67–77.

————. 1981b. *Study of the Career Intern Program. Final Report—Task C: Program Dynamics: Structure, Function, and Interrelationships.* Mountain View, Calif.: RMC Research Corporation.

————. 1982. Ibsen's Baths: Reactivity and Insensitivity: A Misapplication of the Treatment-Control Design in a National Evaluation. *Educational Evaluation and Policy Analysis* 4(3):261–279.

Fetterman, D. M., ed. 1984. *Ethnography in Educational Evaluation.* Beverly Hills, Calif.: Sage.

————, ed. *The Silent Scientific Revolution: Qualitative Approaches to Evaluating Education.* Berkeley, Calif.: McCutchan Press (in press).

Fetterman, D. M. and M. A. Pitman, eds. 1986. *Educational Evaluation: Ethnography in Theory, Practice, and Politics.* Beverly Hills, Calif.: Sage.

Gibboney Associates, Inc. 1977. *The Career Intern Program: Final Report*, vol. 1 and 2. Blue Bell, Pa.: Gibboney Associates, Inc.

19 / Welfare Reform Before Its Time: The Evaluation of the Minnesota Work Equity Project

M. G. Trend

Problem and Client

During the mid-1970s many people in the U.S. Department of Labor and in various state governments were worried about the severe recession. Supplemental benefits for the unemployed had been authorized by the federal government, and nearly one-half of the states had exhausted the reserves from which they paid unemployment compensation benefits. As the recession dragged on, government officials feared that those people who were about to exhaust their entitlements would slide onto the welfare rolls, thereby overburdening the entire public assistance system.

At the same time, talk about achieving true welfare reform was circulating throughout government, just as it is today. Most plans called for some sort of work and training program, in which the federal government would be the "employer of last resort" for those who could not find jobs in the private sector. It was widely believed that such an approach could break the "cycle of poverty" that breeds long-term welfare dependency.

Concurrently, people in the Minnesota state government had been considering a "one stop" eligibility center that would make it easier for people to get help. Because the state bureaucracy was complicated, many folk had difficulty navigating it. The eligibility center was being proposed as a low-cost way of setting things right.

The time was right for the representatives from Minnesota to hold discussions with Department of Labor officials. A modest demonstration program soon swelled in importance and funding until it quietly was touted as a trial balloon for President Jimmy Carter's welfare reform. By now, the nationwide recession was over, the Minnesota economy was booming, and the reform effort would take place under favorable conditions.

The social experiment that eventuated was called the Minnesota Work Equity Program (WEP). The idea behind WEP was to serve a broad mix of low-income clients—people on AFDC (Aid for Dependent Children), General Assistance, food stamp recipients, and those drawing unemployment compensation benefits. Any WEP registrant who was declared "job ready" would be guaranteed employment—either in the private sector (through direct placement or through an on-the-job-training contract with a firm), or in the public sector (on a community work project or CWP).

The CWP was essentially a revival of a 1930s idea—the WPA (Works Progress Administration) project. Program participants who could not find employment in the private sector would be assigned to a CWP. Ideally, the work would be "meaningful." One challenge faced by the WEP agency was to create CWPs in which registrants did something else besides rake leaves.

WEP was a mandatory program for most of its registrants. Early on, protests from organized labor had eliminated unemployment compensation claimants from having to participate. They could volunteer, however, if they wished. Those on other programs (if they were able bodied and were not taking care of small children) had to register for work, bringing them into WEP.

Except for the guarantee of a job and the existence of CWPs, the WEP program resembled the existing Work Incentive (WIN) Program for welfare mothers. For the Department of Labor to evaluate WEP's effectiveness, WEP replaced the WIN program in certain areas. Both programs were run simultaneously, and then "program outcomes" of WEP registrants were compared with those of WIN registrants. That's where Abt Associates Inc. (a private sector evaluation firm based in Cambridge, Mass.) entered the picture. I was working as a senior scientist for the company. That's where I came in, too.

Process and Players

I remembered hearing about WEP while I was working on an in-house project for the Legal Services Corporation. The anthropological content of that effort was nil and I was beginning to get bored. When the president of the company asked me to join the WEP evaluation team, I jumped at the chance.

I had been with Abt Associates since the early 1970s, when the firm hired me out of graduate school. I had started as a field worker on a housing voucher evaluation, and unlike the other anthropologists hired at the time, I had stuck around and worked my way up until I now had managerial and research design responsibilities.

I enjoyed working for the company and liked doing research that I thought would "make a difference." I figured that the WEP evaluation would give me a chance to put into practice what I had learned working on interdisciplinary teams.

I also guessed that the Department of Labor's commitment to the WEP evaluation would grow and that WEP would become a multimillion-dollar effort that would have an impact upon public policy. It seemed to me that the potential was even greater than on the housing voucher studies. Although that research was highly regarded in academic and policy circles, I felt that we had room for improvement.

Any large evaluation involves lengthy planning sessions and visits with the agency sponsoring the evaluation. By the time I joined the project, much of the conceptual groundwork had already been laid. The Department of Labor had devised a set of twelve policy questions. Our research team was to devise a set of research questions whose answers would tell the Department of Labor what it needed to know.

Contract research (as opposed to grant research) is invariably a very controlled activity guided by a detailed analysis plan. Part of my job as director of field research was to design the observational part of the study so that it would mesh with the rest of the effort, which used data from surveys and management information systems. It is tedious business that does not have much payoff until the analysis stage of a project.

The evaluation consisted of a comparison of the new program with an existing program. Thus, the program outcomes of WEP in St. Paul were compared with those of WIN in Minneapolis. We had to collect all information (including observational data) systematically; everything had to be "cross-site comparable." For the anthropologists whom I eventually hired to be on-site researchers (OSRs), this meant that they would have to relinquish much of their traditional autonomy in the field. They were a small part of a large team that consisted mostly of economists and survey researchers based in the Cambridge office. The OSRs were the only regular on-site presence of the company.

To guide the collection of field data, I devised a set of "functions" or bureaucratic behaviors common to the WEP and to WIN. Then, I produced a set of narrative reporting forms or "function logs" and wrote an OSR field manual that showed how to use this material. The

OSRs went through a two-week training period in Cambridge before they entered the field.

I assigned each OSR to a specific post, and each had a desk within a WEP or WIN office. Our site office was located in downtown St. Paul, but individual OSRs—as many as four were employed at a time—covered about one-third of the state because the experiment contained both rural and urban components. I appointed the most experienced OSR to be the field supervisor and office manager. He took care of the day-to-day administration of the field effort, while I commuted once or twice a month between Minneapolis and Boston.

The most immediate worth of the OSRs was to serve as liaison between Abt Associates in Cambridge and various state offices in Minnesota. Especially at the beginning, the OSRs were often asked by WEP and WIN staff members to answer questions about the evaluation. The WEP clients themselves sometimes had questions about the research, particularly the detailed surveys.

WEP was a controversial program in many ways. Representatives from welfare rights groups seized upon the evaluation as proof that human experimentation was going on. The public employees' organizations viewed WEP as a source of scab labor that endangered the well-being of their members. Conservatives did not like the additional benefits and training that the program offered. Liberals disliked the "forced work" aspect of WEP, although work registration was a precondition for receiving benefits from many programs, including food stamps, general assistance, and AFDC.

We had to meet legal requirements to gain access to WEP clients' records. My field supervisor was especially good at obtaining the cooperation of otherwise reluctant state officials. All of these details should have been handled long before the anthropologists arrived on site, but a lot of ball-dropping had gone on. Even if the OSRs had not done research (and later, written reports), I felt they more than paid their way by oiling troubled waters again and again.

In my reading of the evaluation literature, I was struck by how little of the anthropological potential had been tapped. My field supervisor and I were determined to make the WEP evaluation different in that regard. Whenever I was in the Twin Cities, we talked over the research, thought about where we were going, and discussed what else we ought to be doing.

The OSRs soon began functioning as a team. They shared their field notes and worked on "function logs" or reports together. They wrote weekly summaries of their activities and exchanged them with each other, with me, and with the staff in Cambridge. At least twice a month, we held an OSR meeting in our St. Paul office.

In previous evaluations, the company had tended to keep OSRs at a single site. This approach saved travel costs but resulted in single-site myopia, or the anthropologist's firm belief that his or her tribe (or site, or agency) is unique. I tried to forestall this belief by having the OSRs visit other sites randomly. In this way, each OSR was able to get a handle on what was unique to WEP or WIN and what might be a function of, say, the rural location of a particular agency office.

The field supervisor and I also encouraged the OSRs to read the literature from other disciplines, including political science, economics, and sociology. Even though the function logs and the field manual contained some of this material, we wanted the OSRs to become more familiar with what had already been done, particularly in the analysis of formal organizations and in role theory.

We began to experiment with using different methods to tackle research problems that cropped up outside of the core set of research questions. For example, in any social program, clients meet with "gatekeepers" who determine where individuals will be sent or what treatment they will receive. In programs like WEP, social workers have a considerable amount of discretion in deciding who goes where. To understand the implicit decision-making rules by which the WEP gatekeepers operated, we used ethnoscience techniques (card sorts) with WEP staffers to elicit categories of WEP clients, categories of WEP treatments, and the mental rules used to assign particular clients to particular treatments, such as a CWP or a training program.

The OSRs had quickly gained an idea of how WEP gatekeeping worked. We felt that the decision criteria could be made "objective" and tied to the hard data analysis. We wrote up the results of our exercise and filed the memorandum. I hoped that someone would use what we had done because I had already decided that I was going to leave the company.

Much later, when I was in the Cambridge office visiting former coworkers, I was introduced to the analyst who had written the report that linked client characteristics with WEP treatments. He pumped my hand vigorously and told me that he had used our analysis to guide his thinking. Someone had found the bottle with the note in it three years after we had tossed it into the water. I felt good about that small victory.

Another innovation we tried consisted of using randomly selected program participants for a set of WEP case studies. This came about largely because of pressure from an Institutional Review Board (IRB) charged by law with protecting WEP participants from harm resulting from their participation in the program. Even though WEP consisted of an enriched set of alternatives for low-income people, it was controversial with many groups for a variety of reasons.

The local IRB comprised a curious mixture of medical researchers, quantitative social scientists, and activists. Judgmentally sampled qualitative case studies found no champion among the members of the IRB. Their chief objection was that the proposed case study interviews were in depth and hence intrusive. This intrusiveness, the panel members argued, might subject WEP participants to risk (that is, of disclosing self-incriminating information). Some members of the IRB also questioned the usefulness of case studies at all because the total number of selectees would be small, probably less than fifty individuals.

These objections were raised early in the research. The case studies were in jeopardy, and I knew that once one part of a research project began to unravel, there was no way of knowing where things would stop. I did some thinking about the IRB's objections and eventually decided that some of their concerns were legitimate. Except in linguistics, where reliance upon a few key informants seems to pose no threat to the validity of research, the question of key informant representativeness crops up frequently in anthropological studies. Lurking behind all this lies a suspicion of intended or unintended bias.

It seemed to me that the IRB was worried about selection bias rather than small sample sizes. Therefore, my field supervisor and I prepared a special presentation to the IRB that outlined a set of focused case studies that would use randomly selected participants.

The IRB did an abrupt about-face and approved the case studies. My next task was to sell the new design to the OSRs. All but one were anthropologists, and not surprisingly, they were reluctant at first to go ahead with the idea. After all, one of the hallmarks of a good ethnographer is the ability to exercise sound judgement. Random selection ran counter to all they had been taught about the case study method. One of the OSRs asked, "If I draw someone who isn't a good informant, can I replace him with somebody else?"

Sometimes our experimentation came to nothing. For example, a flirtation with systematic natural observation (SNO)—a structured technique involving the use of observational protocols—proved to be a disaster. The OSRs grumbled about the pointlessness of using high-priced analytic help for weeks at a time in scant hope of catching a "rare event." (In this case, we wanted to observe the application of sanctions upon noncooperating participants). After three or four days, I put a stop to SNO, and my flirtation with the technique faded into the lore of the research project.

Because my field supervisor and I were fairly senior members of the research team, we were given "running room" to experiment with different methods. The only stipulation was that our work had to relate somehow to the purpose of the project. It was heady stuff at times, and we enjoyed ourselves. I was especially pleased that all the original OSRs said they wanted to return to Cambridge after the evaluation was over. Half of them actually did, and they had a hand in writing the final reports to the Department of Labor.

Results and Evaluation

The Minnesota Work Equity Program was an early prototype for a series of welfare reform demonstrations, variants of which are ongoing today. Almost all the "new" approaches explained on the news and in the popular press involve a remarkably similar mix of cash subsidies, training opportunities, and jobs. In our study, the differences between WEP and the comparison programs were measurable but modest. The new offering was no panacea.

Some of the CWPs did provide meaningful work (for example, a group of welfare mothers got the chance to become apprentice carpenters), but most were the same old mix of public service janitorial and hospital aide jobs. The real payoff was WEP's enhanced opportunities for the unemployed to pick up skills, rather than forcing people to do "make work." That is a lesson that still has to be learned.

Unlike some of the more recent trial programs where participation is voluntary, WEP provided an example of what welfare reform might look like in the real world. It served a mix of people who varied in their commitment to work. That the outcomes were positive gives me some hope that welfare reform can work, if it encourages human capital investment.

The case studies were published as part of the series of WEP reports. The U.S. Department of Labor was pleased with them and with the way that the on-site presence infused all the reports from the evaluation. The contracting officer recommended that OSRs be used in future evaluations; however, to the best of my knowledge, the later evaluations did not use OSRs to the same extent that we did.

WEP was too far ahead of its time to have much direct impact upon the current (late 1980s) welfare reform debate. In 1980, the administration changed in Washington. WEP ground on and became ancient history, while a much more ambitious effort (involving twenty sites across the nation) was cancelled. At this writing, the administration proposals for welfare reform demonstrations remind me of how little has really been done since the late 1970s.

One reality of this type of applied research is that one eventually must come to terms with the realization that the wheels of progress turn slowly. The policy debates go on interminably. An approximately ten-year-long lag occurs between doing the research and seeing any impact in the public consciousness. In 1985, for example, I saw an article in the *New York Times* about the "new" idea of housing vouchers, an area in which I had worked back in the mid-1970s.

A few months ago, I read a couple of overoptimistic pieces about a "new" welfare reform idea, which will involve WPA-type projects. The articles appeared in two highly regarded national magazines. Their premise—that the poor have gotten a set of bad habits and need "make work" to set themselves right again—is wrong and silly. Still, I am impressed that reporters have a nodding acquaintance with some of the social experiments of the 1970s. The WEP evaluation contributed to that body of knowledge.

The Anthropological Difference

I used to tell other anthropologists in research organizations that they ought to stick around until after the fieldwork is over so they could work on the reports and write articles. I did not follow my own advice in the WEP evaluation, and I left the company about six months before the end of the fieldwork.

My contributions to the published output from WEP consist of authoring the WEP start-up reports and some ghostwriting on the case studies volume. However, before I sat down to write this chapter, I flipped through the WEP case studies. After six years, what strikes me is that the individual stories are alive unlike so much of what came out of the WEP evaluation. The people actually tell what it is like to be on a work-training program and how it changed their lives.

A variety of experiences are depicted (positive and negative), and even a reader with only casual interest in poor people would be interested in how the folk we talked to came to wind up on the welfare rolls. Contrary to the arrogant "Culture of Poverty" theorizing now in vogue, the WEP case studies leave plenty of room for "there-but-for-the-grace-of-God-go-I" musings.

The case studies are the only place in the series of WEP reports where the opinions and experiences of program participants come through clearly, without the filtering and distillation necessary for survey research. At the same time, the random selection process we used avoids the criticism of researcher bias that plagues so much case study work.

The survey-based reports were hampered somewhat by a response rate below the 75 percent level predicted in the research plans. The anthropological research provided another check on the reliability and validity of the analysis.

Perhaps the greatest contributions made by the OSRs was in their agreeing to come back and work as report writers. I've found in the past that there's nothing quite like on-site experience to put a level perspective on research findings. The knowledge gained from on-site research infuses all the WEP reports. Anyone who read them would be impressed by their calm and rather cautious tone and by the way the anthropological analysis of WEP process is intertwined with the economic analysis of WEP impact.

As I noted, WEP did not solve the problem of welfare dependency. The approach had merit and was worth trying again on a larger scale, which it was. As with any social program, WEP worked for some people and didn't work for others. The gains made in employability were modest. The punitive part of WEP (forced work) didn't come about, mainly because sanctions are incredibly hard to apply in real life; the training part of WEP did work, however, and the program paid its own way.

If the anthropologists had not been used on site, I imagine the output would have been survey-based reports with a smattering of econometrics as garnish. Perhaps the evaluation never would have gotten off the ground, given the rough sledding that WEP had initially. (In all my time in the business, WEP was the only project I ever knew about that had *two* start-up reports!)

My field supervisor smoothed things over on-site and prepared the Cambridge staff for meetings with state and local officials whose cooperation we had to have. More than anyone else on the staff, he earned his pay.

So, the anthropological difference consisted of greasing some bureaucratic wheels, helping the home office analysts, and producing a savvy and honest set of reports that included a volume of good ethnographic case studies. Along the way, we experimented with different methodologies and had a good time. With a little different timing, the WEP evaluation might have had more direct impact than it did. The design was certainly elegant enough. I don't think we could have asked for anything beyond this.

20 / The Delivery of Rural Reproductive Medicine

Judith R. Davidson

Problem and Client

Approximately 60 to 80 percent of babies born in the developing world are delivered by traditional birth attendants (TBAs) (Simpson et al. 1981:117; WHO 1979a and 1979b). Although they vary widely in training, range of services provided, age, and even sex, TBAs tend to be community-based middle-aged women, nonformally trained, whose primary health activities are assisting women during pregnancy, childbirth, and the postpartum period. In developing countries, the instruction of TBAs in Western obstetrical skills has been utilized as an economically and biomedically sound method of improving the high rates of maternal and infant mortality and morbidity.

In Peru, instruction of traditional birth attendants in Western techniques of maternity care has been going on sporadically since 1945. In 1979 TBA training became a national priority and training courses were set up in all sixteen health regions. Resources for TBA training were an important segment of a U.S. Agency for International Development (AID) investment of over $17 million provided to the Peruvian Ministry of Health (MOH) for the promotion of community health in rural and semi-urban populations. The target population was estimated to be over 4,284,000 individuals in rural areas and an equal number in semi-urban areas. TBA training was instituted as an economically feasible means of combatting high rates of maternal-infant morbidity and mortality in rural and semi-urban areas (such as squatter settlements on the outskirts of larger cities) that are culturally and geographically isolated from Western healthcare providers and facilities.

During the two-week TBA training course, participants are taught to provide nutritional, hygenic, and birth control counseling. They are instructed on the proper management of basic medicines but are prohibited from giving injections. Other topics included in the course are hygenic birthing methods, prenatal and postnatal patient care, environmental hygiene, first aid, and infant and child nutrition. TBAs are not paid by the MOH but are voluntary community-level health providers. The effectiveness of the course in instructing the TBAs is evaluated by a written examination given at the end. A concluding celebration is highlighted by the presentation of diplomas and a small carrying case containing equipment and medication.

Ministry of Health (MOH) efforts at supervising and maintaining contact with the trained TBAs once they returned to practice in their communities consisted of reports sent by the TBAs to the local health posts; infrequent visits by regional health personnel; and visits by the TBAs to the local health post (MOH 1979). Reports written about a TBA's activities, either by the TBA herself or by the MOH provider working at the local health post, are used to determine the number of patients treated by the TBA per month and the number of patients transferred to healthcare centers. The MOH approach to evaluating the trained TBA entirely focused on the number of patients treated or referred rather than on the quality of healthcare provided.

The MOH measured the success of the program by the numbers of patients treated by trained TBAs. The TBAs' reactions to the course or the patients' reaction to the trained TBAs were not considered by the MOH as important determinants of program outcome. This emphasis on the administrative rather than the grassroots reaction to the program pointed to the direction I would take in designing the evaluation. I presented my approach to the client, director of maternal and child health, Dr. Luis Sobrevilla, as a means of testing the on-the-ground effectiveness of the program in instructing the TBAs to modify their patient care techniques according to program regulations and serve as health educators to their communities.

Process and Players

Once approval of the research approach was obtained, I began to design and conduct a participatory evaluation of the program that focused on the active involvement of MOH personnel in all phases of the evaluation. The intent was to encourage MOH personnel responsible for program implementation to take "ownership" of the evaluation, thereby improving the chances that they would utilize the recommendations drawn from its findings. This was accomplished by seeking input from MOH personnel at each research phase. Final decisions about questionnaire design and site selection came about as the result of discussions held with national-level MOH personnel responsible for the planning of the Primary Health Care Program. At the termination of data collection from each region, national-level MOH personnel, who had played an active role in the design and implementation of the PHC program, were invited to attend conferences during which preliminary results were presented. These conferences accomplished three objectives:

1. Provided an opportunity for national MOH health planners to preview results from the regions.
2. Provided an opportunity for me to listen to their comments on my interpretation of preliminary findings.
3. Provided an opportunity for me to listen to their explanation of national and regional characteristics of the program that developed from political and historical events.

On February 6, 1981, a two-year evaluation of the Peruvian TBA training program was initiated. Funding was provided by a contract from the AID supplemented by economic and logistical support from Occidental Petroleum, Peru. The challenge was to solve the practical problems of testing the training program's effectiveness in up-grading TBA performance and to provide MOH officials with practical and workable recommendations for program improvement that fit into the structure of their training program.

This chapter illustrates the advantages of evaluating the effectiveness of an intervention program from the perspective of program recipients— in this case, the trained TBA and patients. The strategy most commonly used to evaluate the effectiveness of training programs for health workers is to rate their performance by the degree of compliance to program directives determined by observations or tests conducted by professional health personnel. Examples of this approach to evaluation are seen in reports by Baquero (1981), Long and Viau (1974), MacCorquodale (1982), and Rubin (1983). An alternative approach was taken to determine the effectiveness of the Peruvian TBA training program. The assumption underlying the evaluation design was that the effectiveness of the TBA training program was determined not only by whether the TBAs followed instructions but by why they decided to do so. In addition, the evaluation sought to determine the factors underlying patients' reactions to the trained TBAs.

Once the program was instituted by the MOH, its outcome was determined by the trained TBAs' and community members' decisions. The following objectives were formulated from the application of this approach to the determination of the effectiveness of the Peruvian TBA training program.

- Elicit information about the training program's effect on TBA performance.
- Describe the trained TBAs' and patients' reactions to the program.
- Estimate program coverage.
- Describe the administrative features of the program during its operation in the health regions.
- Provide workable recommendations to the MOH that respond to both the TBAs' and community's felt needs and the MOH's budgetary constraints.

To fulfill these objectives a three-phase research strategy was designed that corresponded to the structure and operational and administrative features of the Peruvian primary health care (PHC) system as illustrated in Figure 20.1. On this figure, the inner triangle represents the three administrative levels of the PHC system. The apex represents the central-level bureaucracy, the middle section represents the regional-level administration, and the base represents the MOH health posts located in the local communities.

The relationship between the research design and the structure of the Peruvian PHC system is as follows. The middle triangle represents the three phases of the evaluation design. The operational model of the training program is illustrated by the outer triangle. The left side of the outer triangle portrays the inputs, outputs, and outcomes of the PHC system; these are matched on the right side by the locus of their execution. For example, inputs to the system are planned and executed by national-level MOH personnel; outputs, implementation of training courses, are executed by regional-level MOH personnel; and outcomes, indicated by delivery of services and program coverage, at the community level.

The evaluation had three focal points that corresponded to the phases of the research design.

National Phase

The evaluation began with a thorough search for all documents describing the TBA training program. Since the inception of the program in 1979 there had been some changes in the political party controlling the MOH. As a result earlier documents describing activities at the inception of the program were not available in the reference library of the MOH in Lima. To document its development, individuals who had played an active role in its early history were interviewed. These interviews supplemented available published material, and a history of the development of the program in Peru was written. The norms, regulations,

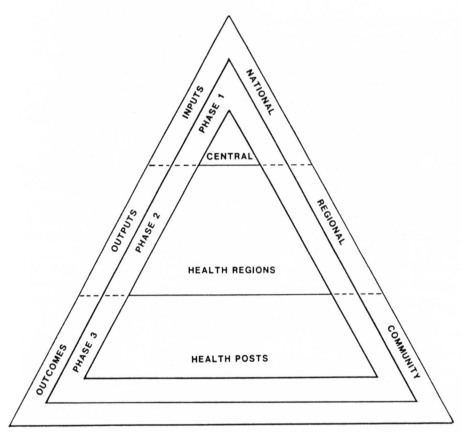

FIGURE 20.1 Evaluation and program design. The innermost triangle represents the administrative models; the middle triangle shows the research phases; and the outer triangle includes the operational model.

goals, and objectives of the program being implemented at the time of the evaluation were obtained from current MOH documents.

Other achievements of this phase were the development of the questionnaires, site selection, and preparation of official letters of introduction addressed to the head of each health region. These letters provided permission to conduct the evaluation at each of the selected health regions and access to MOH regional logistical support.

Regional Phase

Information describing delivery of services was obtained using a semi-structured, open-ended questionnaire administered to a sample of 1,230 patients who had used the services of trained TBAs and a control group of 277 patients who had used the services of untrained TBAs; a second semistructured, open-ended questionnaire was administered to a sample of 250 trained TBAs. The surveys were conducted in five regions that represented the major Peruvian cultural and geographic variation: the Departments of San Martín (high jungle), Ica (south coast), Lambayeque-Amazonas (north coast and highlands), Cuzco (southern highlands), and Ancash (north-central highlands).

The sample of TBAs interviewed during the evaluation was drawn from regional hospital records that contained the names, dates of training, and location of residence of each trained TBA. Identification of patients who had used the services of trained TBAs was drawn from the records of *sanitarios*, MOH community-level health workers, who worked at local health posts. An attempt was made to accurately represent the geographical and cultural diversity within each region of the sample. However, not all communities were being served by trained TBAs. In each community surveyed a sample of five patients treated by each trained TBA was interviewed. A control group was obtained by randomly sampling patients of untrained TBAs from each target community.

To gain an estimate of program coverage, a random sample of women from two communities in the Department of Ancash was interviewed. They were queried about their utilization of the trained TBA working in their community.

Community Phase

The intent of this phase was to find the variables that determined TBA compliance to program directives and patient compliance to the advice given by trained TBAs. To ensure that the results of this phase would be externally valid, data were obtained from two geographically and culturally different communities. The community in the north-central highlands was selected because its socioeconomic and sociocultural features corresponded to the prevalent characteristics of the Peruvian lower class living in urban squatter settlements and rural areas. The lowland indigenous community was chosen because preliminary indicators showed that the results of the TBA training program among these people differed considerably from those of the coastal and highland samples.

This information was obtained through semiformal interviews with trained TBAs and community members. Three months were spent in each of the communities.

Results and Evaluation

Program outcome was determined through an analysis of quantitative and qualitative indicators. Quantitative methods determined the degree to which the trained TBA complied with program directives; they were also used to determine the degree of program coverage. Qualitative methods were used to reveal the factors that determined reactions of trained TBAs and their clients to the program.

Quantitative Indicators of Trained TBA Performance

The proper intervention of a trained TBA during the maternity cycle can mean the difference between a healthy and an unhealthy mother and child. There are three critical stages during which advice from the TBA could potentially alter the health status of the mother and infant: pregnancy, birth, and the postpartum period. To test whether the performance of the trained TBAs had been affected by participation in the training course I selected eight key test variables within these three stages.

Evidence of program merit was obtained by comparing the responses of patients who had been treated by trained TBAs to a control group of patients treated by untrained TBAs. The eight key variables were used as indicators of TBA performance. Analysis of the survey data indicated that in all regions the trained TBAs provided their patients with a higher quality of care, as determined by the eight test variables, than their untrained counterparts.

To estimate the extent to which the TBA is reaching the patient population, surveys were conducted with 357 adult females from the Department of Ancash. These surveys took place in two communities. In one the entire adult female population was sampled, and in a more densely populated area, a random sample of potential patients was taken. In the first community the survey found that only 2 percent of the population used the two trained TBAs practicing in the community, and only 5 percent of the adult female population knew that there were trained TBAs practicing in the community. These TBAs were both women. Community members who had used them remarked that they were not pleased with their services and that they were difficult to contact.

In contrast, interviews with a random sample of 115 women drawn from the second community with a total population of 1,400 adult women found that 20 percent of the survey sample had consulted the two male trained TBAs practicing in the community and 60 percent knew that they were practicing in the area. The popularity of the trained TBAs in one of the communities was not the result of his sex or status as a trained TBA but rather of other factors such as patient satisfaction, personality, and established kinship bonds (Davidson 1984:110).

Qualitative Indicators of Patient and TBA Response

Overall, the survey found a high rate of patient satisfaction. Of the 1,230 informants who had used the services of trained TBAs, only 2 percent replied that they had experienced difficulties with them. Problems mentioned were either logistical or personal (Davidson 1984:127–164). For example, informants complained that they could not find the trained TBA when they needed her. Eighty-five percent of patients interviewed replied that they favored the trained TBA's services over those provided by an untrained TBA.

The survey found that the TBAs were generally pleased with their experiences in the training course. During informal interviews trained TBAs were asked to discuss their training experiences. Difficulties mentioned by trained TBAs were lack of renumeration by the government and patients for their services, conflicts between the demands of their TBA practice and subsistence activities, and limitations placed on their practice by government regulations. For example, they were prohibited from giving their patients injections.

Drawing upon the qualitative and quantitative data collected from the analysis of survey results and informal interviews conducted during the community studies, a set of recommendations was included in the final evaluation report (Davidson 1984:194–206).

The strategy of including national primary healthcare planners in the planning stage for the evaluation design, continually updating them on project findings, and obtaining their input on implications and recommendations was initially highly successful. The evaluation report was translated into Spanish and circulated to each of the seventeen health regions. It was used as a guide for a series of seminars during which regional directors and their PHC staff were instructed on new methods of implementing TBA training. These sessions stressed the need to address the TBAs' and patients' needs when planning for the training, supervision, and evaluation of the program. These events took place in 1983.

In 1984 and 1985, I was asked to return to Peru to evaluate the health promoters' program. The results of this evaluation (Management Sciences for Health ms.) were not as positive. As a result of this study USAID consultants recommended to the MOH that training of all community health workers be discontinued until the entire system could be redesigned. However, political events intervened.

When I returned in 1986 to conduct an analysis of community-based health care (Davidson ms.), I found that the change in political party, from Acción Popular to APRA, meant that the entire philosophy and system of healthcare delivery was in the process of radical change. The intention of the new government was to decentralize healthcare decision-making and allocation of resources. The major objective was to increase regional control and decrease national control. The outcome of this approach will clearly be a greater emphasis on community healthcare workers. However, whether the results of my evaluation will contribute to this process, I cannot say.

The Anthropological Difference

The central point of the evaluation strategy was that, once the training program is operative, its outcome depends upon decisions reached by the trained TBAs and their patients. This perspective guided the development of all phases of the research design. It evolved from exchange theory developed by Blau (1964) and Homans (1968) as well as the cognitive basis of health care as described by Kleinman (1974/1975, 1981).

In practice these perspectives were used in formulating questions for the questionnaires and semiformal interview formats. By using these theories, I was seeking to uncover factors that determined decisions reached by the trained TBAs and their patients. My intent was to assist the MOH in improving its program by uncovering not only whether the program was effective, but more significantly, the reasons behind program success and failure. By using this perspective emphasis was directed at the TBA as a decision-maker. For example, the following are typical questions asked about the TBAs' response to the program. Why did TBAs attend the training sessions? What factors determined their continued attendance for the full two-week program? Once the training course was completed, did they incorporate skills learned in their practice? Did trained TBAs resupply themselves with the materials recommended during the course once their supply had run out?

Responses to these and other questions revealed a multiplicity of factors that determined TBA and patient compliance (Davidson 1984:68–171). Some of these factors were directly related to exchange theory. For example, to perform according to program directives, the TBA had to balance her responsibilities as a poorly paid or unpaid community health resource against subsistence and family obligations. At times, she decided in favor of subsistence and/or family obligations that were in direct conflict with program directives.

Other decisions drew from the cognitive basis of health care; these were based on the patients' and TBAs' perception of their appropriate sociocultural role characteristic of their specific segment of Peruvian society. For example, parts of the training program were in direct conflict with popular healthcare beliefs. The trained TBA's responsibility was to operate as a change agent. However, in the process the trained TBA could lose patients if she insisted that the patient follow recommendations in conflict with healthcare beliefs.

Other aspects of the unique contribution of anthropology to the design and implementation of this evaluation were a recognition of the effect of the community, as a unit, on the outcome of the program and the recognition of the varied cultural base of Peruvian indigenous cultures and its impact on program implementation and ultimate outcome.

The effect of these two factors on program outcome was clearly indicated by evidence accumulated during the two community studies as well as by specific questions on TBA recruitment used on the questionnaires. A poignant example of the impact of the community on program outcome came from the study conducted among the indigenous lowland community of Bajo Naranjillo (Department of San Martín). Due to the lack of appreciation for community structure, regional MOH personnel forced the selection of an unsuitable candidate for training. The end result (Davidson 1984:147–154) was that the community refused further attempts by regional MOH personnel to participate in the TBA section of the primary healthcare program.

References

Baquero, Huberto, et al. 1981. Ecuador: TBA Training Program, Supervision, Evaluation and Follow-up Services. *Public Health Papers* 75:9–26.

Blau, P. M. 1964. *Exchange and Power in Social Life*. New York: Wiley.

Davidson, Judith R. 1984. An Anthropological Evaluation of Teaching Reproductive Medicine and Primary Health Care to Traditional Birth Attendants in Peru. Unpublished Ph.D. dissertation, University of California, Los Angeles.

———. 1986. Analysis of the Health Sector Peru, (ANSSA), Health and Community Participation in Peru. Unpublished manuscript, Stony Brook, N.Y.

Homans, George. 1968. Social Behavior as Exchange. In Edward E. Le Clair, Jr., and Harold K. Schneider, eds., *Economic Anthropology*. New York: Holt, Rinehart and Winston.

Kleinman, Arthur. 1974/1975. Cognitive Structures of Traditional Medical Systems: Ordering, Explaining, and Interpreting the Human Experience of Illness. *Etnomedizin* (Germany) 3:27–49.

———. 1981. The First Five Volumes (editorial). *Culture, Medicine and Psychiatry* 5(1):3–5.

Long, Croft E., and Alberto Viau. 1974. Health Care Extension Using Medical Auxiliaries in Guatamala. *Lancet* 1 (7845–7857):127–130.

MacCorquodale, Donald W. 1982. Primary Health Care in the Dominican Republic: a Study of Health Worker Effectiveness. *Journal of Tropical Medicine and Hygiene* 85:251–254.

Management Sciences for Health. 1984. Evaluation: Health Promoter Program. Unpublished manuscript, Ministry of Health, Peru, January–June 1984, vol. 1 and 2.

Ministerio de Salud (MOH), Lima. 1979. Modelo Normativo Para La Capacitación de Parteras Empíricas. Escuela de Salud Pública del Peru, Dirección General de Programas de Salud, Dirección General de Salud Materno-Infantil y Población, Lima.

Rubin, George, Charles Chen, Yolanda de Herrera, Vilma de Aparicio, John Massey, and Leo Morris. 1983. Primary Health Care Workers: The Rural Health Aide Program in San Salvador. *Bull. Pan American Health Organization* 17 (1):42–50.

Simpson, Herbert, et al. 1981. Traditional Midwives: Controversial Community Health Workers. *Development Digest* 19 (1):115–128.

World Health Organization (WHO). 1979a. Training and Utilization of Auxiliary Personnel for Rural Health Teams in Developing Countries: Report of a WHO Expert Committee. *Who Technical Report Series* (Geneva), no. 633:1–35.

———. 1979b. *Traditional Birth Attendants: A Field Guide to their Training, Evaluation and Articulation with Health Services.* Geneva: WHO.

Index